6 The Pen and the Sword

1601   1609   1620

Newsweek Books New York

Editor Christopher Hibbert

HEPATICI COGNITIO

1628   1630   1631   1640

6   The Pen and the Sword

1644

1649

1661

ISBN: Clothbound edition 0-88225-068-x
ISBN: Deluxe edition 0-88225-069-8
Library of Congress Catalog Card No. 73-81688

Printed and bound in Italy by
Arnoldo Mondadori Editore – Verona

1666   1667   1667

1683   1688   1685   1698

Contents

Introduction

The seventeenth century was a time of continuous war —dynastic, religious and civil—wars fought for territory, for trade and for control of the sea. In China, in the violent upheavals that led to the overthrow of the Ming dynasty by the Manchus, huge areas were laid waste; and in the floods that engulfed the province of Hunan, when the dikes of the Yellow River were cut by the imperial army, over two hundred thousand people were drowned. In India the last of the great Moguls, Aurangzeb, who went to war with an iron disembowelling claw on his arm, led trailing hosts, half a million strong, into the Deccan in his relentless endeavor to extend the frontiers of his empire. In Japan there was civil war which ended in a fearful conflict beneath the ramparts of the castle of Ōsaka where the son of the great warlord, Hideyoshi, who had gained control over almost the entire Japanese archipelago, lost his inheritance to the Tokugawa shoguns. In Persia, Shah Abbas the Great vigorously renewed his people's war with the Ottoman Empire, driving his cavalry into provinces which his predecessors had lost, slaughtering the Sultan's troops, until Persia's boundaries had once more been pushed back as far as they had been in the days of Ismael I.

Elsewhere, in every part of the world, representatives of all the leading mercantile powers in Europe, sometimes peaceably, often by force, were expanding their colonies and trading posts, their settlements and missions. By the middle of the century the Portuguese were well established in Africa, at Macao in China, in Ceylon and all down the southwest coast of India from Bombay to Quilon. The Dutch had numerous trading posts in the East Indies, in Formosa, Siam and Japan. The Spanish occupied the Philippines as well as their huge empire in South America. The French, who had founded their settlement at Quebec in 1608, were enlarging their dominion in Canada and would soon move down the Mississippi toward the Gulf of Mexico,

establishing the first European settlement in Arkansas in 1686 and claiming Louisiana, an area much larger than the present state, in the name of Louis XIV. The English, with posts in India, in China at Canton, in Java, Sumatra, southern Arabia and the West Indies, had been extending their territories along the North American Atlantic seaboard ever since they had built their first permanent settlement at Jamestown in 1607, and were pushing deeper and deeper into the hinterland, north toward the Kennebec and south toward the Savannah. In 1660 Trimountaine was renamed Boston after the town in Lincolnshire from which several of the chief settlers came. In 1664 New Amsterdam became New York. A few years later, on the other side of the world, the English buccaneer and navigator, William Dampier, began to explore the northwest coast of Australia.

This rapidly expanding contact with an outside world hitherto unknown not only infinitely increased the wealth of Europe but also permanently enhanced the quality and pleasures of European life. Some idea of the extent of this enhancement may be suggested by the large number of oriental words which were at this time introduced into the English language, such as—selecting a few at random—tea, coffee, chinaware, chintz, gingham and curry. As it was in trade, so it was in art. Chinese porcelain and Japanese lacquer work, Mogul paintings and mosaics inspired generations of English artists; while translations of Arabic fables and of the works of Confucius reminded Europeans that there were civilizations more ancient and, in some respects, more enlightened than theirs.

In Europe no war was more savage, devastating or prolonged than the Thirty Years War which raged over almost the whole of Europe until the Treaty of Westphalia was signed in 1648. It was a war which left Germany exhausted in medieval disunity, with Brandenburg the only important Calvinist principality still in existence, and which postponed for two centuries the formation of a united national state. Like Germany, Italy, too, still remained the mere "geographical expression" which Metternich was so derisively to call it. Yet north of the Alps the creation and consolidation of powerful national states, following the disruption of Christendom by the Reformation and the Counter-Reformation, was the most important political development of the century. Of all these states, whose claims to absolute authority were justified by such philosophers and jurists as Hobbes and Grotius, France emerged as the most powerful, governed by a succession of the century's most remarkable men—Henry IV, Richelieu, Mazarin and Louis XIV, the Sun King himself, who was able to declare without exaggeration, "Monarchs are absolute Lords and have full authority over all people."

At the beginning of the century Spain still deserved those lavish expressions of regard which King James I of England bestowed upon her; but toward its end, her endeavors to bring about a Counter-Reformation in northern Europe having failed at enormous cost, her vitality was being drained away by her Protestant rivals in colonial expansion, the English and the Dutch. In fact, the Dutch, that painstaking and determined people who had combined to make a formidable power out of the Low Country provinces which had rebelled against Spain, were to enjoy a golden age of military and naval strength and commercial riches. And the English, at the same time, were to garner more benefits from these violent years than any other nation in Europe. After revolution, civil war, the execution of the King, the rule of Cromwell, the restoration of the Stuart dynasty and the deposition of James II, they were finally to emerge with their differences overcome, their liberties secured, with the promise of vast wealth and a worldwide empire. For their neighbors across the North Sea the seven-

teenth century was also a time of glory. The Danes under Christian IV were without question the most powerful nation in Scandinavia, dominating immense territories, supremely influential in all the affairs of northern Europe. While the Swedes, inheritors of that power and influence, were to dazzle and alarm their contemporaries under the leadership of Gustavus Adolphus, the most brilliant soldier of his time, the master of the Baltic.

The Europe of these new national states was comparatively small, less than half the size of the Europe whose problems the statesmen of 1814–15 were to attempt to resolve at the Congress of Vienna. At the end of the Thirty Years War, when its population in many areas had appreciably declined since the beginning of the century, Europe comprised an area of less than four million square miles. Although limited then as now by the Mediterranean in the southwest, the Atlantic in the west, and the Arctic circle in the north, its limits in the east and southeast were far from being so definitely and conveniently defined. Vienna, indeed, which Metternich was to present to his fellow statesmen and diplomats as the pivotal center of a stabilized Europe, was almost a frontier town; and the frontier beyond its gates was constantly liable to fluctuate. Not many miles down the Danube to the east the dominions of the sprawling Turkish Empire began.

The Moors were sent back to Africa from Spain by Philip III's minister, the Duke of Lerma, in 1609–10; but it was to be many more years before the Turks were driven back toward the Bosphorus. Throughout the seventeenth century they were, on the contrary, continually threatening to advance still further west. Already they controlled an enormous area from Belgrade to Athens, from the Adriatic to the Black Sea, an area more extensive by far than the Kingdom of France. They had been severely checked in the Gulf of

Lepanto in 1571 at the last great naval engagement between oared galleys; and on land in 1683 the "invincible" armies of the Ottoman Sultan were defeated by John Sobieski, King of Poland, outside besieged Vienna. But the Turkish threat to Christian Europe was even then not past, as events in the next century were to show.

Northeast of Vienna, beyond the Pripet Marshes, lay another alien race outside the European pale. It was Christian not Moslem; but its Christianity came from the Byzantine, not the Latin Church, and its contacts with the West were at once tenuous and tentative. Russia was still a sadly primitive country, populated by ignorant peasants, as mysterious and remote to Western Europe as Westerners were mysterious and remote to them. No one considered them as Europeans, least of all themselves. It was Tsar Peter's outstanding achievement to open up for them that "window on the west" which was to alter the course of European history.

Peter the Great left Moscow for his tour of Western Europe almost exactly a century after Shakespeare began work on *Hamlet*. Between these two events, the first and last of those described in this volume, there appeared in the world a multitude of men uniquely gifted in the arts of war and government, original as scientists and philosophers, and brilliant as painters, sculptors, writers and architects. A century before the genius of the world seemed to be centered in Italy where the Renaissance first burst into flower.

Yet in the seventeenth century genius seemed universal. If England had cause to take pride in her great writers, in Shakespeare, Bacon, Milton, Donne and Dryden, France could boast of Molière, Racine, Corneille and Pascal, and Spain of Cervantes and Lope de Vega. While Seville gave birth to Velásquez and Murillo, there arose in the Low Countries a whole school of masters from Rubens to Van Dyck, from Frans Hals to Rembrandt and de Hooch, from Vermeer to Aelbert Cuyp. At the same time Poussin, Claude le Lorrain and the brothers Le Nain were at work in France. While Inigo Jones and Christopher Wren were responsible for some of England's most beautiful buildings, Le Nôtre, Le Vau and Mansart gave to France the glories of Versailles, and Bernini so beautifully embellished St. Peter's in Rome. Soon after Monteverdi, director of music at St. Mark's in Venice, wrote *Orfeo*, one of the landmarks in the history of the opera—*la nuova musica*—first heard at the court of the Medici grand dukes of Tuscany some years before, Purcell produced his first opera, *Dido and Aeneas*, in London. In the year that Galileo died in his villa outside Florence, Newton was born in a manor house in Lincolnshire. From La Haye came Descartes; from Amsterdam, Spinoza; from Leipzig, Leibnitz. The procession of great names is endless. More justly perhaps than any other, the seventeenth century may be termed a century of genius.

CHRISTOPHER HIBBERT

A Play for all Seasons

The tragic legend of Denmark's Prince Amleth had fired the imaginations of European storytellers long before England's famous playwright, William Shakespeare, began work on his Revenge of Hamlett Prince of Denmark *in 1600 or 1601. In fact, the tale of Hamlet's bloody demise was already a familiar folk legend when Saxo Grammaticus, a Danish scholar, first committed it to paper in 1186, and its popularity had not diminished four centuries later when Thomas Kyd produced his melodrama based on the tale. Drawing heavily upon Kyd's action-filled but otherwise inconsequential drama, Shakespeare created what is certainly his most famous tragedy and quite possibly the most famous play in world literature. In the centuries since* Hamlet *was first performed, its title role has been coveted—and attempted—by nearly all leading actors.*

No play has had a more enduring impact on the world than Shakespeare's *Hamlet*. It has been acted in every country where there is a serious interest in the theater, and leading actors the world over have been eager to play the part of the melancholy Prince. In the chronicles of writing and performance for the stage, *Hamlet* has become a part of world history.

The saga of the Danish Prince Amleth was first recorded in the twelfth century by the Danish scholar Saxo Grammaticus, but it has its origins in Scandinavian legend. In Saxo's story the murder of Amleth's father by his uncle is common knowledge. Amleth pretends to be insane to save his own life until he can avenge the murder. Revenge, when it comes, is bloody and violent; while the members of the court are celebrating a false report of Amleth's death, Amleth tricks them into drunkenness, sets fire to the hall, kills his uncle and proclaims himself king.

In the late sixteenth century an English play about Hamlet appeared in London. That play, which was probably written by Thomas Kyd, was a bloody, old-fashioned melodrama, complete with a ghost that went about wailing "Hamlet, revenge." The play was in the repertory of the Chamberlain's Men—one of London's two leading acting companies—for some time. In fact the type of melodrama it represented was spoofed in another play produced by the same company:

> A filthy whining ghost
> Lapt in some foul sheet, or a leather pilch,
> Comes screaming in like a pig half sticked
> And cries, *Vindicta*–Revenge, Revenge!

This English *Hamlet* was the play that Shakespeare rewrote in creating his own play.

Documented records of Shakespeare's tragedy begin in 1602, although the exact date of its composition is unknown. The date 1601 is usually given, but the author may have begun work on the play in 1600. In July, 1602, "a booke called the Revenge of Hamlett Prince Denmarke, as it was latelie Acted by the Lord Chamberlayne his servantes" was "entered" at Stationers' Hall in London. The practice at the time was for new books, including the texts of plays, to be sent to the headquarters of the Stationers' Company, whose members—all the booksellers and most of the printers in London—had the sole right of publication.

The application for the right to print *Hamlet* did not give the author's name. It did, however, clearly indicate that the play was already popular, and it identified the company of actors performing the play as the Chamberlain's Men. Of this troupe or "fellowship" Shakespeare had been a leading member and a shareholder for eight years. Shakespeare's writing skill—more of an asset than his acting—and the great ability of Richard Burbage, the troupe's leading player, had won renown and prosperity for the Chamberlain's Men. They were favored by Queen Elizabeth and had the acclaim of the general public. A rhymed epitaph that appeared after Burbage's death in 1618 named "young Hamlet" as one of his principal roles.

Thus we know that the most famous of Shakespeare's tragedies started with every advantage. Its author had been well established by his histories and comedies, and by the tragedy *Romeo and Juliet*. Further, the play was performed by a renowned company headed by Burbage.

.It became immediately apparent that *Hamlet* was one of those rare works of art with nearly universal appeal. The play was great melodrama, with blood and violence and pageantry. But it was much more, for Shakespeare had taken an old, familiar plot and had shifted the emphasis from external events to Hamlet's character. And the man he revealed—paralyzed by gloom and indecision, torn between the flesh and the spirit, with shifting moods, uncontrolled passions, sharp insights and haunting fears—proved frighteningly real not just to seventeenth-century audiences but to every later generation.

Yet, while *Hamlet* has impressed and gripped audiences down the centuries, it is nonetheless a play of its own period. It is the first of the four great

The Globe Theater in London: for many years the home of the Chamberlain's Men, a theater company of which Shakespeare was a leading member.

Opposite The print of Shakespeare used as the frontispiece to the First Folio edition of his plays, published in 1623.

Elizabeth I at
Blackfriars, surrounded by
her guard of honor.

The Earl of Essex, one-time
favorite of Elizabeth I.

Shakespearean tragedies that reveal an increasingly dark and pessimistic view of human nature. Shakespeare was to write light romantic pieces after that phase, but he never returned to the old gaiety of his "high fantastical" comedies, which had their happiest, finest—and final—hour in *Twelfth Night*, which was almost certainly produced in 1601.

The first years of the seventeenth century in England were dominated by the twilight of the reign of the great Queen Elizabeth. The glory of Gloriana was being dimmed by her years, and her heart had been bruised, if not broken, by a shattering event. In February, 1601, her former favorite the Earl of Essex had led a foolhardy rebellion. With him was a clique of malcontents, including Shakespeare's early patron, the Earl of Southampton.

The challenge to the Queen's sovereignty found little public support and failed miserably. Essex was convicted of treason and beheaded; Southampton, lucky to escape with his life, was imprisoned in the Tower of London. Some of the insurgents had paid Shakespeare's company a special fee to revive *Richard II* at the Globe Theater, and even—as the Queen later alleged—to play it in the streets. Their purpose was to show that the deposition of a monarch could be successful—and it was absurdly stupid of the players to accept their bribe. There was an official inquiry into the company's conduct, but they were not penalized and they were quickly returned to royal favor. A subsequent remark of the Queen's —"Know ye not that I am Richard the Second?"— indicated that the wound had been deep.

Elizabeth's death came in March, 1603. The nation mourned and wondered. The Protestant succession was assured—there would not be a revival of civil and religious war to ravage public life with blood and hatred. But none could be sure how King James VI of Scotland would behave when he became also King James I of England. Doubts and fears gathered, and thus *Hamlet* was born in stormy weather, in a country under a cloud.

Even amid the eager, ardent and creative energy of the Elizabethan Age there had been a cult of melancholy. It had been more of a fashionable pose than a considered philosophy, but during the reign of the new king there was a growing wave of bleak pessimism. In his *History of the World* Sir Walter Raleigh noted that "the long day of mankind draweth fast towards an evening and the world's tragedy and time are near at an end." Raleigh was a prisoner—and probably knew that he was doomed —when he wrote his *History*, but bishops and clerics who were not in danger also preached decay and disaster. In one of his sermons, John Donne, Dean of St. Paul's, told his listeners that the sun was "fainter and languishing, men less in stature and shorter lived. No addition, but only every year new sorts of worms and flies and sicknesses which argue more and more putrefaction." Other divines urged the saving of souls before the darkness thickened.

Those dismal forebodings came after *Hamlet* was written. By then Shakespeare had entered a period in which his despair about human character and

destiny was far more prominent than his faith in charity and the saving power of mercy. That view is found in his last plays. If something was rotten in the state of Denmark, there was also a smell of corruption in the English air—and Hamlet's bitter commentary on life anticipates a generally felt insecurity.

The settled philosophy and faith of the Middle Ages had cracked. To question authority in Church and State once had been strange and sinful; it was now familiar and fashionable. The stage of national life had become full of questioning Hamlets.

Had *Hamlet* been no more than a projection of sad skepticism, it could never have pleased as it did. It has lived by the dramatic values of its fast-moving story and still more by the character of the Prince, so quicksilver in his moods, so sharp of wit, so profound in reflection, and, above all, so ready with the perfect phrase and the perfectly chosen word. Whatever were the failings of the new reign and the degradation of court life, the English language reached its summit of power and richness in the Authorized Version of the Bible, which was suggested by and dedicated to King James. The old Anglo-Saxon or Anglo-Norman English had a special strength, and the classical culture of the Renaissance brought new

Above left James 1; he took the Chamberlain's Men under his patronage and plays were often performed at court.

Above right The third Earl of Southampton, an early patron of Shakespeare.

15

The title-page of the
Second Quarto of *Hamlet*.

Far right William Kemp,
a famous Shakespearian
comedian, from a woodcut
of 1600.

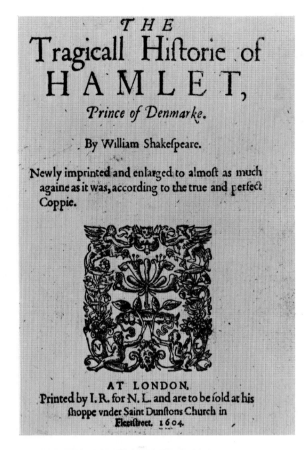

THE
Tragicall Hiſtorie of
HAMLET,
Prince of Denmarke.

By William Shakeſpeare.

Newly imprinted and enlarged to almoſt as much
againe as it was, according to the true and perfect
Coppie.

AT LONDON,
Printed by I. R. for N. L. and are to be ſold at his
ſhoppe vnder Saint Dunſtons Church in
Fleetſtreet. 1604.

Richard Burbage,
the leading player of the
Chamberlain's Men. He was
the first actor to play the
role of Hamlet.

decoration to its sinewy frame. Hamlet is a university student with a gift of golden words. He commands a thundering eloquence in his parley with the ghost. He can be as brief as poignant: "The Rest is silence." And he dies with a sigh, not a swan song. His part was written in the dusk of Elizabethan glory, and in the high noon of the English language.

There is no question that the play pleased its audiences. In fact, *Hamlet*'s reception was so gratifying that a "pirated" version was thought to be worth printing in 1603. There was then no copyright of plays, and the manuscripts were keenly guarded by the companies for which they were written in order to prevent performance by rivals. If a piece were popular, a bogus text could usually be dishonestly obtained by bribing one of the minor players. Such players were known as "hired men" to distinguish them from "sharers," who took the chief roles. The hired men's wages were very low, and they could be bribed to provide rough scripts based on memories of parts taken by themselves or others. There were also shorthand writers who took surreptitious notes at performances in order to get out a text.

The pirated version of *Hamlet*, a truncated travesty of the play, was known as the First Quarto. The Quarto named Shakespeare as the dramatist, and therefore either he or his company decided to print the full and genuine text. Doing so involved the risk of its being used by other teams of players, but since the play had been published with a text grotesquely unfair to the author, it was decided to issue a correct version. In 1604, therefore, the Second Quarto—which described the play as "Newly imprinted and enlarged to almost as much againe as it was according to the true and perfect Coppie"—was issued. There were two reprintings in 1611.

In 1623 John Heminges and Henry Condell, Shakespeare's fellow sharers in the Chamberlain's Men, printed a slightly abbreviated form of the Second Quarto, omitting four hundred lines out of four thousand. They were probably using a playhouse text in which some cuts had been marked, for the complete version occupies the stage for nearly four hours—or nearly double "the two hours' traffic of our stage" mentioned by Shakespeare in his prologue to *Romeo and Juliet*. Uncut, *Hamlet* is the longest of Shakespeare's plays.

The unauthorized first edition of the text stated that the play had already been performed both in and out of London, and it is certainly true that *Hamlet* appealed not just to the regular playgoers or to the students at Oxford and Cambridge. In 1607, when Captain Keeling of the East India Company's ship *Dragon* was sailing east with two other vessels, *Hector* and *Content*, they were becalmed off Sierra Leone. There Keeling recorded in his diary that he entertained Captain Hawkins of *Content*. There was a fish dinner and then he had "Hamlet acted abord me: which I permitt to keepe my people from idlnes and unlawful games, or sleepe." That they managed to improvise a stage on the tiny ships of the period is remarkable. So is the fact that the Captain had taken a copy of *Hamlet* with him. The performance by the crew, organized for the sake of discipline rather than in devotion to drama, must have been extremely crude. The impact of *Hamlet* had indeed been wide.

There is no record of command performances of *Hamlet* at court, even though King James constantly made requests to see other plays. If *Hamlet* was never in demand at court, that is understandable. James had married a Danish wife, and neither the story of the murder and revenge nor the remarks about the drinking habits of the Danes were complimentary to the Queen's nation. But the play remained in the repertory of the King's Men (the name the Chamberlain's Men had taken upon the accession of James I).

English actors frequently toured in Europe, where

they had a high reputation. As early as 1586, the Earl of Leicester had taken players with him when he was with an army in Holland, and the Shakespearean clown William Kemp was among them. Fynes Moryson (1566-1630), a Cambridge scholar and traveler, met English actors at Frankfurt. "The Germans," he wrote, "not understanding a word they said, flocked wonderfully to see their gesture and action." The English standard of performance was thought exemplary. In 1626 an English company led by John Green played *Hamlet* in Dresden. They used a shortened version: *Der Bestrafte Brüdermord, Prinz Hamlet ans Dannemark.*

English theaters, closed by the Puritans for nearly twenty years during the civil war and the Commonwealth, were reopened after the restoration of the monarchy in 1660. *Hamlet* was one of the first plays to be revived. The diarist Pepys noted that Thomas Betterton played the Prince "beyond imagination" in "the best part I believe that man ever acted."

In recent years classics have been subjected to the whims of directors who want to prove their ability by giving old plays a new look. *Hamlet* has been dressed in the costumes of many periods, including our own. It has received new interpretations and been staged according to strange theories. Through all that, it has held its position at the summit of English drama, continually examined by scholars while continually fascinating the general public. More than any of Shakespeare's plays, it has justified Ben Jonson's promise of the author's survival, "not for an age but for all time."

IVOR BROWN

Thomas Betterton, a well-known actor after the Restoration of 1660. Hamlet was one of his favorite roles.

Left The title-page of John Donne's *Sermons*, published in 1640.

John Donne, poet and divine.

Amid declining political fortunes,

English writing

Hamlet was only one of Shakespeare's great masterpieces, and Shakespeare only one of a large group of outstanding English dramatists who were writing in the period 1590–1625. Their dramatic achievements were comparable to those of the great dramatists of fifth-century Athens, but were far more concentrated.

The most notable characteristic of this literary output is the rebirth of tragedy. Shakespeare's great works, such as *Hamlet, Macbeth, King Lear* and *Othello*, do not stand alone. Christopher Marlowe (1564–93), the father of Elizabethan tragedy, was the most important dramatic influence on Shakespeare, an influence transmitted through his *Tamburlaine, The Jew of Malta, Dr Faustus* and *Edward II*, all great plays in themselves. Other lesser figures, dwarfs beside Shakespeare and Marlowe, but major dramatists by any other standards were men such as Cyril Tourneur (*c.* 1575–1626), John Webster (*c.* 1580–

Detail of Ben Jonson, English dramatist.

c. 1625), John Marston (1576–1634) and Thomas Kyd (1558–94). Many of their tragedies, which often end with a stage literally littered with corpses, seem almost comic to the modern theatergoer, but to contemporaries they expressed a meaningful sentiment—if only a profound cynicism about the way in which authority corrupts. Although the settings were often Italian, the feelings were universal.

The dramatic achievements of the age were not confined to tragedy. Shakespeare was a great comic writer, and others such as Ben Jonson (1573–1637) were not far behind him in ability. Again

Detail of Sir Philip Sidney.

there was a host of lesser figures. The greatest achievements of tragic writing were all completed by about 1625, but comedy continued to develop until the end of the century, with only a brief pause during the puritanical years of the Commonwealth, when drama was banned. The Restoration of 1660 brought with it a new, light, highly sophisticated form of comedy.

Structurally, too, theatrical art was progressing rapidly. The rhetorical character of medieval mystery plays was fading rapidly away, and being replaced by increasing attempts at realism. The highly stylized masque became a separate form of art from the play. Instead of merely reciting their lines the new breed of professional actors such as the Lord Chamberlain's and the Lord Ad-

miral's Men, attempted to bring life into the characters whom they were portraying. The specially designed theaters, which were beginning to be built in the late sixteenth century, made it possible to use more elaborate scenery than previously.

In other fields of writing, also, the Elizabethan age was one of distinction. Sir Philip Sidney (1554–86), who was killed at the Battle of Zutphen, exemplified the Renaissance ideal of aristocratic culture. Edmund Spenser (*c.* 1552–99) left fragments of a great masterpiece in *The Faerie Queene*. Shakespeare's *Sonnets* are regarded by some as his highest achievement. But perhaps the outstanding literary figure of this period was the poet and preacher John Donne (1573–1631), whose metaphysical imaginings are a verbal equivalent of the distortions and exaggerations of Mannerist and Baroque art.

Cervantes

Outside England at this time, there was no equivalent to this sudden literary flowering. One book of the period, however, is a notable exception.

While *Hamlet* was being performed for the first time in London, an impoverished fifty-six-year-old Spaniard who had once been a soldier and had lately

Cervantes; soldier, slave and author.

been in prison was writing "just such a book as might be begotten in a jail." The Spaniard's name was Miguel de Cervantes Saavedra and the book was *Don Quixote*, the first modern novel. Cervantes' work was in the tradition of the picaresque romances that had been popular in Spain since the middle of the sixteenth century, when the anonymous *La Vida de Lazarillo de Tormes y de sus fortunas y adversidades* was published. *La Vida* had been followed by the equally popular works of Mateo Alemán, Agustín de Rojas and Francisco Lopez de Ubeda, whose *La Picara Justina* appeared in 1605. Indeed, the Spaniards have been credited with inventing the picaresque novel—a genre that takes its name from the Spanish word for rogue, *picaro*.

Don Quixote was much more than a picaresque novel, however. Cervantes' work was soon recognized as the greatest social romance of the early seventeenth century. The Spaniard's highly moralistic masterpiece succeeded not only in ridiculing the picaresque novel and its chivalric sentiments, but also in demonstrating the follies of prejudice and the real dangers behind the exaggerated contemporary regard for pure blood and nobility of birth—

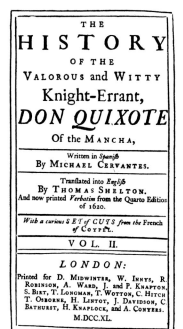

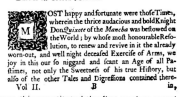
Don Quixote; a satire of the picaresque romance, this constituted the first modern novel.

Spain produces a literary masterpiece

a regard that was coupled with widespread disdain for work. Cervantes himself led a hard and vigorous life. He joined the army in 1568 and served in Italy, where he was badly wounded at the Battle of Lepanto in October, 1571. On his return to Spain he was captured by Barbary corsairs and taken to Algiers, where he was sold as a slave to a Greek renegade. Ransomed after five years, Cervantes returned to his homeland in 1576. He tried and failed to make a living as a playwright and eventually found employment as a collector of provisions and stores for the Spanish Armada of 1588. After the fleet's defeat, he was retained as an ill-paid and overworked commissary to the galleys—but his unbusinesslike methods soon led to his imprisonment. Out of that experience grew Cervantes' great literary panorama of Spanish society, *Don Quixote*, which was published in 1605. In 1614, a spurious sequel to *Don Quixote* appeared, and a year later Cervantes himself published an authentic second installment.

On April 23, 1616, Cervantes died in Madrid ; on that same day Shakespeare died in Stratford-on-Avon, England. Like his contemporary, Shakespeare may also have been a soldier—and may even have fought against Cervantes' countrymen in the Netherlands. Indeed, Spain and England were at war for most of the two authors' lives, and the rivalry between the two countries continued at the time of their deaths.

Portugal

After his successful invasion of Portugal in 1581, Spain's Philip II promised to recognize the constitutional rights of the Portuguese people, particularly those of the influential hidalgos. He agreed to summon the Cortes regularly and to create a Portuguese privy council with responsibility for Portuguese affairs. The country's possessions in Brazil, Africa and Asia were to be held by Portugal, which was to be considered not as a conquered province but as a separate kingdom, joined with Spain in a mutually profitable political union.

Few of Philip's promises were observed: the Cortes was summoned only once; the government of the country was left to the

The Escorial. Built by Philip II, this combination of palace, monastery and tomb served as the administrative center of Spain's world empire.

grasping favorites of the Spanish court; and the union with Spain —known in Portugal as the "Sixty Years of Captivity"—led to incessant involvement in wars with Spain's maritime enemies.

Spain's declining power

Despite the size of her empire, Spain's power at the beginning of the seventeenth century was already in decline. The defeat of the Armada in 1588 had exposed the incompetence of the Spanish navy and had given Spanish self-esteem a severe shock. Since that time it had become increasingly clear that Spain no longer had the strength to maintain the position she had presumed to occupy in the world. The continuing war with England was but one of the constant strains on her resources.

Toward the end of his reign, Philip II added to his country's fiscal burden by intervening in France in support of the Catholic League, a group that sought to unseat Henry of Navarre. The Duke of Parma was ordered to march across France to help raise the siege of Paris, and Don Juan del Aguila was directed to land in Brittany at the head of 2,000 men. The siege of Paris was successfully raised, as was the siege of Rouen; but Parma, Philip's most valued servant, was wounded during an attack on Caudebec and died on December 2, 1592. Subsequent Spanish victories—the

capture of Doullens and Cambrai by the Count of Fuentes, Parma's successor, and the reduction of Calais and Amiens—counted for little when weighed against Henry of Navarre's superior diplomatic skill. And by the Treaty of Vervins, signed in May, 1598, Philip was obliged to recognize the failure of his schemes in France and to return all his conquests except Cambrai. By now it was clear that Henry had beaten all opposition and was accepted as King of France by all. Even the Duke of Brittany, the most persistent of his enemies, was forced to sue for peace.

Philip III

Philip II died at the Escorial a few months after the Treaty of Vervins was signed and he was succeeded by his son Philip III, a pious, extravagant, incapable monarch who was content to leave the government in the hands of the worthless Duke of Lerma. The unscrupulous Duke encouraged the King's extravagances while acquiring a vast personal fortune and involving his impoverished country in disastrous foreign entanglements. Fearing that they might support a Moslem invasion of Spain, Lerma expelled the Moriscos (Spanish Moors) from the country. His move was almost as damaging to Spain as Louis XIV's expulsion of the Huguenots would later be to France; for the half-million Moriscos forced into

exile by Lerma were among the most skilled members of the community.

Hoping to strike a blow against England in 1602, Spain landed an army in Ireland to bolster the cause of the Earl of Tyrone. The intervention was wholly unsuccessful, and by the time Don Juan del Aguila, the Spanish general, had evacuated Kinsale, Spain's finances were all but exhausted.

The accession to the English throne of James I, who "naturally loved not the sight of a soldier nor any violent man," saved Spain from further expensive involvement with England ; for Elizabeth's successor achieved a peace settlement between the two countries in 1604. Nothing could save Spain from the loss of its possessions in the Netherlands, where Dutch rebels, who were supported by England and subsidized by France, had been resisting all attempts to crush them for over thirty years. On April 9, 1609, a treaty was signed that recognized the independent Dutch Republic.

Philip III of Spain.

Revolt of the Netherlands 1609

*The revolt that erupted in the Spanish Netherlands in 1568 pitted a small band of vastly out-
numbered, militantly Protestant Dutch nobles against the armies of Spain's Catholic King, Europe's
mightiest monarch, Philip II. The contest was a lopsided one, and Philip's victory over the Dutch
troops led by William of Orange should have been a swift one. Instead, the fighting dragged on for
forty years before a temporary truce was agreed upon in 1609. William of Orange had been
assassinated in 1584 and Philip died in 1598—but the dream of an independent Dutch state lived
on. Sporadic fighting continued for forty years after the truce, however. Not until 1648, by the
terms of the Treaty of Münster, was the former Spanish possession divided into the independent
Dutch Republic in the north and the "obedient" southern provinces (later known as Belgium).*

The Dutch nation achieved its independence
through a war that lasted for eighty years—from
1568 to 1648. If a single day can claim to be the
turning point in that long struggle, it is probably
April 9, 1609, the day when Spain was compelled
to sign a twelve-year truce with the Dutch rebels
and thereby recognize that the war had reached a
state of complete deadlock. The truce acknowledged,
de facto, what forty years later was to be recognized
de jure: that the Dutch Republic was an independent
state. Before the final Treaty of Münster was signed
in 1648, there were to be military threats to that
independence from Spain and more serious threats
from France. Frontiers were to be adjusted by
military action but subject only to these relatively
minor changes in territory and law, 1609 marked
the emergence—through political revolt and armed
conflict—of a new state in Europe, unique in its
constitution, its social structure and its economy.

In its earliest phase, the resistance to Philip II of
Spain, who had succeeded his father Charles V as
sovereign of the Burgundian Netherlands in 1555,
came from the great aristocrats. Charles had
scarcely abdicated when the trouble began. The
high Netherlands nobility resented Philip's assump-
tion that he "ruled" their territories and could treat
them as he liked. They protested against the presence
of Spanish troops on Dutch soil, the enforcement of
the Inquisition by persecuting edicts, the rational-
ization of the Netherlands bishoprics and the general
disregard of their traditional feudal rights and privileges. Of the three leaders, Egmont, Hoorn and
William, Prince of Orange, it was the latter who
rapidly developed the habit of command and the
exercise of authority. Yet even Orange, desperately
trying to maintain reasonable relations with Philip
and also—after the King's departure for Spain in
1559—with his regents and deputies, could not
prevent the spread of more violent protest. Some five
hundred lesser nobles banded together in a league
that was by no means inclined to moderation. Neither

were the fanatical Protestants who went on a wild
spree of iconoclasm in the churches of Antwerp and
other cities in 1566.

Philip's answer was to send the Duke of Alva to
suppress the revolt in 1567. Orange fled, Egmont
and Hoorn were executed, and thousands were
burned or killed. Alva subsequently proposed a
turnover tax, known as the "Tenth Penny," that
turned the powerful merchant class in cities like
Antwerp, Ghent and Bruges against Spain. Nevertheless, Alva's brutal measures seemed to be working
when, in 1572, a band of Dutch rebels—ordered out
of Dover harbor by Queen Elizabeth I—fell upon the
Dutch port of Brill and succeeded in capturing it.
These "Sea Beggars" then went on to take the nearby
communities of Flushing, Middelburg and Zierik-
zee. They swiftly established control over the entire
Scheldt estuary and the approaches to Antwerp.
That region was not only the center of Spanish
government in the Netherlands but also the largest
commercial entrepôt in the world. And although
Alva successfully laid siege to Haarlem, the dogged
resistance of Leyden and Alkmaar led to the
liberation of most of Holland and Zeeland.

In 1573 Alva retired to make way for two successors, Luis de Requesens and Don Juan of Austria.
Neither succeeded in quelling resistance nor in
stemming the growing mutinies among the 60,000
unpaid Spanish troops stationed in the Netherlands.
Between 1578 and 1579—amid growing Spanish
confusion—Orange consolidated the rebel forces
and strengthened their grip on the northwestern
Netherlands. Unfortunately for him, religious quarrels between Dutch Catholics, moderate Erasmians
and extreme Protestant groups like the fanatical
Calvinists of Ghent made national unity impossible;
the Prince's opportunity for an early victory was
lost amid factional squabbling.

In 1577 Philip sent Alexander Farnese, later
Prince of Parma, to join Don Juan. Farnese was not
only one of the greatest military commanders of the

Obyt Anno 1592. 3 Decemb.

Alexander Farnese, Prince of
Parma and Governor of the
Netherlands; he was one of
the military geniuses of
his age, but was unable to
hold Spain's northern
possessions together.

Opposite Detail of *The Treaty
of Breda* by Velásquez. This
highlighted the importance
of the United Provinces in
international affairs.

The blockade of Bommelia by the Spanish, 1585. The seeds of Dutch discontent grew in the late sixteenth century despite Spain's military might.

century, he was also an adroit diplomat. By military genius and skillful bribery, Farnese reunited a large part of the south and east for Spain, and in 1579 he signed the Treaty of Arras with the leaders of the southern provinces. That treaty was, in effect, an answer to the Union of Utrecht—an accord signed by most of the northern and some of the southern provinces and towns that is regarded as the foundation charter of the Dutch Republic.

From 1578 to 1589 Farnese pushed north, recapturing most of present-day Belgium—including the great cities of Ghent, Bruges and Antwerp—for Spain. He reached the region where the Rhine, Maas and Lek rivers cross the Low Countries from east to west before his progress was checked by Philip's orders to divert troops to the 1588 invasion of England. Just before Antwerp fell, the rebels' great leader, Orange, was struck down by an assassin. Orange was succeeded by his son Maurice, who proved to be an even greater military commander. With the political help of another republican leader, Jan van Oldenbarneveldt, Maurice regained much of the territory to the south and east that Farnese had captured, but he could not break the siege of Ostend. Its surrender to Spinola, another brilliant Italian commander in the pay of Philip II, ended the first half of the war and made the truce of 1609 inevitable.

Little of real consequence happened after hostilities were resumed in 1621. In a protracted and dreary struggle, the Dutch, under Maurice's successor, Frederick Henry, managed to capture 's Hertogenbosch, Maastricht and the surrounding country. Neither a French alliance nor the marriage of Frederick's daughter Mary to James, Duke of York, enabled them to do more. The 1648 Treaty of Münster irrevocably divided the Netherlands into

the obedient provinces of the south, which remained loyal to Spain, and the Dutch Republic, which became a monarchy in 1813.

Nineteenth-century historians assumed that the rebellion was Protestant and liberal, and that there was something about the ethos of the "Teutonic" north that predestined it to lead the Netherlands out of the decadent, Catholic, persecuting Spanish Empire. The explanation is obviously defective. In the early stages—and indeed as late as 1578—the revolt drew much of its strength from the south; the southern city of Ghent was, from the beginning, a violent, unrepentant center of Calvinism—and Calvinism itself entered the Netherlands from the south (from France, via the Walloon provinces). The original center of Orange's resistance movement was in

Right Hugo Grotius, the father of modern international law, with friends, by Rubens.

22

Brabant, or Brussels, a city that lay far south of Holland and Zeeland. The Sea Beggars drew much of their strength from Flanders, Brabant and Wallonia, and many southern Catholic nobles were as strong in defense of their privileges as their poorer northern neighbors—until they were bribed back into loyalty by Farnese.

Such obstinate facts caused the most famous twentieth-century historian of the revolt, Peter Geyl, to reject the religious or "racial" explanation of the rising in favor of a quite different one. The Netherlands, he argued, had already formed a natural cultural unity before the revolt; the country was on its way to becoming a political unit before the fighting began. Thus the revolt began as a medieval, feudal, noble protest and ended as a conquest of the north by Protestant forces working through the Sea Beggars. The north was able to fight off Spanish attempts at reconquest because it was protected by a defense line of great rivers that even Farnese failed to breach.

Geyl's interpretation has become virtual orthodoxy, although after forty-odd years it seems oversimplified. Unquestionably the rebels were helped by geography. Yet other factors must be taken into account. For one, the era was one of siege warfare, not mobile warfare. Southern cities like Ghent, Bruges and Antwerp were well fortified and capable of self-defense. For another, the pattern—even in the north—was inconsistent; the northern city of Haarlem fell, but Amsterdam remained pro-Spanish and Catholic until 1578, when it fell to the rebels by an internal coup d'état. The truth is that Antwerp and the other southern cities succumbed through muddle, bribery and loss of morale—rather than through absolute indefensibility.

Nor should one ignore another important feature of the revolt that does not fit Geyl's theory of a united Netherlands disrupted solely by Spanish military force. The fact is that even before Philip's accession there were marked differences of social structure between south and north. The south was more prosperous, more commercial, more industrial—and yet more subject to feudal, aristocratic influence—than the north, which was a poorer society, dependent upon shipping and fishing. From the beginning of the revolt in 1567, merchants, manufacturers and workers began to move north, sensing that the north was likely to be safer and less exposed to the risk of princely or aristocratic looting than the south was. Perhaps ten per cent of the southern population—and a far higher percentage of its most dynamic members—emigrated during this period, and by the 1590s they were prominent among the professors, printers, artists, bankers, clothiers, silk spinners, shipbuilders and overseas traders in Amsterdam, Haarlem, Leyden, Middelburg and many other ports and cities of the north.

The southern aristocracy, immobilized by their investments in land and property, could contribute little to the revolt. Shamefaced, they stayed put and allowed themselves to be bribed into renewing their loyal pledges to Spain. On the other hand, there can be no doubt about the fanatical sincerity of the

Frederick Henry Prince of Orange; it was ironic that Holland's struggle for liberty should be led by German nobles such as the princes of Orange.

southern Calvinists, most of whom came from the lower or middle classes.

There was little homogeneity among the classes that supported the revolt, and it is difficult to determine the motives that drove them on. Simple hatred of Spanish occupation and Inquisitional persecution was widespread among the middle and upper classes. (Among other things, persecution, war, dynasticism and all the costs that accompanied them were bad for business—and Dutch society was already a business society.) At the other end of the scale, frustration and mistrust were increased by a new phenomenon of the age—unprecedented inflation, which afflicted aristocracy and working men alike. Nobles living on incomes derived from more or less fixed rents found themselves caught between rising costs and falling receipts at a time when court jobs and army appointments were going to Spaniards. And as industry deserted the old guild-dominated towns for the Flanders countryside, a growing force of workers found itself turned adrift, workless and starving. As a result, the extremes of Dutch society were united in their discontent and unanimous in their support of both political and religious dissent. They were soon joined by the potentially less vulnerable and certainly more circumspect middle class, whose members were disturbed by the prospect of damaging and unlimited Spanish taxation. This class took control of the new Republic.

It is that combination of social classes and political motives which distinguishes the revolt of the Netherlands from the feudal protests, Protestant rebellions and peasant uprisings that occurred in France, England, Germany, Italy, Spain and Scandinavia in the late sixteenth and early seventeenth centuries. The Dutch revolt represents the one successful rising of a mercantile republic against the centralized,

Franciscus Gomarus: leader of the Calvinist extremists.

A Dutch merchant with his wife in Java. The Dutch colonial empire, like that of England, grew during the seventeenth and eighteenth centuries, while those of Spain and Portugal stagnated.

Right The Mayor of Delft. Dutch domestic life, after independence was officially acknowledged by Spain, became far more prosperous than it had previously been.

The Rise of the Dutch Republic to 1648

- ◯ Holy Roman Empire
- ⬤ United Provinces
- ◯ Remained Spanish Netherlands

Dutch open dikes 1573
Alkmaar
Amsterdam
Haarlem
Besieged by Alva 1572-73
The Hague
Assassination of William the Silent 1584
Leyden
Utrecht
Defeat of Sir Philip Sidney 1586
Zutphen
Rotterdam
Delft
Brill
Breda
Bruges
Antwerp Sacked 1576
Ghent
Nieuwport
Maastricht
Brussels
Louvain
Liège
Mons
Rhine River
Cateau-Cambrésis
FRANCE

monarchical absolutism typified by the states of early modern Europe—Spain, France, England and Prussia. Curiously, the Dutch example did not spread. (John Adams, scraping the bottom of the barrel for money to finance the American Revolution, appealed to the spirit of comradeship between the American "federation" and its Dutch "originals" —and got nowhere.)

The chronicle of the Republic's economic and cultural history is an altogether different story. Before about 1590 the northern provinces were poorer than their southern neighbors, but after 1590 they rapidly overtook them. Amsterdam soon replaced Antwerp as the world's foremost entrepôt, and the Dutch *fluit*—an unarmed, cheap, sea-going barge—introduced a technological revolution in shipbuilding. The Dutch *fluit* fleet soon established a virtual monopoly on the trade in grain, timber and naval stores from the Baltic to Europe.

In the early seventeenth century Dutch merchants opened new markets in Russia, Greenland, Newfoundland, India, Java, Sumatra and Australasia. At New Amsterdam (renamed New York after its capture by the English) and at the Cape of Good Hope, the Dutch left colonies that helped to shape the character of future settlements. In India, Ceylon and the East they founded a great trading company, the East India Company. And in North and South America and the West Indies the Dutch West India Company flourished for a time.

Dutch colonial history has been emphasized in Western history books, yet statistically it was never as important as Dutch trade within Europe. The

"new drapery"—carried by Belgian emigrants from Ypres to Leyden, and then to Norwich and Colchester—revolutionized Europe's textile trade, replacing old, heavy, expensive cloths with bright, light, cheaper textiles. Antwerp silk weavers and linen bleachers carried their skills to Amsterdam and Haarlem, and cohorts of merchants and bankers followed King William and Queen Mary to England. In ensuing decades, Dutch bankers helped to shape the structure and finance of the Bank of England, and the loans by which England financed her wars—including the American Revolution—were underwritten by men named Vanneck, Van Notten, and Capadose.

Almost every country in Europe profited from Dutch immigration. From London to Rome and Danzig to Warsaw, Dutch settlers used their engineering skills to clear swamps and marshes and to build dams, locks and canals, water works and pumping systems. Colbert employed Dutchmen in Bordeaux to reclaim land and build textile factories, and in Sweden Dutch immigrants negotiated contracts with the crown that gave them a virtual monopoly of iron and copper mining, the manufacture of munitions, the cutting of timber and the export of tar, hemp and rope. Export of Dutch capital and skill to less-developed economies is a recurrent feature of economic life in the seventeenth century.

Along with the economic tide went ideas, philosophy and works of art. Grotius was the spokesman, advocate and historian of the patrician governing class, but his principles—among them *mare liberum*, or freedom of the seas—were adopted by England and later by the entire civilized world. (Indeed Grotius' claim to the title Father of Modern International Law has never been challenged.) Philosophers like Descartes, Spinoza and Locke took refuge in the relatively tolerant climate of Holland.

Rembrandt, the greatest of the hundreds of Netherlands artists whose works have become part of Europe's cultural heritage, lived not far from Spinoza in Amsterdam's Jewish quarter. Dutch art, like many Dutch innovations, grew up under strong Italian influence, yet it developed its own unique and unmistakable style. Seascapes, domestic interiors, flower paintings, portraits, landscapes—all demonstrate a miraculous absorption of detail into broad and satisfying patterns that has rarely been equaled before or since.

The capacity for combining detailed observation with significant generalization links seventeenth-century Dutch artists with their scientific contemporaries—men like Leeuwenhoek, Boerhaave, Huyghens and Stevin—who brought scientific methods to microscopy, biology, zoology, medicine, astronomy, architecture, ballistics and navigation.

Economic decline set in with the eighteenth century, as competition from larger states, high defense costs and heavy taxation combined to check Dutch prosperity and diminish Dutch power. But in their heyday, Dutch capital, Dutch enterprise and Dutch technology—all by-products of the Dutch revolt—served as a powerful driving force, propelling a predominantly agrarian, semifeudal Europe toward industrial revolution and socio-economic modernity.

CHARLES WILSON

The ratification of the Treaty of Münster, 1648, which finally gave Holland independence from Spain.

Lacking a commonly held higher

The United Provinces

The Dutch wars caused the decline of Antwerp and its replacement by Amsterdam and Rotterdam as the country's leading ports. But this was only one aspect of the changing balance between the north and the south. By the time that the Twelve Years Truce was signed in 1609, it was clear that the independent United Provinces were richer and better able to profit from the available opportunities for trade than the south, which remained loyal to Spain. The Jews, who had been driven from Spain and Portugal, made Amsterdam into a thriving commercial center, and the city's bourse rapidly developed into the world's first stock exchange as merchants flocked there to raise money for their journeys abroad. Although its industry was highly productive, the real success of the United Provinces was dependent on trade. It was largely as a result of the rebellion against Spain that this commercial success became possible, for the original wealth of the United Provinces was built on plundered Spanish shipping. The East India Company, which was founded in 1602, and the West India Company, which was founded in 1621, were both private joint-stock companies, but they operated with the energetic support of the government.

Each of the seven provinces was governed by its own States, and delegates were sent to the States–General of the United Provinces. The princes of Orange held the office of Stadholder in most of the provinces, but their real power was based on command of the army and navy. It was largely due to Maurice of Nassau (1567–

1625), who became Prince of Orange in 1618, that the House of Orange was able to establish itself in such a dominant position in the state. The States–General had little authority as the States of the individual provinces could ignore its decisions. There was almost continuous tension in the States–General between the local landed aristocracy, the merchant aristocracy of the towns and the House of Orange.

The Synod of Dort

Political disagreement was aggravated by religious quarrels. The University of Leyden, which had been set up in 1575 by William of Orange to teach Calvinist doctrine, had rapidly developed into one of Europe's most distinguished universities. It became the scene of a dispute between those, led initially by Jacobus Arminius (1560–1609) and after his death by Hugo Grotius (1583–1645), who believed in man's free will, and those, led by Franciscus Gomarus (1563–1641), who believed that salvation and damnation were predestined by God. The Arminian controversy, which was to be paralleled throughout Europe, among Roman Catholics as well as Protestants, was particularly fierce in Holland. It soon became linked with politics.

The political rivalry between the Stadholder, Maurice of Nassau, and the Landsadvocate of the province of Holland, Johan van Oldenbarneveldt (1547–1619), was expressed in religious terms ; the former supported Gomarism, the latter Arminianism. Oldenbarneveldt succeeded in passing laws favorable to the Arminians but was unable to enforce them without military help, which Maurice refused to supply. Olden-

barneveldt tried to raise a small army in the province of Holland, which supported him, but Maurice simply invaded the province and took the leading Arminians prisoner in 1618.

The States–General, despite the

Maurice of Nassau.

opposition of Arminian Holland, summoned a Church synod at Dordrecht (Dort), and Arminian ideas were formally condemned by the delegates, who included representatives from England, Scotland, the Palatinate and Switzerland. With his military authority buttressed by the synod's decision, Maurice was able to strengthen his hold over the country and the States–General. Oldenbarneveldt, who represented the main challenge to his authority, was executed on a trumped-up charge of treason.

Grotius was sentenced to life imprisonment, but managed to escape in 1621 and fled to France where he became the leading international jurist of his age. His main works, De Jure Praedae, (On the Law of Prizetaking) (1609), and De Jure Belli ac pacis, (On the Law of War and Peace) (1625), which tried to base the law of nations on principles of natural rather than divine law, are the foundations of modern international law.

Tyrannicide and royal power

The quarrel, which so concerned Grotius, between nations that could not accept a common higher authority was only one of the issues in dispute among lawyers and theologians in the century that followed the breakdown of the idea of a Christian commonwealth. No less important was the debate on the extent of royal power. This

problem was made more acute by the religious disputes of the day. In the event of religious disagreement between a prince and his subject, should the prince be allowed to enforce his own views? Should the subjects of an irreligious or heretical prince be allowed to depose him? If they were not powerful enough to depose him should they kill him?

These questions obsessed scholars in the early seventeenth century. Both Machiavelli and Bodin had skipped lightly over the problems, but in 1599 the Spanish Jesuit Juan de Mariana (1536–1623) published De Rege et Regis Institutione, (On the King and the Institution of Kingship), in which he appeared to express approval of the murder of Henry III of France. Despite condemnation from the General of the Order and many others, regicide soon came to be an accepted doctrine among the Jesuits. The controversy was made fiercer by the fact that many Protestants believed that it was permissible to assassinate a Roman Catholic but not a Protestant prince, and vice versa.

France's ascendancy

France, to whom the House of Savoy would one day lose both Savoy and Nice, was ruled by Henry IV, the most remarkable ruler of his time. The son of the Duke of Vendôme and Jeanne d'Albret, Queen of Navarre, he was educated as a Protestant and distinguished himself in the religious wars in France. On the death of his mother in 1572 he became King of Navarre, and following the assassination of Henry III in 1589 he became King of France.

Ten years of fighting intervened before Henry, who had become a Roman Catholic convert, could claim his inheritance. From that time on, Henry, aided by his friend the Duke of Sully, concentrated his considerable talents upon restoring the fortunes of France. Riding over all opposition and ignoring all criticism, Henry drove through reforms of the administration, finances, industry and the army, and beautified Paris.

In his efforts to weaken the power of the Hapsburgs, the French King entered into a series of alliances with the Protestant princes of Germany, the King of Sweden, various Italian states, the

Amsterdam in 1652, the successor to Antwerp as Europe's entrepôt.

The execution of Henry IV's murderer, Ravaillac.

Swiss cantons and the Duke of Lorraine. After the death of his first wife, Margaret of Valois, sister of Henry III of France, Henry married the formidable Marie de' Medici and thus gained the favor of her uncle, the Grand Duke of Tuscany. By the time of his assassination in May, 1610, Henry had prepared France for the fulfillment of her great destiny. Cardinal Richelieu, minister to Henry's son and heir Louis XIII, and Richelieu's successor, Cardinal Mazarin, were to achieve that destiny.

On May 14, 1610, a Roman Catholic fanatic assassinated Henry IV and the controversy over tyrannicide was reignited. But in a sense, the murder of Henry led to the abandonment of favor for regicide and helped to strengthen ideas of totalitarian government. When, in 1612, a French Jesuit, Martin Becanus, published an attack on royal authority it was immediately condemned by the papacy and the University of Paris. Throughout Europe monarchical ideas were strengthened by the horror that was felt at Henry's assassination, because of the almost universal admiration in which he had been held during his later years.

James I

One of the foremost advocates of monarchical ideas was the new King of England, James I, the son of Mary Queen of Scots. James began a pamphlet war on the subject of royal power in 1607, but he had already written *Basilikon Doron* (*A Kingly Gift*) in 1559, the work in which he presented his high views of royal authority. James was a man whose learning and scholarly habits were only matched by an inability to govern, which led critics to call him "the wisest fool in Christendom." James entertained grandiose but vague notions of peacefully uniting the whole of Europe and establishing himself and the pope as joint presidents of a great council of the Church. James' ambitious design far exceeded his rather limited talents and powers, however, and seventeenth-century Europe remained

Prince Henry on the hunting field. Heir to the English throne, he died young.

as perversely fragmented as it had been at any time in its history.

From the beginning of his reign in England James made clear his support for the doctrine of the Divine Right of Kings. This rapidly brought him into conflict with Parliament and particularly with the House of Commons, whose Puritan members disliked both James' ideas on royal power and his emphasis on episcopacy as a divine institution. Many of them would have preferred a Presbyterian Church and a state in which royal power was subordinate to that of Parliament. This did not mean that they favored democracy; they merely sought to enhance their own position and authority.

If James had shown the same ability to handle Parliament as Elizabeth had done, the Civil War might have been avoided, but the strength of his views was only equaled by the weakness of his character. James preferred to write diatribes against witchcraft and tobacco than to interest himself in the day-to-day administration of his kingdom.

The country was run by a succession of incompetent favorites —James had a penchant for handsome youths—of whom the most notorious was George Villiers (1592–1628), Duke of Buckingham, who was to be James' most unfortunate legacy to his son. Even more unpopular in England than Buckingham was James' growing friendship with Spain. Philip III's skillful diplomat, the Count of Gondomar—whose task was to keep James from aiding the Protestants in their quarrels with Spain and to prevent English attacks on Spanish possessions in America—helped maintain the amicable relationship. Negotiations were eventually entered into for a marriage between James' son Charles and Philip's sister.

James' eldest son Henry, Prince of Wales, idolized by the country, might have been a more capable ruler, but he died in 1612, and Charles, who showed most of James' weaknesses without possessing any of his intellectual ability, became the heir to the throne.

Scholarship

James' legacy was not wholly bad. He was a patron of scholars and sought to persuade figures in the world of learning to live in England. Among those who took up his invitation was Isaac Casaubon (1559–1614), a leading classical scholar. Another was the scholarly but greedy Marco Antonio de Dominis (1560–1625), who had been Roman Catholic Archbishop of Spalato (Split). He came to England both in the hope of re-uniting the Roman and English Churches—a project dear to James' heart—and in order to become rich. James rewarded him with the deanery of Windsor, but de Dominis was disappointed and returned to Rome where he thought he would be made a cardinal. Instead he died in the hands of the Inquisition. James tried to encourage Grotius and Paolo Sarpi to come to England, but in these attempts he failed.

Other princes, too, encouraged scholarship, and it became a sign of distinction for a ruler to be surrounded by men of learning. The purpose of this was partly to recruit widely respected names to take part in the pamphlet controversies of the time. Men such as Isaac Casaubon, Cardinal Robert Bellarmine (1542–1621) and Bishop Lancelot Andrewes (1555–1626) used their European reputations in pamphlet warfare.

Many of the pamphlet controversies of the day led to advances in scholarship, particularly in historical and legal subjects. Men such as William Camden (1551–1623) and William Dugdale (1605–86), who spent their lives researching into local history; Joseph Scaliger (1540–1609), also showed the value of chronology as an aid to history, and the Jesuit Bollandist hagiographers, who produced lives of the saints free of pious fables, made important contributions to historical study. But the efforts of scholars did not preclude continued exploration and settlement of the New World.

The Pilgrims at Plymouth 1620

Unlike their predecessors, who settled in Virginia at the end of the first decade of the seventeenth century, the religious dissidents who boarded the Mayflower in September 1620 had no patron and no significant financial backing. Those expatriate Englishmen—most of whom had recently sought, and failed to find, ecclesiastical equanimity in Holland—sailed without a royal charter and without commercial backing. Their voyage was undertaken amid considerable uncertainty and at long odds—and when half the 102-man company died within six months of their arrival, Plymouth Colony appeared doomed. Indeed, the Colony never did prosper, and it was ultimately absorbed into the thriving Massachusetts Bay Colony—but not before America's most famous colonists had firmly established religious diversity and, to a degree, religious toleration as a fact of life in the New World.

From September 6 to November 9, 1620, the merchant ship *Mayflower*, usually employed in the Anglo-French wine trade, sailed west across the Atlantic Ocean toward the coast of North America. On board were 102 men, women and children bound for a new life in a new world. (According to William Bradford, leader of the *Mayflower* company and the governor of Plymouth Colony, the original passenger list totaled 102. Two children were born during the voyage.)

The *Mayflower*'s passengers were predominantly poor men, drawn from the ranks of small craftsmen, artisans and petty tradesmen. Many of them came from Leyden, Holland, where they had made a meager living in and around the cloth industry. All were English—and although they were poor, their main reason for leaving Europe was not to improve their economic lot but to secure religious freedom. They had emigrated from England and settled in Holland to escape religious persecution, seeking and finding in Holland the right to organize their own church. But in Leyden other vexations had arisen: the immigrants feared that their children would quickly absorb Dutch ways, lose their attachment to the English community and abandon the "Pilgrims" church.

The Pilgrims were a community centered upon a church. Like many other Englishmen of their time, they had grown discontented with the Church of England. The majority of its critics had remained within the Anglican Church, pressing for reforms; the Pilgrims were part of a small, weak minority which had decided that it could no longer profess allegiance to a corrupt Church. Following the lead of their ministers, a number of persons from Scrooby, in Nottinghamshire, had separated themselves from their parish churches and formed their own congregations. Their act was blatantly seditious—a challenge to Church and State alike—and rather than risk prosecution, the separatists had fled to Holland in 1607. Holland too had posed problems, and the immigrants had therefore boarded the *Mayflower*, hoping that they would soon be beyond the reach of the English government—yet free to remain English in the New World.

In early November of 1620, the *Mayflower* reached Cape Cod. New England was not the Pilgrims' intended destination; their original plan had been to settle themselves in a remote and empty part of Virginia, which was already an English colony. The settlers attempted to sail free of the New England coast and proceed south, but the currents and winds hindered them and they returned to Cape Cod. On November 11, their ship lay safely at harbor. The Pilgrims had decided to settle in New England.

Winter was near, and the settlers were justifiably apprehensive about its coming and about the desolate look of the nearby coasts. William Bradford, their great leader and chronicler, noted in his journal the "violent and savage hue" of the "wilderness." Reconnoitering parties were put ashore to search for a suitable place to begin the long business of building a new settlement, but it was several weeks before such a place was found. The *Mayflower*, cruising down the inner coast of the Cape, reached a sheltered harbor. The inlet was safe for shipping, and its shores had "divers cornfields and little brooks"; all in all, "a place fit for situation." There the settlers would establish Plymouth Colony.

The long search for a suitable site for their future colony had been only one of the Pilgrims' troubles. Since they were outside the jurisdiction of Virginia, some of the passengers—those recruited in London, who were not members of the Leyden church—claimed that no government existed and that no one could exercise authority over them. Bradford and the other Pilgrim fathers resolved that dilemma by drafting the famous Mayflower Compact. In signing that document, the vast majority of the adult males on board the *Mayflower* pledged their obedience to an elected governor and to any laws on which they might agree. In effect, control was given to the

The seal of the Plymouth Colony; it was used on official documents.

Opposite A reconstruction of the Plymouth Colony as it appeared in 1627.

29

Boston

Cambridge

Greenwich

Southampton

Plymouth

Main emigrant areas

Secondary emigrant areas

William Laud, who became Archbishop of Canterbury in 1633. His rigid intolerance of Puritanism caused a wave of emigration to New England.

Below left The port of Southampton; one of several ports on the south and east coast of England from which emigrants set sail for America.

Below right The *Mayflower*, the ship in which the Pilgrim Fathers sailed to the New World.

Leyden group, the dissenting faction was suppressed, and the colony's chances of survival were enhanced.

Unity was necessary. The first years of the colony's existence were hard and cruel ones, as famine, disease and privation—all potential invitations to anarchy —overtook the little society. Half the *Mayflower*'s original passengers were dead by the spring of 1621, and the colony did not achieve even the most modest sort of security until two years later. Yet its internal life proceeded smoothly. The religious community of the Pilgrims acted as a stabilizing force, and so did their social homogeneity. After a few years the colony became a self-governing settlement—one in which there was a simple and unselfconscious legal and political equality.

During those first difficult years, the struggling colony received immeasurable assistance from several indigenous Indian tribes, notably the Wampanoag. Their chief, Massasoit, signed a mutual aid pact with the settlers in 1621. Legend credits Squanto, sole survivor of the Pawtuxet Indian nation, with teaching the colonists how to catch and dry herring, tap maple groves for their sugar, and plant the native corn—Indian style, four kernels to a mound. Squanto had been captured by an English slaver in 1614 and sold to a Spanish master, had escaped to England and, in 1618, had returned to his homeland—to find all the members of his tribe wiped out by a smallpox epidemic. Squanto's trans-oceanic travels had given him a knowledge of the English language and English customs that was to prove of inestimable value to Bradford and his company.

The Pilgrims, touched and astonished by the Indians' aid, reciprocated by inviting Squanto and ninety-odd members of Massasoit's tribe to the most famous alfresco buffet in American folklore—the first Thanksgiving dinner. That feast, held in mid-October of 1621 to celebrate the completion of the colony's first harvest, featured native turkey, duck, geese, deer, corn bread and wild berries. The Indians, obviously caught up in the spirit of the occasion, stayed for three days.

The Thanksgiving celebration was the lone bright spot in a year otherwise noted for famine, skirmishes with unfriendly Indians and uncontrolled epidemics —known collectively as the "General Sickness." The *Mayflower* passengers were not unique in their sufferings, however; Virginia's early settlers (1584 and 1607 at Jamestown) had had similar experiences. It was the radical nature of the Pilgrims' religious attitudes, their poverty and their lack of support from England that set them apart from other early American colonists. Virginia was the creation of English gentry and merchants, who financed voyages of colonization and supported New World colonies for commercial reasons. Massachusetts Bay, the third English colony in North America, had both a royal charter and financial backing from several quarters. Plymouth Colony, on the other hand, was the only North American settlement to be established with little aid from England and no influential friends.

Plymouth never became a particularly thriving colony. It remained a society of traders, small farmers and fishermen—poor and unpopulous. In 1630 the colonization of Massachusetts by the Puritans began in earnest, and that colony soon surpassed Plymouth in size and importance. In 1691 the Pilgrim Colony was absorbed by its large and powerful neighbor (more or less willingly, since the two shared similar religious and political systems). The memory of Plymouth's founding remained a vivid one, however, and the story of those poor and humble settlers —who sailed three thousand miles across the storm-tossed Atlantic to find religious freedom and suffered in the wilderness to build their new homes—became a not unimportant part of American legend.

By the end of the seventeenth century, that legend had already become a politically useful tool in New England. The Pilgrims and the Puritans were frequently depicted as a poor, harassed minority that had fled the persecution of kings and bishops to secure freedom in the New World. There, at their own expense, they had built simple but godly societies that were antipathetic to monarchs—unless they were good Protestant ones who left them alone—and

to bishops, of any religion whatsoever. New England was naturally sympathetic to Cromwell, to the Parliamentary side in the English civil war and to the nonconformists exiled upon the return of the Stuarts. Their plight corresponded perfectly with the Anglo-American nonconformist tradition—a tradition that had its roots among the middle classes, was suspicious of ecclesiastical hierarchy, aristocracy and monarchy, and was devoted to representative assemblies that opposed any flavor of absolutism or princely power, whether exercised by kings or their ministers.

New England was only one region of America, and the Plymouth settlers were only part of a much larger migration of Englishmen to the New World—one that rapidly produced settlements along the entire eastern seaboard. For the most part, those migrants were humble people: indentured servants, young men and women from the lower sections of

Colonists landing in Virginia; in 1607 the first permanent English colony in the New World was established at Jamestown in Virginia.

Left Indians celebrating a victory; in the early years, the Pilgrim Fathers received invaluable assistance from local Indian tribes.

31

An Indian village, showing corn production. The Indians taught the colonists how to plant the native corn.

Factors Favoring Colonization

 Improved navigation and sailing skills make new continent accessible

 Innumerable navigable rivers and excellent harbors

 Climate like western Europe with adequate rainfall

 European food crops thrive in America Native crops for trade and home use

Early Settlements in North America 1603-42

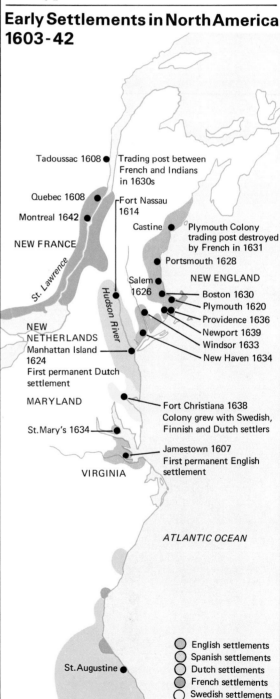

Tadoussac 1608 ● — Trading post between French and Indians in 1630s

Quebec 1608 ● — Fort Nassau 1614

Montreal 1642 ●

Castine — Plymouth Colony trading post destroyed by French in 1631

NEW FRANCE

Portsmouth 1628

Salem 1626 — NEW ENGLAND

St. Lawrence

Hudson River

Boston 1630
Plymouth 1620
Providence 1636
Newport 1639
Windsor 1633
New Haven 1634

NEW NETHERLANDS
Manhattan Island 1624
First permanent Dutch settlement

MARYLAND — Fort Christiana 1638 Colony grew with Swedish, Finnish and Dutch settlers

St. Mary's 1634 —

Jamestown 1607 First permanent English settlement

VIRGINIA

ATLANTIC OCEAN

St. Augustine ●

○ English settlements
○ Spanish settlements
○ Dutch settlements
● French settlements
○ Swedish settlements

society, artisans and craftsmen. The hopelessly poor and degraded did not come. Nor—naturally enough—did the aristocracy, the gentry and the great merchants. A few men of property made the long voyage, but the colonial upper classes were largely recruited from within. In the process, many of the practices and institutions linked to the privileges of the European and English upper classes disappeared. Hereditary aristocracy was never introduced, nor was the concept of a professional army. Land tenure was simple in America, for the feudal complexity of European practices was rejected. Entailed estates were all but nonexistent, and attempts to introduce "quit rents" (rents paid in lieu of feudal services) and to link landownership to institutional privileges were largely unsuccessful.

The most remarkable alteration of all occurred in the area of religious toleration. During the first decades of the seventeenth century, the New World witnessed the breakdown of the concept of religious uniformity, a dream that was still cherished in most of the monarchies of Europe. European states had largely acted to choke off the proliferation of religious sects after the early years of the Reformation, but in the seventeenth and eighteenth centuries religious groups sought and found great opportunities in America. Maryland was settled by Catholics from Protestant England; New England, of course, was colonized by Puritans and Separatists; Pennsylvania by Quakers fleeing Anglican repression; and Nova Scotia by Huguenots seeking security from French religious absolutism.

That massive migration was a remarkable phenomenon. By the end of the eighteenth century it had given America a reputation for profound and widespread religious tolerance. Such tolerance had not always been there—it was the growth of sects that forced its emergence. And grow they did—for once relieved of the weight of effective established churches, the original denominations rapidly splintered and multiplied. Old and New Light Congregationalists and Presbyterians, Baptists, Separate Baptists, Rogerenes, Methodists, Shakers and Quakers, Dunkers and Amish, Huguenots and Anglicans—all testified to the disintegration of European ideas of religious orthodoxy. The multiplication of sects evidenced the weakness of institutionalized religion and also lessened the formal influence of ministers and priests in government.

Diversity was also noticeable in the population of the New World. The French and the Spanish had their own national settlements—the former in Canada and the Ohio Valley, the latter in Florida and the Caribbean—but these were weak and fail-

An illustration from a discourse of 1636 outlining the heresies of two weavers.

Above left A seventeenth-century cartoon showing wrangling sects tossing a Bible in a blanket.

Below left The first church in Salem. Salem was founded in 1626 by discontented members of the Plymouth Colony.

Detail from a Puritan tombstone at Dorchester, Mass. The heavy symbolism of death reflects the tradition of Puritan religious severity.

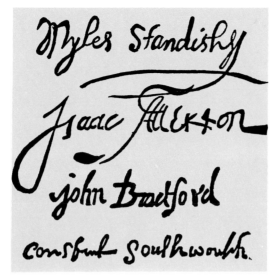

Miles Standish, a leading member of the Plymouth Colony, although he was not a Separatist but a member of the Church of England.

Above right Signatures to the Mayflower Compact which served as the Pilgrim Fathers' constitution in the New World. It was signed on November 21, 1620, before the landing at Plymouth.

ing. After 1620, non-English settlers came to the English colonies in increasing numbers. The Ulster Scots—called Scotch Irish in America—and the Germans—known as the Pennsylvania Dutch—were the two largest groups; by 1790 they comprised eighteen per cent of the colonial population. Catholic Irish, French Huguenots, Swiss and Salzburger Protestants, Jews from southern Europe, Lowland and Highland Scots, and the remnants of early Dutch and Scandinavian colonists made up another twelve per cent. All these foreshadowed the variety of national groups that flooded into nineteenth-century America.

By the eighteenth century, colonial society was moving in the direction of struggle and protest—conditions that normally release social energies and,

for a time at least, increase political opportunities for all classes. England had allowed her American possessions large political freedoms while trying to enforce a certain degree of economic control, and that policy had produced strong local political institutions. Those institutions naturally opposed Britain's restrictions on colonial economic development, and for decades the royal governors of the colonies were forced to contend with strong and restive representative assemblies.

The growth of the representative assembly was an essential American development—one that could trace its origins back to the Mayflower Compact. Springing from privileges given to the early colonies in their charters (which were intended to grant a limited form of municipal self-government), the

Right An early-seventeenth-century map of America with Indians decorating the border.

The South East Prospect of The City of Philadelphia By Peter Cooper *Painter*

assemblies had gradually arrogated parliamentary rights and immunities. Many of their members were fully conversant with the most extreme and advanced theories of eighteenth-century English politics and were as capable of using them as any English radical.

The final struggle came after 1763, when the British crown, suddenly aware of the need for a revised colonial policy, decided to increase its regulation of American governments. The result was an intensification and universalization of the conflict between autocracy and personal liberty that had prompted the emigration of the Pilgrims more than a century earlier. Americans claimed to stand for the rights of man against the crimes of tyrants—for the people, and against their kings.

The largest non-English immigrant group shared none of the freedom or opportunity that the New World supposedly offered. That group consisted of more than half a million black slaves, nearly twenty per cent of the total population of North America in 1790. The economies of the southern colonies—and their profitable crops of tobacco, rice, indigo and cotton—were supported by the labor of men and women who were regarded as chattel and whose numbers were augmented each year by a thriving slave trade.

Henceforward the rhetoric of Americans would emphasize the differences between Europe and America. The Reverend Ezra Stiles proclaimed that Divine Providence "was making way for the planting and Erection in this land the best policied Empire that has yet appeared in the World. In which Liberty and Property will be secured." That empire, he asserted, would be renowned for "liberty civil and religious" and for "Science and Arts."

His opinion won widespread support among Europeans, for with the American Revolution, the New World had taken its place on the stage of history. Its institutions, and the prevailing opinions of its statesmen, placed it firmly in the "party of humanity"—the camp of the Enlightenment. Given time, the Old World might even catch up with the New.　OLIVER WALSTON, ADRIAN BRINK

Philadelphia. The territory of Pennsylvania was granted to William Penn in 1681, and Philadelphia rapidly grew to be the leading town and port.

Left The first Quaker temple in Philadelphia. Most of the early settlers in Pennsylvania were Quakers.

Quakers being tortured in London in 1656.

Religious war in Europe

Religious differences in America did not lead to war; in Europe they did. The inevitable battleground for religious disputes was central Europe, where the Roman Catholic Hapsburg dynasty maintained a weakening hold over a vast empire in which Protestants were growing in numbers, power and ambition. Several times in the early years of

Engraving by Jacques Callot from Les *misères et les malheurs de la guerre* (1633).

the century war seemed imminent. In 1608 there had been an ominous riot in Donauwörth, a free city northwest of Munich on the Danube, and in its wake the *Reichshofrat*, a council of imperial advisers empowered to adjudicate in disputes within the vassal states, deprived Donauwörth of its rights and decreed that its

church, which had been taken over by the Protestants, should be handed back to the Roman Catholics.

War threatened again in 1610, when the death of the childless Duke of Cleves-Jülich left various provinces along the Upper Rhine without a ruler. To prevent a clash between the two Lutheran contenders for the dukedom, Emperor Rudolf II sent in an occupying force whereupon one of the claimants became a Roman Catholic and the other declared himself a Calvinist. Eventually they agreed to divide the territories between them, and war was once more averted. But nobody could doubt that another crisis would soon arise elsewhere.

That crisis seemed to be approaching in 1617, the centenary year of the Protestant Reforma-

tion when, in an effort to increase religious ferment, the Archduke Ferdinand of Styria announced his claim to the Bohemian throne of his cousin, the Emperor Matthias, who was dying without an heir in Vienna. Ferdinand, who had been brought up in a Jesuit college, was known to detest Protestants and to have done all that he could to root them out of Styria. He was a friendly, fat, good-natured man with a red face and a passion for hunting—the most improbable of zealots. But a zealot he was and a politician of cunning and determination.

The elevation of this devout Roman Catholic to the throne of Bohemia aroused the fear of every Protestant in the country. In 1609 a threatened uprising of Bohemian Protestants forced Ferdinand to grant them a measure of toleration, but they had reason to complain that the toleration accorded them in theory was denied them in practice, and that the disabilities from which they suffered under Matthias were becoming persecutions under Ferdinand. Led by Count Thurn—a nobleman who had been educated in Italy and who, having once been a Roman Catholic was now more Calvinist than Lutheran—they decided on rebellion. They demanded the execution of two leading Roman Catholic ministers, Jaroslav Martinitz and William Slavata, and called for the immediate establishment of an emergency Protestant committee.

Martinitz and Slavata sent an urgent appeal to Vienna for help, but before their messenger reached the capital the Protestants seized

control of Prague. A mob marched to Hradshin Palace, seized the two ministers and dragged them toward a high window and threw them down into the Palace courtyard. With the "defenestration of Prague," the Thirty Years War began.

The Winter King

In February, 1613, King James I's pretty, high-spirited daughter Elizabeth had married Frederick V, the Elector Palatine, one of the foremost Protestant princes of Germany. Five years later, after the "defenestration of Prague," in defiance of the Emperor, Frederick rashly accepted the crown of Bohemia from the Protestants of Prague—and thereby divided the Empire along religious lines.

Elizabeth, who was admired for her beauty and vitality and revered as the "Queen of Hearts," was extremely popular in England. When the Emperor's troops marched against her husband's supporters in Prague, her plight aroused the country's deepest sympathy and led to loud demands for her protection. The defeat of Frederick's troops at the Battle of the White Mountain in the winter of 1620 was followed by the fall of his former capital, Heidelberg, and he and Elizabeth were obliged to seek shelter in The Hague at the court of Prince Maurice of Orange and Nassau. The defeat of Frederick left Bohemia at the mercy of the Hapsburgs and effectively marked the end of Bohemia as an independent state.

The "defenestration of Prague" which signaled the start of the Thirty Years War.

Frederick of Bohemia and Elizabeth: "the Winter King" and his Queen.

the Thirty Years War

The Thirty Years War

Although the fighting in the Thirty Years War took place on German soil, the main protagonists were not German. The fall of Heidelberg was not the end of the fighting; Frederick was supported by Ernest von Mansfeld (1580–1626), a talented mercenary soldier. From outside Germany, too, there was support for the

Cavalry making a sortie from a hilltop fort.

Protestant cause as few foreign princes wanted a Hapsburg victory. Christian IV (1588–1648) of Denmark attempted unsuccessfully to help the German Protestants.

It appeared that a Roman Catholic and Hapsburg victory was inevitable, and that what Charles V had unsuccessfully attempted—the conversion of the Hapsburg Empire into a unitary Roman Catholic state—might become a reality. This was as unwelcome to the Roman Catholic princes of the Empire as it was to the Protestants because they too would have lost their power. The most anxious of the Roman Catholic princes was Maximilian (1597–1651), Duke of Bavaria, who had led the army that had driven Frederick from the Palatinate. Maximilian's gains from the war, including the repayment of large sums lent to the Emperor Ferdinand at a high rate of interest, would have been threatened by an easy imperial victory.

In 1629 when Ferdinand issued an edict ordering the restitution of all Church property that had been secularized since the Peace of Augsburg in 1555 and outlawing Calvinism, he must have been confident of victory. But, within a year, the Emperor's confidence was to be shattered by the interference of Sweden.

Italy—a geographical expression

Like Germany, Italy was what Metternich would later call "*ein geographischer Begriff*"—a geographical expression. In the south lay Naples, the capital of a kingdom that included Sicily and Sardinia and formed part of the vast possessions of the King of Spain. The extensive Duchy of Milan was also part of the Spanish Empire. Milan's neighbors—apart from Venice to the east and Switzerland to the north—were the Duchy of Mantua ruled by the Gonzaga family, the Duchy of Modena governed by the House of Este, the Duchy of Parma which was in the hands of the Farnese, the Republic of Genoa to which Corsica belonged until it was sold to France in 1768, and the Piedmontese possessions of the House of Savoy.

Venice

The only powerful non-Spanish states in Italy were the papacy and Venice. The papacy, deeply absorbed as it was in its own affairs, offered little challenge to Spanish control of Italy. Venice, however, weakened though it had been by the loss of much of its empire to the Turks and much of its trade to the nations on the Atlantic seaboard, still retained its independence. In 1570 a 60,000-man Turkish army led by Selim II had landed on the island of Cyprus which the Venetians had held since 1489. The invaders soon occupied most of the island, took the city of Nicosia and slaughtered over 20,000 of its inhabitants. Famagusta held out for nearly a year, but in August, 1571, it too was forced to capitulate. The Turks, breaking the terms of the capitulation flayed the governor alive and despatched his skin stuffed with straw to Constantinople. The loss of Cyprus prevented the Venetians from deriving any lasting benefit from their victory at Lepanto. During the early decades of the seventeenth century, Venice's independence was challenged from two sides. After continuous quarrels with the papacy over disputed territory and over the traditional independence of the Patriarchate of Venice, Pope Paul V (1552–1621) placed the city under an interdict. The Doge and Senate, advised by the distinguished scholar Paolo Sarpi (1552–1623), refused to give way. For a time it seemed possible that the Republic would abandon Roman Catholicism, but eventually the dispute was solved through the mediation of Henry IV. Venice was able to

Claudio Monteverdi.

get rid of the Jesuits, and the Venetian Inquisition was to remain under the control of the main judicial authority, the much feared Council of Ten.

In 1618 a more serious threat was uncovered. For decades Venice had feared attacks from Spain, and it now appeared that the Spanish were attempting to take over the city. The Council of Ten acted with great speed to destroy the conspiracy, and several hundred pro-Spanish citizens were executed. During the early seventeenth century Venice remained a diplomatic center of unrivaled importance. Protestant princes kept permanent embassies there which they could not do elsewhere in Italy; espionage and intrigue flourished; executions and plots became commonplace, but Venice retained its highly valued independence. Indeed, culturally it was at its finest. The splendor of the ceremonies connected with St. Mark's led to a concentration on suitable music.

Although the birth of opera as an art form cannot be traced to Venice—the earliest known opera, *Dafne* (1597), was written by Jacopo Peri (1566–1631), a Florentine—the greatest early master of the art was Claudio Monteverdi (1567–1643), director of the music at St. Mark's, whose *Orfeo* (1607) and *L'Incoronazione di Poppea* (1642) are the outstanding operas of the period. The world's first opera house, the theater of St. Cassian, was opened at Venice in 1637. As a madrigal composer, too, Monteverdi was without peer, while his church music was little less distinguished.

Padua University

Venice's intellectual and cultural distinction was partly due to the University of Padua, whose excellence persuaded the Venetian Senate not to found a university in Venice itself. The astronomer Galileo Galilei (1564–1642) taught at Padua from 1592–1616, and his open support for the Copernican system led to his condemnation. The relative mildness of the Venetian Inquisition encouraged scientific speculation. The arrest of the Pantheistic philosopher Giordano Bruno (1548–1600) by the Venetian Inquisition, which handed him over for execution to the Roman Inquisition, was an isolated incident. Although there were other centers of scientific advance in Italy, and in Rome the Academy of the Lynxes was founded in 1603 as a society for scientific research, Padua was the most distinguished, and biologists and anatomists at Padua did much of the ground work that made possible Harvey's discovery.

Gulielmus
(Magnus ille)
Harveus

Harvey Explains the Circulation of the Blood

1628

The seventeenth-century scientific "establishment" was committed to the theories of Aristotle and his follower—although much later—Galen. It was accepted that blood was manufactured in the liver and distributed from there to all the body's organs. Disagreement was close to blasphemy, but one quiet, conventional, conservative—and stubborn—doctor disagreed. By close observation and experimentation, William Harvey demonstrated the function of the heart and how blood really circulates—and helped set in motion the "Scientific Revolution."

In medicine, physiology and in the way men think about the world around them, and of themselves in relation to their environment, 1628 represents a watershed. It was a year of wars and preparation for wars, when immediate concerns were centered around victory, defeat and survival. Yet, almost unnoticed, the major catalyst of change that made its appearance that year did not originate with kings, princes or generals; it was a slim volume, published in Germany, written by an aging court physician in England. It discussed the circulation of the blood and, almost in whispers, demolished a whole way of thought and feeling.

Before the impact of Galileo and Newton, William Harvey laid down the guidelines of the scientific method in practice and demonstrated the need for accurate, patient observation leading to logical interpretation. He showed that, in a sense, science owes nothing to the past, nothing to the accumulated common wisdom of the ages, but everything to sharp eyes and a clear brain. He was, despite his high social position, one of the first of anti-establishment scientific figures, for he took on not only the ensconced doctrines of the Church and of the medical establishment, but also dared to fly in the face of the newly rediscovered ideas of the Renaissance which found inspiration in the writings of the authors of antiquity. He was one of the very first to demonstrate the use of observation and unprejudiced thinking in scientific inquiry. Today we live with the results not only of his factual discoveries but of the method he had made his own. And he also discovered the true nature of the circulation of the blood, an immense step on the long journey that brought medicine and physiology to its present shape.

Harvey overcame three major forces in his society thereby arousing our sympathy and fellow-feeling: political instability, educational developments and the conscious internationalism of science. All three bring pressures to bear not only on the way people think, on what has been described as the embodiment of science, but also on the all-intrusive daily round that has to be survived. A man in fear of his life tends to think in terms of the immediate.

Harvey's world experienced a time of social and political upheaval. It started with the glow of the Elizabethan era and ended during the Protectorate. The year of Harvey's birth coincides with Drake setting out in the *Golden Hind* to circumnavigate the globe in 1578; he died in 1657, a controversial scientist in social limbo, surrounded by material possessions, leaving an estate of over £2,000. He was a man of the court, a man deeply touched by the rising professionalism of the middle classes through his involvement with the College of Physicians, a scientist whose debates resounded across the whole civilized world. Paradoxically, he was also a very mediocre diagnostician.

Change attended Harvey from the beginning. He was born in Folkestone, the son of a sheep farmer who became prosperous by developing a postal service to London. Later, Harvey's brothers were to achieve eminence as merchants in the City of London. Till the end of his days, the family stayed close-knit; Harvey died in one of his brothers' houses. In 1588 he entered King's School, Canterbury, which had just come through a series of major convulsions. From being a cathedral school it expanded after the dissolution of monasteries in 1539 to become what would today be called a liberal arts college. To complete the story of upheavals, the first headmaster was dismissed for "riott and dronkynness," the second died after two years, but between him and the third one Harvey did obtain probably as good an education as it was possible to have in England.

The next step up the educational ladder was Gonville and Caius College in Cambridge, which

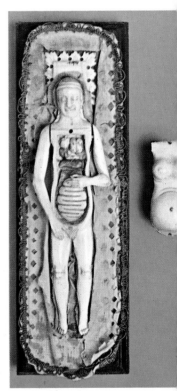

A seventeenth-century Italian anatomical figure. During his studies at Padua University Harvey acquired the professional approach that eschewed received theory and philosophy for pragmatic research and observation.

Opposite William Harvey. His patient research, resulting in discovery of the cardio-vascular system, revolutionized the current theory of medicine.

had itself recently obtained a new charter through the efforts of the redoubtable Dr. Caius, among whose many accomplishments was a calculation proving that Cambridge was founded 1,267 years before Oxford (both were in fact founded in the early twelfth century). Despite a course of study we today would hardly recognize as medical, let alone scientific, Harvey was given a medical scholarship, but—not unreasonably—after three years decided to continue his studies in Padua.

In Padua of the early seventeenth century the university, despite all manner of differences, was similar to its modern counterparts. It had descended from the original of all universities, that of Bologna started about 1088, through the migration of students who had wearied of town-gown confrontations. By Harvey's time Padua could boast 3,000 students, a tolerant and liberal outlook under the protection of Venice, and therefore opposition to papal oppression. Teachers of the caliber of Peter of Abano had shown the way toward the scientific renaissance to come. Here students lived in halls of residence, according to nationalities—a practice still surviving on the Continent—and attended dissections. They were being prepared for a professional middle-class life, rather than for the Church. Harvey's contributions as a scientist have their roots in Padua.

The bombshell that a conventional fifty-year-old court physician and luminary of the College of Physicians eventually dropped into the midst of the scientific establishment of the day drew its force not so much from the facts it contained. After all, medical men had for hundreds of years been arguing about pieces of anatomy and physiology, their patients tamely dying since, despite all the talk, medical care tended to do more harm than good. The essence of Harvey's argument resided in a rejection of philosophy, and what is more, of a newly found philosophy. The pained outcry of scientific contemporaries was the local equivalent of a revisionist's reaction to Mao's claims of truth. Harvey himself went a long way to realize the reasons for this. In the manner of a prudent practitioner, he thought and experimented. He used his position at court to treat the herd of royal deer as experimental animals. He discussed his ideas carefully and let them emerge slowly through a series of lectures, the Lumleian, given to the College of Physicians. He also took the trouble to have the treatise, now entitled *De Motu Cordis* (*On the Motion of the Heart*), printed at Frankfurt in 1628 and in decent obscurity, and remarked that, "I not only fear that I may suffer from the ill will of a few, but dread lest all men turn against me." He was, in all matters outside his work on the heart and circulation, a deeply conventional, conservative man, and his judgment on the reception of his ideas was substantially correct. Yet by that time, at least in England, even physicians had other matters on their minds and the furor sputtered to a standstill.

To understand Harvey, we have to try to look at the world from the point of view of a highly educated scientist and medical man of the early seventeenth century. What he saw, at least in the invigorating atmosphere of northern Italy and western Europe, was a liberation from the intellectual supremacy of the Church and its medieval habits of thought. He was allowed to think and speculate, but his justification was not the scientific revolution which was yet to come. Galileo was a mere dot on the horizon, and the rationalist, quantitative approach of Newton and his progeny was not even a dream. In fact, it was an enemy, for the new revolutionary philosophies drew their inspiration and justification from the rediscovered writings of Greek and Latin authors.

It had developed that in anatomy and physiology self-consistent, fairly logical but generally wrong frames of reference had been drawn up. The reasons were understandable, if we realize that virtually no mechanical aids of any kind were available. The naked eye, a knife and some tourniquets were all the existing laboratory equipment. In medicine, the leading light had been Galen, a physician who had practiced around A.D. 130 and whose influence lasted well into the seventeenth century. By the standards of his time, Galen was an outstanding physician and anatomist who yet had the misfortune of not having enough cadavers to dissect. So, in the absence of anything better, he had to make theory fill the gaps.

The great physiological difficulty that Galen, his precursors and followers had to face was to explain facts that appeared intractable. The problem was to

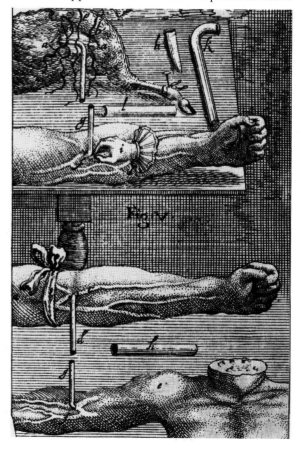

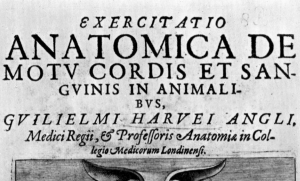

EXERCITATIO
ANATOMICA DE
MOTV CORDIS ET SAN-
GVINIS IN ANIMALI-
BVS,
GVILIELMI HARVEI ANGLI,
Medici Regii, & Profefforis Anatomiæ in Col-
legio Medicorum Londinenfi.

FRANCOFVRTI,
Sumptibus GVILIELMI FITZERI.
ANNO M. DC. XXVIII.

Above Further illustrations from the frontispiece to Galen's collected treatises.

Left The title-page of Harvey's treatise on the circulation of the blood, 1628. Fearful of the consequences to himself of this subversive discovery, Harvey took care to publish in distant Frankfurt. In the event political strife put an end to the ensuing scientific controversy in England.

the right questions, for the frame of reference was wrong—not simply illogical, but wrong. The wrongness was introduced by Aristotle in classical times, for he postulated the existence of four humors, which have survived to the present as descriptions of personality: sanguine, phlegmatic, melancholic and choleric. These four were not emotional states, but rather actual, if intangible and unseeable, presences that had consequential effects on how the body worked. The modern parallel would be the atomic structure which until recently nobody had seen, but the belief in which enabled a satisfactory picture of the world to be built up.

By Galen's time the four humors were simplified to three, "natural," "vital" and "animal" spirits. These formed the conceptual basis of Galen's medical philosophy, providing between them a reasonable explanation of the cardio-vascular (heart and associated pipework) system. Thus the liver made blood and, supplying the veins, distributed it to the body's organs, the heart among them. The venous blood entering the heart continues as arterial blood to the lungs, where it becomes purified. The apparent flow of blood in the veins was attributed to a two-way movement.

Two essential points in this description help to place it in some perspective. First, as far as a doctor's patient was concerned, it did not matter in practice. No treatment did or could take into account the true nature of the cardio–vascular system, and, even if it did, would have had no therapeutic tools at its disposal. Thus, arguments were truly scientific and philosophical rather than functional. Beneath them lay notions about, the nature of the divine will—for did not God create all parts of the body as perfectly as possible? Such ideas contained in themselves a hint that too much inquiry came dangerously close to blasphemy; indeed in the thirteenth century Ibn an Nafis, an early critic of Galen, refused to perform dissections for religious reasons.

The other side of the argument had a more lasting effect and continued beyond Harvey. It was, simply, that the heart—and subsequently the newly discovered circulation—was not associated with any function that blood, whether gently undulating or vigorously circulating, may perform. Harvey himself, once he had proved circulation, did hint at the possibilities that blood might be the means of transporting materials around the body and might therefore be in some way associated with the spreading of disease, but he went no further. Up to his time, the heart was thought to be part of the respiratory system. One view held that the lungs were like the cooling fins of a refrigerator—they served to keep the body temperate. Another ingenious idea originated with Leonardo da Vinci, who thought, on the contrary, that the flow of blood in the heart created so much friction that the body might derive its heat from it.

Despite a theoretical basis which by its very nature insured that significant discoveries could

give an explanation of where the essence, the very self, of an individual resides. Galen inclined to the brain, in opposition to Aristotle, who located it in the heart. But, central organ or not, the heart was clearly an important part of the anatomy. For example, the heart obviously moved in some way; it was connected to a massive pipework that also could be felt to throb; and, as every battlefield bore witness, large quantities of blood were manufactured and stored somewhere. Moreover, the blood was warm. By Galen's time it was also evident that there were two sorts of blood, which today we call arterial and venous blood. They differ in color because, as we now know and as Harvey could not, even after his discovery, color change in blood is due to the presence or absence of oxygen. In other words, blood primarily transports oxygen from the lungs to the tissues and carbon dioxide from the tissues to the lungs. In Galen's time the very idea of oxygen would have been inconceivable, yet the difficulty remained that blood of one color somehow had to turn into blood of a different color. How does one sort of blood turn into another? What is blood for? And what does the heart do? These were questions that had to be answered if the nature of man's body was to be understood. Unfortunately, as later experimentalists were to appreciate, Nature only answers if the right questions are asked.

Galen and all those who followed him over the next fourteen hundred years or so could not ask

Harvey demonstrating to
Charles I. As Physician
in Ordinary to the King his
involvement with the court
caused Harvey to neglect his
duties at St. Bartholomew's.
His Royalist sympathies were
later to bring him into
disfavor with Parliament.

not be made because the right questions could not be asked, anatomical observations went ahead. The two most important were the discovery of valves in the venous system that, it was subsequently found, allowed blood to flow in one direction only. This observation is linked to the name of Cesalpino of Pisa at the end of the sixteenth century. Further, it was more than suspected that there was some circulation of the blood to and from the lungs. This idea was probably first conceived by Leonardo da Vinci, but was published by philosophers such as Servetus, burned at the stake in Geneva for other reasons, and the greatest anatomist of the time, Vesalius, in his book on the fabric of the human body which appeared in 1543. The greatest barrier against jumping to the right conclusions in all these cases was the problem of how blood gets from the right side of the heart to the left, since it obviously cannot simply seep across.

Thus, Harvey set out as a careful observer to clarify a technical point. The logic of his own observations drove him to become a scientific revolutionary who greatly contributed to the overthrow of the Galenic theory of medicine. In his seventy-two-page book he starts by observing, correctly for the first time, that the heart has two separate movements: a contraction—the systole—and a relaxation—the diastole—and that these movements are syncopated. Thus, when the heart is contracting, the arteries dilate to let the blood through. Reasoning based on observation convinced him that the heart was a muscle and indeed that it acted as a pump. The trouble arose when he considered the amount of blood involved, for even

his inaccurate experimental measurements sufficed to show that all the blood going through the heart could not possibly be made by the liver, as stipulated by Galen, in a given time. In effect, the amount of blood going through the heart would have to be greater than the total quantity contained in the body. The same blood must therefore be circulating. This is where the valves come in, since they prevent anything but a unidirectional flow in the system.

The vexatious question of how blood from the right side of the heart commutes to the left was also finally answered. It does so through the lungs, through the pulmonary circulation. This Harvey proved by a simple, logical and gruesome experiment on a hanged man. If the passages from heart to lungs were tied off and one side of the heart transfused with water nothing happened, but once the arteries and veins were untied, the whole lot—water and blood—came through, proving that there was some means of transport within the lungs. The physical passage between arteries and veins Harvey could not discover. This had to wait until the middle of the seventeenth century when the Italian anatomist Marcello Malpighi, now in possession of a microscope, found the capillaries connecting the ends of arteries with those of the veins in a frog's lung.

Malpighi's proof roughly coincides with the general acceptance of Harvey's ideas after an initial outcry. Indeed, by that time, medical authorities were claiming that Harvey was not, after all, the first discoverer. How rapidly his ideas influenced medical teaching is a matter of some argument; for a considerable time the anti-

Galenic tenets promulgated by Harvey were not part of the medical student's curriculum.

To the young Harvey returning from Padua, all this was still in the future. In London he must have appeared as a well-educated, somewhat conventional man, whose family was beginning to make its mark in solid commercial circles. His first appointment was at St. Bartholomew's Hospital, which after forty-eight years' existence decided that a physician would, after all, be needed. As it turned out, Harvey was a dubious bargain, for his later involvement with the court and his journeys to accompany members of the aristocracy cut heavily into the time he could devote to the hospital. Matters came to a head in one of those bitter series of memoranda and resolutions that characterize famous institutions, but the upshot was a strengthening of the physician's position as opposed to the surgeon's.

In 1618, Harvey became Physician Extraordinary to James I. Subsequently he became Physician in Ordinary to Charles I, and later Senior Physician in Ordinary. Throughout his life he was a Loyalist—he accompanied Charles on a number of battles during the Civil War and stayed with him at Oxford between 1632 and 1646. "The King," said Harvey, ". . . is the foundation of his kingdom, the sun of the world around him. . . ." The Parliamentarians did not agree; they looted Harvey's house in London and later fined him £2,000. Under the circumstances he was reasonably lucky.

Harvey's second major contribution to medical science was his *De Generatione Animalium* (*Essays on the Generation of Animals*), published in 1651. Although, like the book on circulation, it contains a great deal of acute and careful observation and shows that Harvey had a good appreciation of the circulation within the placenta, this is an area where the lack of a microscope was proving insurmountable. *De Generatione* is a compendium, a summing up of existing knowledge, which cannot be compared with the influence of *De Motu Cordis*.

After Oxford fell in 1646, Harvey returned to London where he took renewed interest in the College of Physicians, of which he had been a member since 1604. It availed him little. He was now an old man of sixty-eight; his short-lived marriage during the early days of the century had produced no child. He spent his time wandering among the houses of his brothers, silent and increasingly eccentric. He was helped by a preparation of opium which he kept in his study to take to alleviate the pain of the severe gout from which he was suffering.

On June 3, 1657, he lost his power of speech, and in the words of the chronicler John Aubrey, "He knew then there was no hopes of his recovery . . . his Apothecary . . . lett him blood in the Tongue, which did little or no good; and so ended his dayes."

In Harvey's time, the complex and fast methods of communication existing today were absent.

Scientists wrote letters to each other and occasionally published books. Thus it is hardly surprising that the factual content of Harvey's discovery took many years to filter into accepted medical practice. Once established as a part of common knowledge, reinforced by the subsequent availability of the microscope, it allowed the development of accurate anatomical and physiological knowledge over the next two centuries. Harvey's discovery, together with his power within the medical establishment of the day and the slow progress made by surgery, insured the supremacy of physicians over surgeons until the advent of the pioneers of the nineteenth century and the subsequent surgical feats of today.

Harvey's contribution to the general condition of human thought is perhaps not a precise one, but is highly important. Unlike Galileo, he had no need to retract his views or advance quietly when the authorities were looking the other way. Yet he is one of the first representatives of a breed of well-educated, middle-class, obstinate thinkers and doers who, having made up their minds, held to their own views whatever the opposition. They were revolutionaries despite themselves. They had little quarrel with the structure of society and little realized that their ideas and their ways of thinking, would do more to change society and its works than all the potentates and revolutionaries put together. Harvey made his discovery and stuck to it; he could have said with Fouché, the survivor of a later and bloodier revolution: "*J'ai vecu*," "I survived".

PETER FARAGO

Illustration from a seventeenth-century medical textbook by John Banister of Glasgow, showing instruments such as Harvey used. A pig is being dissected while a monkey awaits its turn. Laws limiting human dissection, however, forced Harvey to work in secret.

English colonialism

For several years after the sailing of the *Mayflower* in 1620, few Englishmen were adventurous enough to make the dangerous and fearfully uncomfortable Atlantic crossing. The prospects on arrival were bleak, and only those whose religious faith was certain, whose sense of adventure was acute, whose ambition was intense or whose debts were overwhelmingly pressing chose to hazard their future by making the long journey. As the colonies prospered, however, new companies were founded and new charters were granted. And as the determination of William Laud to impose uniformity upon the Church of England increased in intensity, the number of emigrants also increased. By the mid-1630s depopulation had become a serious social problem in several areas of England, and the government was obliged to issue proclamations against emigration. Those edicts notwithstanding, more than 60,000 people left England between 1630 and 1643, and a third of them settled in New England.

At first the English government and the Church were glad to see the Puritans leave the country, taking their heresies with them. America was thought of as a useful depository for tiresome, nonconforming Protestants who would otherwise stir up trouble at home. The American colonies, in the words of Peter Heylin, the Archbishop's senior chaplain, were "like the spleen of the natural body, not unuseful and unserviceable to the general health by drawing to it so many sullen, sad and offensive humours." Within twenty years of the *Mayflower's* departure that spleen had become too full. There was a real fear in England that the offensive nature of the religion practiced in the American colonies—which had previously been of little interest and had consequently gone unchecked—would spread to the home country. It was decided that an Anglican bishop would have to be dispatched to New England and that troops would have to go with him to force the colonists to mend their ways and join the one true Church. This drastic proposal came to nothing, however, for there were troubles enough at home.

But even if a bishop had been dispatched there can be no doubt that his mission would have met with small success, for Puritanism was by now an essential element in New England life, and New England was becoming increasingly independent of the old. The New England Company, which had been organized in London in 1628 to provide a refuge for discontented Puritans as well as a profit for the shareholders, had been transformed into the Massachusetts Bay Company shortly thereafter. Within a matter of months the government of the extensive territories controlled by the Company was transferred from England to America, and it was soon established that no one could aspire to the privileges of a freeman unless he accepted the Puritan creed and conformed to Puritan morality. In 1634 with the growth of the colony a representative system was introduced. And since it was only freemen who could name "assistants"—the men who in turn named the governor—political power was firmly lodged in Puritan hands from the beginning. It would have taken more than a lone Anglican bishop to wrest it from them.

Religious intolerance

Although the emigrants had gone to America in search of religious freedom, they had, upon arrival, been remarkably intolerant of those who would not accept their own faith. Moreover, their elected leaders had been less than indulgent in their treatment of the sinners in their midst. Baptists were penalized, and in all of the New England colonies acts were passed to exclude or punish Quakers. The death penalty or various forms of mutilation were imposed for idolatry, blasphemy and adultery. A man who denied the existence of the Devil might have a hole bored in his tongue with a hot iron, and offenses as venial as smoking and wearing unseemly clothes were also considered crimes.

Yet cruel and absurd as their intolerance now seems to us, neither the Puritan colonists nor the zealots from whom they had fled were in conflict with the commonly held views of their time. Religious toleration was considered scarcely more acceptable in the first half of the seventeenth century than it had been in the days of Erasmus and Montaigne, for religion was not thought of as a private matter between God and a man's conscience, but was inextricably bound up with society and politics. It kept a king's subjects in obedience—and because it did so it became the direct concern of the state. (Such a view was not unique to England and its American colonies; it applied with even greater force on the Continent of Europe where the fundamental issues had not yet been resolved.)

The issue was not simply one of conflict between Roman Catholics and Protestants. On the Roman Catholic side for example, there were two rival defenders of the Church of Rome, two forces propagating the Counter-Reformation from different standpoints. There were the Capuchins, an order of friars who had broken away from the Franciscans and were particularly influential in France; and there were the Jesuits, members of the Society of Jesus founded by the Spaniard Ignatius Loyola in 1534. On the Protestant side there were also two main movements, the Lutherans and the Calvinists. Those rival factions were as essentially different as the two men from whom they took their names—the earthy, ebullient, self-critical German monk and the austere, polite, reserved French scholar. John Calvin's teaching represented more than a new theology; indeed, what Calvin proffered was a new political theory. He envisaged a theocratic state in which the full

Complaints against Puritan laws banning selling on Sundays.

The Orthodox true Minister,   the Seducer and false Prophet.

A seventeenth-century contrast: the orthodox true minister (left), and the seducer and false prophet.

mirrors the conflicts of the Old

privileges of the Church were reserved for those of proved godliness, a society in which pastors and laymen alike were subject to scrutiny and control by a council representative of the community and answerable to no one but God. It was a teaching that formed a direct challenge to monarchic government, one that allied itself to the growing forces of republicanism. Its followers were natural enemies of popery—and if there was one thing a Calvinist disliked as much as a papist it was a Lutheran. From the beginning of the seventeenth century the quarrel between Protestant and Roman Catholic had been threatening to erupt into war and when war did come at last in Europe, the reciprocated antipathy of the Calvinists and the Lutherans added to its protracted bitterness and tragedy.

Witchcraft

The intolerance that characterized religious disputes was to some extent due to the political differences enshrined in the different religious confessions. Less rational was the hatred that was felt for witchcraft. In an age of widespread scientific advance there erupted an irrational belief in demonology both among the few who practiced witchcraft and among the many who feared its practice and sought to extirpate it by punishment. The witch craze reached its height in the first half of the seventeenth century. Both in relatively civilized countries like France and in more backward ones such as Austria witchcraft beliefs became for a brief period almost universal; to express a disbelief in witchcraft was to invite

The hanging of witches in Essex.

the accusation of being a witch.

The cause of this phenomenon was probably in large measure the religious hatred and warfare that sprang up between Roman Catholics and Protestants; it cannot be completely accidental that it coincided with the French religious wars, with the Thirty Years War and with the English civil wars, all of which had strong religious roots. As religious fanaticism declined so did the accusations of witchcraft. But religion was not the only cause; social discontent played a part, and there was an element of mass hysteria in many of the wilder accusations. The hysteria was particularly apparent in the famous case of the French priest Urban Grandier in the 1630s. He was accused of being possessed by the devil, and the nuns of the convent of which he was chaplain all showed signs of possession also.

The existence of belief in witchcraft is an important reminder that even an apparently rational society often has a strong element of the irrational within it. Other societies have not been immune to similar flights from the rational, as the persecution of Jews in early twentieth-century Russia and Nazi Germany shows.

The French colonize Canada

After the failure of their early attempts to found colonies in parts of America occupied by the Spanish and the Portuguese, for a time no further French efforts were made. But Henry IV, perhaps influenced by the English example, encouraged a Protestant settlement at Port Royal in Acadia (now Annapolis Royal, Nova Scotia) in 1605, and a further settlement in Quebec was made by Samuel Champlain (1567–1635). The success of these settlements encouraged others to try. In 1629 Cardinal Richelieu founded the Company of New France to regulate and finance the North American colonies. The colonists were able to support themselves by farming, while the export of furs, which they acquired by barter with the Indians rather than by themselves hunting, provided prosperity. But French colonization was far slower than English. While England encouraged religious noncomformists whether Roman Catholic or Puritan to

Onondaga Fort in the Iroquois country, one of Champlain's settlements.

emigrate, the French tried to prevent Huguenots from settling in their colonies. By about 1640 there were probably 35,000 English colonists in North America but only about 3,000 French. In the West Indies, too, English settlement was far more rapid than French.

Despite the vast spaces available for settlement, the English and French colonists were very soon at war with each other. Port Royal was captured by the English in 1627, and Quebec in 1629. Although both were returned in 1632, the rivalry between England and France in the colonies was to continue and indeed to become fiercer as time passed.

The Dutch, too, having thrown off the Spanish yoke were beginning to look abroad. As early as 1605 the Dutch seized Amboyna in Malaysia from the Portuguese. Their colonization spread rapidly thereafter, particularly in the East.

Louis XIII

The course of seventeenth-century monarchy in France was one of increasing absolutism. After the

horrors of the sixteenth-century wars of religion, Frenchmen appeared to be willing to accept any intrusion of royal power into their lives—a practical demonstration of the ideas of the sixteenth-century French theorist Jean Bodin. Henry IV began the trend to totalitarian government. He refused to summon the Estates–General, which he regarded as a threat to his power. He did not abolish the local privileges of taxation in Normandy and other areas but he made sure that the taxes were paid in full. Nor did he object to the legal privileges of the *Parlement* of Paris provided that it did not conflict with his wishes.

After Henry's assassination the monarchy was hardpressed. Marie de' Medici, the regent for the new King, Louis XIII (1601–43) was unable to prevent the loss of royal power to local lords. A meeting of the Estates–General in 1614 (the last to be summoned before 1789) ended in confusion. In 1617 the King declared himself of age, a declaration that his mother refused at first to accept. There was a real danger of civil war between mother and son. The Huguenots, too, were becoming restless. It was not until 1624, when Louis appointed Cardinal Armand du Plessis de Richelieu (1585–1642) as his chief minister, that peace became possible. It was Richelieu who was to be the real builder of French absolutism. The Cardinal at once set about reestablishing the authority of the central government in military, political and religious affairs. Abroad, too, he sought to strengthen France by opposing the traditional enemy of the French monarchy, the Hapsburgs. It was inevitable that his policies would make him enemies, and in 1630 he determined to overcome the opposition in France.

The last Estates-General held by Louis XIII in 1614.

The Day of the Dupes

1630

In an attempt to gain power over the stubborn but indecisive King Louis XIII, a royal cabal including the Queen Mother, the heir presumptive to the throne and a group of powerful nobles plotted to kill Richelieu, the King's minister. Told of the plot by the erstwhile assassin, Richelieu foiled it. An aftermath was Louis' decision to rely on Richelieu and quell any pretentions to power on the Queen Mother's part. France was thereby finally freed of the royal family feuds that for so long had torn the fabric of national unity.

In literature, seventeenth-century France is known primarily for its theater. More gripping than any drama, however, is the real-life conflict known as the Day of the Dupes. Considered by some to have been one of the thirty or so momentous days of history that made France what it is, and by others as a red-letter day in the history of modern Europe, this truly French drama required the minimum of physical action and the smallest of casts. In fact, there were only three principal characters in the play, the denouement of which was to determine the very existence of an effective French monarchy, by freeing it from the influences of family feuds and the power of the great nobles.

First, there was the King, Louis XIII, a man who was not robust and indeed was constantly threatened by tuberculosis, which hung over him like the sword of Damocles and made him even more nervous than he was by nature. For all his timidity, Louis was stubborn and determined to be truly regal. He trusted no one for long, which made relationships difficult. Moreover, being on the whole more interested in men than women, he tended to select his favorites from his male entourage and abandon them when his inclinations cooled, which was rather an insecure basis for politics.

Although he was only twenty-nine in 1630, he had been married for fifteen barren years to Anne of Austria. This marriage was strangely prophetic of that of his descendant, Louis XVI, who was to dabble in manual occupations like metalwork, rather than in the arts of seduction and gallantry and who likewise was to have so many inhibitions that his wife became his enemy.

Louis XIII longed to be physically tough and delighted in campaigning, which took him away from the women he feared and into the restless activity that had become his essential way of life. His relations with Richelieu, his Chancellor, were unstable and charged with emotion. Louis enjoyed domination by this clever man, especially since he was a prince of the Church, for Louis was also pious. However, in contradiction to what Alexandre Dumas was to suggest about this relationship in *The Three Musketeers*, Louis asserted his royal authority and was seconded in this by the Cardinal who, far from trying to outwit the King, depended utterly upon Louis for his very survival.

Like all geniuses, Richelieu was a complex being. Thirteen years older than his master, he had had a checkered career, always motivated by the need to wield power. Attached to the Queen Mother at Blois, he had tasted the delights of proximity to the royal family, but favor from the mother meant dislike from the son, and this he judged damaging to his ultimate ambitions. Therefore he had exiled himself to his own diocese and for a time had become a conscientious bishop. But ambition would not allow him to remain in obscurity and Richelieu began to realize that if he were ever to make himself irresistible to the King he would have to wear the cardinal's hat and rise on the crest of ecclesiastical power. His determination received its reward in 1622, when he was made Cardinal, and in 1624, when the King asked him to lead the royal council. Some idea of the Cardinal's conception of his new role is provided by the promise which he made to the monarch on attaining high office, "to employ all my diligence and all the authority which it pleased your Majesty to bestow upon me in bringing down the Protestant Party, in humbling the mighty, in leading your Majesty's subjects back into the paths of duty and in exalting your name among foreign nations to a level it richly deserves." Thus, by 1630 he had become the King's right-hand man, utterly devoted to the throne and the national unity it must ultimately symbolize.

Armand Jean du Plessis, Cardinal and Duke of Richelieu, by Philippe de Champagne.

Opposite Louis XIII attaining his majority, by Rubens. The highly strung Louis reacted to his forceful mother, Marie de' Medici, by placing himself under the domination of her former protégé and rival, Richelieu.

A sketch of Louis XIII marching toward La Rochelle, the Huguenot stronghold captured in 1628 as part of Richelieu's campaign to strengthen the French monarchy by eradicating heresy and regionalism. Richelieu, who personally supervised the siege, accompanies the King.

An allegorial portrayal of the extirpation of Heresy and Rebellion: Richelieu plucks a caterpillar from the *fleur de lys*.

In 1630 Marie de' Medici, the Queen Mother, was fifty-five. Florentine by birth, she had a difficult life with her husband, Henry IV, who had constantly and openly preferred his mistresses and humiliated her by his attitude and behavior, which were difficult to tolerate because she was both passionate and sentimental. Since then, she had enjoyed power during her own regency and had undergone the bitter experience of relinquishing that power in favor of her son. The wound was the more painful since her intelligence was far beneath her emotional capacities. By no means an astute politician, Marie had failed to retain her

hold securely over her "ungrateful" son. For his ingratitude she had only herself to blame, because, during his formative years, she had clearly favored his brother Gaston, to such an extent that Henry IV often reproached his wife for being totally indifferent toward the Dauphin. These reproaches proved to be in vain, for Marie would intervene with the governess only to recommend even more severe beatings. In 1630, Louis still recalled this unhappy past and its accompanying injustices, and could never forgive his mother. The mother sensed this and yearned more desperately than ever for his royal favor, and this, in its turn, made the King increasingly disgusted with her. Richelieu recognized the problem, for he too had had disagreeable experiences with the Queen Mother and judged her not only to be bad for the King but also for France.

For some time the peace and internal security of the realm had been put at risk by family rivalries and political intrigues in high places, almost all centered around one person. Of the surviving children of Henry IV, there remained at court only one, Gaston, Duke of Anjou, who was still his mother's favorite and led a useless, dissipated existence. But he was approaching his majority and, since Louis XIII was still childless, was regarded as the most probable heir to the throne. The absolute incompatibility between Louis and Anne seemed to guarantee that this state of affairs would continue into the forseeable future. True, after the Duke of Luynes had forcibly persuaded the young King to consummate his marriage, there had been a miscarriage, but after this the royal pair appeared to have had no intimate relations. To heighten the tension, Gaston was now of marriageable age. His children might therefore turn the line of succession toward the Orleanist branch—a prospect unpalatable to most Frenchmen. It happened that Henry IV (and

indeed Marie de' Medici too) had planned that Gaston should marry the wealthy and noble Mademoiselle de Bourbon-Montpensier. This union would keep an important alliance as well as a considerable fortune within the confines of the royal family. After much initial hesitation, Richelieu concluded that the interests of the monarchy and the realm would best be served by accepting the late King's advice on this matter.

As usual, Richelieu's policies were opposed by the clique of nobles surrounding the Duke of Anjou, including the powerful Prince of Condé, who wished Gaston to marry his daughter; by the Count of Soissons who wanted the rich Montpensier heiress for himself; and by Anne of Austria who hated the Cardinal and, being without child, did not wish to be eclipsed by a future sister-in-law. At this point another enemy, Gaston's tutor, d'Ornano, began to be blatant in his arrogance and, suspecting that he was encouraging Gaston to be rebellious, Richelieu had d'Ornano confined at Vincennes. This act inflamed the princely cabal, but the Cardinal stood his ground and, when Gaston approached him about his tutor, explained that the arrest had been necessary to his (Richelieu's) safety and that of the realm. Richelieu's safety was indeed a problem, as immediately subsequent events showed. Eager for revenge, the cabal made plans to assassinate the Cardinal-Minister at his country house of Fleury, in the forest of Fontainebleau. The scheme appealed to the women too, especially to Madame de Chevreuse who, wishing Gaston to marry Anne of Austria should the sickly Louis XIII die, persuaded one of her lovers, the foolish young Count of Chalais, to play a central role. Six days later, the Count incautiously revealed the plot to his uncle and then, on his uncle's advice, to Richelieu. The Cardinal listened quietly to the Count's confession, and then told him that he was forgiven. The other conspirators gathered at Fleury and Richelieu, offering them the hospitality of his house, went quickly to Fontainebleau Palace, where he confronted Gaston in bed. Richelieu placed himself at the Duke's disposal and fell silent. Gaston, obviously shaken that the plot had miscarried, dismissed the Cardinal with his thanks.

Obviously, the matter could not end there. Angered by yet another example of the reckless plotting inspired by the royal heir, Richelieu promptly offered his resignation, which Louis declined. However, the heir to the throne was of course unassailable. The ensuing reconciliation, though touching, was quite insincere, the brother promising to revere "as one does a father" his king and sovereign lord. The Queen Mother was asked to act as guarantor in the change of heart. She was delighted. Weeping copiously, raising her eyes and hands to the heavens and asking her Creator for the concord, greatness and happiness of her two sons, she conjured them in the name of the Almighty to remain forever united and love each other with all their hearts. Richelieu, who

had a taste for the theatrical, enjoyed the scene which, in a sense, he had written in advance. Furthermore, he was probably the only sincere member of the group, desiring as he did that the royal trio, on whose cooperation he really depended, should indeed be reconciled once and for all.

He was not deceived, of course; the realist in him prevailed. Continuing therefore to maintain relations with the heir presumptive, he nonetheless took the opportunity to warn this dangerous scion of the royal house that he was being misled by bad counselors. For Richelieu knew that the plot was by no means extinguished and so, when the court moved to Nantes, he decided that Gaston's marriage should be hastened and the cabal exposed. On July 9, 1626, the Count of Chalais was arrested. Richelieu decided that he must be made an example of, and retracted his pardon. The Count's royal accomplice and friend now knew that all things would be revealed and that the best course of action open to him was to throw himself upon the Cardinal's good will. He consented to be wed and was created Duke of Orleans. Chalais was beheaded in a particularly revolting, brutal and clumsy manner.

In 1627–28 Richelieu, who was by temperament and inclination a soldier rather than a cleric, successfully besieged La Rochelle and thus dealt a blow to the fractious Protestant minority at home; but foreign affairs were now presenting problems and, once the Protestants had been dealt with, he departed with his King to campaign in Italy. There the Duke of Savoy had claimed Montferrat for his granddaughter, niece of the late duke of that territory; but the Dowager Duchess of Lorraine claimed the same dukedom, and Spain joined in to help Savoy. France could not stand aside while these complicated political maneuvers were taking place, and in the winter of 1628–29, Louis XIII and his army crossed the Alps. Austria joined against France and hostilities continued until September, when a truce was concluded. Richelieu then hoped that Father Joseph, his indefatigable emissary, would obtain from the

A contemporary engraving of the Luxembourg Palace, scene of the drama that determined the existence of effective monarchy in France.

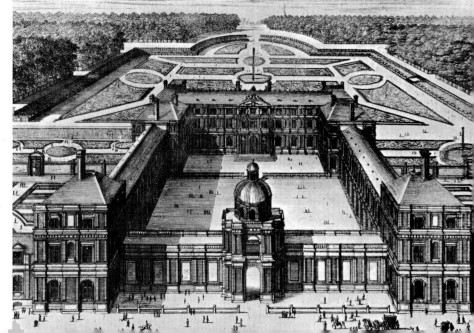

A portrait of Louis XIII by Vouet. Although under the influence of others all his life, Louis, by throwing his weight behind Richelieu in his confrontation with the Queen Mother, changed the internal balance of power. Henceforth the French monarch was absolute.

Austrian Emperor a suitable treaty at Ratisbon.

Released temporarily from military duties, the King, who was suffering from dysentery, left the army and in July, 1630, returned to Lyons, where he became rapidly more unwell until, by the end of September, he was near death. Both queens, Marie, his mother, and Anne, his wife, tended the tormented monarch with exemplary devotion, a situation which gave them certain advantages. For example, Marie, who had begun to detest Richelieu more than she had ever done before, persuaded the ailing monarch to agree to dismiss his minister. On the morning of September 20, the doctors decided that the King would not survive the day, but late in the afternoon the intestinal abcess that had been causing his distress burst of its own accord and the patient escaped peritonitis. Richelieu was relieved, if only because his own survival depended on the survival of his master.

Slowly the royal party came back to Paris in a barge along the Loire River. All was cordial between the Cardinal and the royal family, who had to admit that there was merit in his foreign policy—an opinion borne out in October when Mazarin, who was already acting as agent, managed to arrange a peace in Italy more favorable than the one achieved at Ratisbon. Home at last in the capital, Marie de' Medici went to the Luxembourg Palace and, since the Louvre and the Palais-Cardinal (Royal) were not at that time

habitable, Louis set up his quarters in the Rue de Tournon, near the theater now known as the Odéon. Richelieu installed himself close to the Queen Mother in the Petit-Luxembourg. The dominant trio were thus within a few hundred yards of each other in the heart of Paris. On November 10, 1630, at an early hour, Richelieu called upon the Queen Mother to present his compliments and was surprised to learn that she was not receiving, being in conference with the King. His suspicions aroused, the Cardinal immediately resolved to be bold. Aware of a back passage by way of the chapel, he entered the Queen's apartment to the great astonishment of its two occupants.

The air inside was heavy with expectancy, for the exposition was already complete. No doubt now that the Queen Mother had been settling his destiny, Richelieu thought, for the pallid Louis appeared both cowed and sheepish, while the stout Queen Mother was flushed with obvious triumph. Richelieu said quickly, "I am sure you are discussing me. Admit it, Madame." Marie attempted to deny the charge, then, reversing her ground said defiantly, "Oh well, yes, we were indeed discussing you, most ungrateful and troublesome of men," and began to reproach the Cardinal not only with bad policies, but with improprieties in his private life as well. This was followed by a torrent of abuse, seasoned with court gossip and various anecdotes. The King had a strong sense of what constituted proper royal behavior and he had heard enough. "Madam, what are you doing? What are you saying?" he asked with annoyance. She rounded sharply upon him, accusing him of preferring a mere "servant" to herself. Meanwhile, his nerves now stretched to the utmost, the Cardinal was on his knees, weeping profusely. The Queen screamed at him and then a minute later burst into tears herself. Louis was upset too, not enjoying the struggle for the possession of his soul that raged around him. Paler than ever, he asked the Cardinal to withdraw, saluted his mother and left the room.

As he passed through the Cour d'Honneur, the King encountered Richelieu again, this time bowing obsequiously, but Louis paid no attention to the minister and entered his coach without a single word. The Cardinal was now thoroughly worried, especially when his closest advisers recommended that he flee. Le Havre, of which he happened to be the governor, offered the most hopeful prospects of safety, for there he could immure himself in the massive fortress and weather out the storm. Still, he could not make up his mind. Meanwhile Marie's spies had observed the royal coldness toward the Cardinal and hurried to assure her that there was nothing more to worry about. People were even offering their services for the new cabinet, purged of the Cardinal's influence. However, the significant action was taking place a few leagues to the west.

Having reached his temporary residence in the Rue de Tournon, the King gave vent to his pent-up emotions. In the afternoon, feeling calmer, he decided to seek the peace of his hunting lodge, one day to be famous as Louis XIV's great Palace of Versailles. As he set forth, Louis wondered if the root of all the trouble and the most menacing danger, not only to himself but to France, was not his mother's influence. He made his decision, and signaled that Richelieu should join him at the country palace. There the two had another

emotional scene, in the course of which the King expressed full confidence in the Cardinal-Minister. The great drama was over. What a curious reversal of hopes and fears! Near-dismissal in the forenoon; complete restoration of his powers in the afternoon. Richelieu was never to forget that exhausting day, when the three dominant personalities in French politics battled for mastery and, in the end, his monarch assured him: "Stay close to me and I will protect you from all your enemies."

It is significant that it was Louis XIII who rang down the curtain on the drama and on July 10, 1631, dared inform his mother that she must change her attitude toward the Cardinal and his policies. Marie and her party were now a laughing stock. Inflamed with anger, unwilling to forget the humiliation of that terrible day, when both parties had misinterpreted the King's wishes, she decided to seek the relative peace of the frontier area to the north and then passed into Holland, finally ending her days in melancholic retreat at Cologne in Germany. Meanwhile her chief rival was made a duke by his grateful master. France had turned an important corner in her history. The balance of internal power had shifted significantly. No longer would a sovereign be subjected to endless family feuds. No longer would a minister of the crown wonder whether his power was insubstantial and whether the court cared about the nation he was endeavoring to serve to the best of his ability. It is true that the uprising of the Fronde was soon to come with its further discordant scenes and armed violence, but they only served to make the new monarch more determined to assert his authority when he came to maturity. Indeed, standing back from the canvas of the whole seventeenth century, one can see that the sun had already begun to break through the clouds of dissension and disunity on the Day of the Dupes.   JOHN LAURENCE CARR

Above The uprising of the Fronde: the Prince of Condé gives battle at St. Antoine, July 2, 1652. This was the last attempt of the French nobility to oppose the court by armed resistance.

Left Marie de' Medici, Dowager Queen of France. Until her death she plotted vainly against Richelieu.

Richelieu establishes the absolute power

The rule of Richelieu

As a result of his victories over the Queen Mother and her allies in the Day of the Dupes, Richelieu's already substantial power was enlarged. Although Louis XIII did not like him personally, the Cardinal could rely on his continuing support. If Louis XI and Henry IV were the founders of French absolutism, if Bodin was its architect and Louis XIV its ultimate expression, Richelieu was its builder. It was Richelieu who made the absolutism of Louis XIV possible.

Richelieu's domestic policy was founded on the destruction of all privileges that conflicted in any way with those of the crown. "Reason of State" was the motivation for almost all his actions, and he thought that the state's highest interest could only be fulfilled by giving the government absolute power. Everything else was subordinate to that aim. Richelieu's ambition was for the state rather than himself, and Louis' recognition of that was the basis of his continuing power. Richelieu and his chief adviser, the Capuchin friar Father Joseph (1577–1638), who was far more interested in mysticism than in politics, lived in a state of almost total detachment from the life of the court.

The nobility and the Huguenots

The two main obstacles to Richelieu's plans were the residual power of the nobility and the independence of the Huguenots. The Huguenots were a smaller problem than the nobility because they practically constituted an independent state within the state, while the nobility were an important part of the establishment, without whose support the government could not easily act. The main center of Huguenot power was the city of La Rochelle, which was captured in 1628, largely because of the inept handling of an English relief attempt led by the Duke of Buckingham. But the destruction of Huguenot power was merely political. Richelieu did not attempt to prevent the Huguenots from worshiping in their own way, and he did not revoke the basic charter of their rights, the Edict of Nantes.

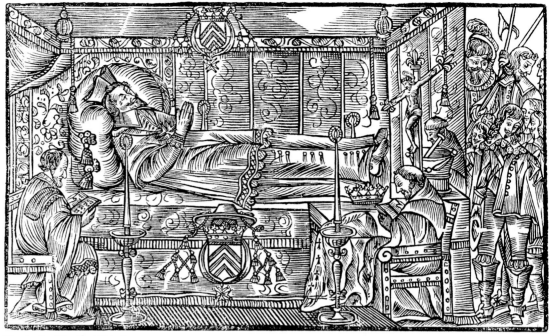

The death of Cardinal Richelieu.

The attack on the nobility was more far reaching. The whole aristocratic ethos had to be changed. Richelieu began the movement toward changing the old territorially based aristocracy into a court aristocracy, whose life was centered on the life of the court, a trend that was to be continued successfully by Louis XIV. In order to achieve this, legislation was necessary. Duelling was banned; the power of the provincial governors was reduced; the fortifications of castles that were not essential for the country's defense were removed. Even the greatest families of France felt the effect of his edicts. The main feudal offices of state, such as the High Constableship of France, which carried enormous power, were either abolished or drastically reduced in power. Inevitably, such changes provoked an aristocratic reaction, and there were several ineffective attempts by nobles to regain their lost privileges by rebellion; these were put down with great brutality. Richelieu was able to use the rebellions as an excuse for further attacks on aristocratic power. Instead of spending time on their country estates, the nobles were encouraged to come to court and compete for offices—usually honorific —in order to give them something to do.

The main effect of the change was felt in the provinces, where *intendants* appointed by the crown became the chief officials. The power of the *intendants* was directly dependent on the crown, and they were immediately responsible to Richelieu. As a means of reducing local autonomy, they proved highly effective. Under Richelieu, France became the first large country in modern Europe in which the central government could make its autonomy felt everywhere.

Foreign policy

Richelieu's foreign policy was far more complicated. The basic aim was simple enough: to reduce the power of the Hapsburgs, both in Spain and in Austria. But the aim was enormously complicated by the need to do this without strengthening the Protestant cause in Germany too much—Richelieu was, after all, a prince of the Roman Church. The Cardinal sought to use the Protestants in the Thirty Years War by giving them large subsidies to attack the Hapsburgs. The Swedes, in particular, benefited from this policy. The success of Richelieu's policy was shown in 1639, when one of his anti-imperial allies, Bernard of Saxe-Weimar, died, leaving Alsace to France. Eventually France was dragged into the fighting, but the victory over the Spanish at Rocroi in 1643, six months after Richelieu's death, showed that French arms were equal to French diplomacy.

Yet, despite the brilliant success of his domestic policy and the destruction of Hapsburg hopes in Germany, Richelieu's policy was expensive and left France financially weak. Louis XIV inherited financial problems which even the ability of Colbert could not overcome. Indeed, finance was to prove an endemic problem in the sort of society that Richelieu and, later, Louis XIV sought to create. Large handouts to client rulers abroad, the upkeep of huge armies and expensive prestige projects, such as the rebuilding of much of the University of Paris, exhausted all the resources that Richelieu could find.

It is even possible that had Richelieu lived longer he would have been overthrown. In 1642, the Marquis of Cinq-Mars (1620–42), a favorite of Louis XIII, attempted to do so, and only at the last moment did the King show his support for his minister. The words that he used, "We have been together for too long to part now," show a grudging rather than an enthusiastic favor. After the Cardinal's death, the King showed little respect for his memory.

The rule of Mazarin

The day after Cardinal Richelieu died, on December 5, 1642, King Louis XIII issued a circular-letter to France's *intendants* and other leading officials, ordering them

of the French monarchy

The siege of the Huguenot city of La Rochelle by the French fleet in 1627.

to send their regular reports to another cardinal, Jules Mazarin. Mazarin, who was originally Giulio Mazarini, was the son of a Sicilian father and of a mother who was related to the ancient Roman family of the Colonnas. He was born in Abruzzi in 1602, educated by the Jesuits in Rome and at the University of Alcala in Spain, and before he had reached the age of thirty he had distinguished himself as a diplomat in the service of Pope Urban VIII. In 1634 Mazarin became papal nuncio at the French court, where his ingratiating charm and brilliant intellectual attainments so recommended themselves to Cardinal Richelieu that he was persuaded to abandon his former employer and enter the service of Louis XIII. He became a naturalized Frenchman, and was elevated to the cardinalate in 1641 (after his triumphant success in establishing Louis XIII's sister, the Duchess of Savoy, in the regency of Savoy after the death of her husband). A year later, at the age of thirty-nine, he succeeded Richelieu as France's chief minister.

Mazarin was an ambitious and avaricious man—cunning, devious and intuitive. Well aware that the sickly and lethargic Louis XIII did not have long to live, the Cardinal concentrated on winning the trust and affection of the King's wife, Anne, daughter of Philip III of Spain. Anne was a neglected wife as well as an attractive and responsive woman, and Mazarin had no difficulty in winning her trust and, indeed, her devotion. Upon her husband's death in 1643 she was appointed regent,

and Mazarin's position as supreme minister remained secure.

Jansenism

The close cultural links between parts of Europe that disagreed both in politics and in religion can be seen in the widespread belief in witchcraft and also in the theological disputes that racked the Churches during the seventeenth century. The controversy over predestination that had led to the Synod of Dort was not ended by it, even in Holland, where the fierce persecution of Arminians continued almost until the end of the seventeenth century.

In the Roman Catholic Church, too, the problem was alive. During the sixteenth century, Jesuit theologians such as Luis de Molina and Leonhard Lessius (1554–1623) had taught a doctrine similar to that of Arminius, while the Dominicans had upheld a more Augustinian doctrine of Grace, stressing man's helplessness and original sin. The Jesuits were soon accusing the Dominicans of Calvinism, while the Dominicans replied by accusing the Jesuits of Pelagianism. In an unsuccessful attempt to settle the dispute, which was rapidly bringing the whole Roman Catholic Church into disrepute, Pope Clement VIII (1536–1605) set up the Congregation de Auxiliis to examine the whole question of Divine Grace, and his successor, Paul V, attempted—equally unsuccessfully—to ban all discussion of the subject.

In 1640 the debate burst out with renewed force. A huge

volume, the *Augustinus*, by the recently deceased Bishop of Ypres, Cornelius Jansenius (1585–1638), was published. It claimed to present Augustine's views on Grace, but was in reality a thorough attack on Jesuit teaching over a wide range of subjects. The Jesuits got five propositions from the *Augustinus* condemned by Pope Innocent X (1574–1655) in 1653, but, particularly in France and the Netherlands, the book found many supporters. Gallicans and enemies of the Jesuits found a common cause in the book's defense. The center of the opposition was a highly talented group that was associated with the nunnery of Port Royal, whose spiritual director, Jean Duvergier de Hauranne (1581–1643), Abbé of St. Cyran, had been Jansenius' closest friend. The main line of defense was that the doctrines attributed to Jansenius by Innocent X could be found nowhere in the *Augustinus*. Jansenism became an increasingly important theological controversy as the century progressed, and as late as 1715 had to be condemned in the most energetic terms in the bull *Unigenitus* by Pope Clement XI (1649–1721), and Louis XIV suppressed the nunnery of Port Royal in 1709. By that time the original issues had largely been overtaken by others: the attitude of Jansenists toward the papacy and the crown had now become more important than their views on Grace. Some Marxist historians even claim to see great significance in their views on society. As a result of *Unigenitus* most of the Roman Catholics in Holland abandoned their obedience to the papacy and set up the Old Catholic Church, which still exists.

Pascal

Among the supporters of Port Royal, the Arnauld family held the most prominent place, but the most interesting individual figure was the mathematician and philosopher Blaise Pascal (1623–62). In 1656 and 1657 he published a series of *Letters written to a Provincial* which were a highly destructive and very popular attack on Jesuit moral laxity as well as a defense of Jansenist ideas. The *Provincial Letters* were immediately recognized as a masterpiece of controversial journalism, as well as a brilliant, if occasionally tendentious, account of the issues in the controversy.

Pascal's importance went far beyond the *Provincial Letters*. As a result of a sudden violent conversion, which he called "the night of fire," Pascal began to compose a major work of Christian apologetics. This was based on an appeal to the heart, which has "reason that reason does not know." His notes for this book were published in 1670 and are known as the *Pensées (Thoughts)*. Both the beauty of their style and their psychological insight have made the *Pensées* a popular book ever since. Pascal's mathematical work on conic sections, his invention of a crude barometer and of a simple balancing machine made him an important figure in the history of mathematics and invention also.

While the Jansenist controversy was disturbing French religious and scholarly life, the Thirty Years War had continued with unabated fury in Germany.

Blaise Pascal, mathematician, philosopher and religious writer.

The Rape of Magdeburg

Defying their Catholic Emperor's edict of 1629, the Protestant residents of the fortified Prussian city of Magdeburg refused to cede control of their community to Ferdinand II's son, Leopold. The enraged Emperor promptly laid siege to his arrogant fief, hoping to take by force what he had been unable to win by fiat. His actions provoked a continental religious war that ultimately involved Sweden, France and Bohemia, as well as the German princes of Hesse, Saxony and Brandenburg. England, Denmark, Spain and the Netherlands were eventually drawn into the struggle—and long after Magdeburg fell, the political conflagration that had been kindled there was still raging. The religious antagonisms that the struggle provoked ended all hopes for a wider Counter-Reformation, divided Germany for decades and shifted the European balance of power.

A German soldier of the mid-seventeenth century.

Opposite Gustavus Adolphus, the Lion of the North. German Protestants came to rely increasingly on Swedish armies to help them against their Catholic rivals during the Thirty Years War.

The attack by the imperial German army on the Prussian city of Magdeburg began in the last days of March, 1631. The city, which guarded a crossing point on the Elbe River, was strongly fortified on its land side and was further protected by islets in the river. As one of the richest cities in Prussia, it was believed to be adequately supplied with gunpowder and generously provided with food.

Originally, Magdeburg had been a Roman Catholic archbishopric, but during the Reformation it had fallen into the hands of Lutherans and had acquired a Protestant administrator (or bishop). In 1629 the Catholic Emperor Ferdinand II—victor of the German civil war that began in 1618—issued an imperial edict calling for the restitution of former Roman Catholic properties. The wealthy archbishopric of Magdeburg was assigned to Ferdinand's young son, Leopold. When the city refused to accept the edict, Albrecht von Wallenstein, then the imperial commander-in-chief and an extraordinary soldier and Bohemian tycoon, received orders to occupy Magdeburg on Leopold's behalf.

For seven months in 1629 Count Wallenstein, leading six thousand men, laid siege to the city. His efforts were in vain; the 30,000 citizens of Magdeburg successfully defied their Emperor. Wallenstein, unpopular because of the independent attitude he adopted toward the Emperor, withdrew and was later dismissed. Johan Tserclaes, Count of Tilly, the septuagenarian general of the army of the Duke of Bavaria, took over the command of all the imperial armies. He was an experienced and victorious general who had not only defeated the Elector Palatine at the Battle of the White Mountain in 1620 at the outset of the German civil war, but had also easily defeated the King of Denmark, Christian IV, when the King came to the aid of the German Lutherans. As a boy, Tilly had been intended for the priesthood, but he had elected to become a professional soldier instead.

In the decade after White Mountain the military scene changed completely. By 1630, peace no longer reigned in Germany; the siege of Magdeburg rapidly ceased to be an isolated military operation and became part of a general war. On June 26, 1630, King Gustavus Adolphus of Sweden landed in Pomerania and announced that he was coming to the rescue of his fellow Protestants. While Gustavus Adolphus strengthened his base on the Oder River in northern Germany and reinforced his troops, Christian William, the Protestant administrator of Magdeburg who had temporarily taken refuge in Sweden, reentered the city at the end of July, 1630. Supported by Swedish soldiers, he declared that he would defend the archbishopric with the help of God—and the King of Sweden—against all his enemies. But the ultimate safety of the city depended on the coming of the King of Sweden himself, since Magdeburg lay isolated among the neutral territories of John George, Elector of Saxony, and George William, Elector of Brandenburg. Although they were Protestants, these electors had never declared war on their Emperor.

Count Tilly was assigned the task of stopping the Swedish advance into Germany. The aging Field Marshal regarded it as important not merely to secure the strategic Elbe crossing at Magdeburg but, because his Roman Catholic army was short of supplies in this largely Protestant area of Germany, to lay hold of the ample provisions said to be stored in the city. Nevertheless, he was torn between concentrating on confining Gustavus Adolphus to his bridgehead on the Oder and storming the isolated fortress of Magdeburg, which had declared itself to be the first Swedish ally. Thus, in November, 1630, Count Gottfried zu Pappenheim, Tilly's second-in-command, began a renewed investment of Magdeburg, while the Field Marshal himself led darting attacks on the lines of the Swedish King.

Gustavus Adolphus recognized his responsibility for the safety of Magdeburg, but he believed (early in 1631) that the city could hold out without his army's assistance for several months. It was, after all, well fortified and well supplied, and the King had sent one of his ablest subordinates, the fanatical

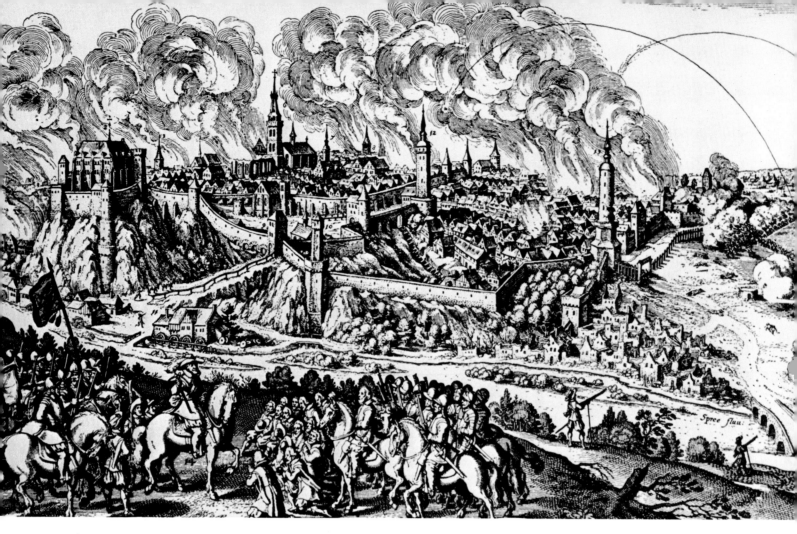

Above The siege of the town of Bautzen in 1620.

Below The Battle of Lützen, fought on November 6, 1632, where Gustavus Adolphus was killed.

Lutheran Dietrich von Falkenberg, and a garrison of 3,000 men to organize its defenses. Meanwhile Gustavus Adolphus himself, with a trained and equipped army of about 13,000, advanced up the Oder, assaulting the important city of Frankfurt and conquering the nearby town of Landsberg.

The burghers of Magdeburg were far from eager to defend their city to the death against the over-whelming forces now assembled before them. They had already withstood over a year's investment by the imperial armies, and they were not particularly loyal to their Protestant administrator from Brandenburg. (Indeed, the burghers had recently looked to the more powerful electorate of Saxony for a ruler.) But they were obliged to yield to the pressure of Dietrich von Falkenberg, who was utterly determined to hold the city until his Swedish master came to the rescue.

Pappenheim, however, was as determined to capture Magdeburg as Falkenberg was to defend it. On May 7, the islets having already been occupied by imperial forces, Pappenheim attempted to storm the city from the river side. By May 9 the situation had grown desperate for the defenders, and the burghers were clamoring for surrender. Early in the morning of Tuesday, May 10, Falkenberg addressed the city fathers, urging them to fight on. But it was too late; Pappenheim, without orders from Tilly, renewed the assault—and this time he was successful.

According to the laws of war in those days, a city that had refused a summons to surrender could be put to the sword—and some 25,000 citizens perished as Magdeburg was pillaged by the imperial soldiers. It was impossible for Tilly to restrain his mercenaries, but he did see to it that the cathedral itself—which harbored thousands of refugees including the wounded Protestant Bishop Christian William—and five other city churches were preserved from destruction. The rest of the city caught fire—apparently by accident—and was burned to ashes. Four days after the assault Tilly was at last able to call off the plundering, and the bodies of the dead were thrown into the river to prevent plague. But whatever booty his men may have acquired amid the dreadful scenes of fire, rape and slaughter, the immediate military object of the siege was not attained. For Tilly did not obtain the provisions he sought to feed his army.

Tilly at the siege of Magdeburg.

Gustavus Adolphus and his army were sixty miles away at Potsdam when word of the sack of Magdeburg reached him. After his successes on the Oder, he had gone to Berlin to compel his brother-in-law, George William, Elector of Brandenburg, to join him as an ally. With the help of Brandenburg he had hoped to save Magdeburg. Now it was too late.

The thrill of horror that swept through Protestant Europe at the news of the sack of Magdeburg was tempered by fear in Germany. Whereas those princes more distant from the scene were inclined to look upon the King of Sweden as their only savior, the neighbors of Magdeburg were impressed by the ruthless efficiency of the imperial army.

Tilly himself had misgivings about his success. "Our danger has no end, for the Protestant Estates will without doubt be only strengthened in their hatred by this," he reported to one of his masters, the Duke of Bavaria. Gustavus Adolphus at once recognized the advantage of the situation. In January, while on his way to Frankfurt, he had signed an open treaty of alliance with Catholic France. The

The assassination of Wallenstein, which took place after he had been dismissed from the Emperor's service.

Wallenstein, who began the siege of Magdeburg for the Emperor.

Below right Tilly, who succeeded Wallenstein as the leading imperial general.

A mid-seventeenth-century German gun.

John George of Saxony had been attempting for some time to create a third force in Germany—one capable of mediating between the Swedes and the Emperor—and early in 1631 he summoned a convention of Protestant rulers to his capital, Leipzig. The convention agreed to raise an army and issued a manifesto to the Emperor Ferdinand outlining the Protestant grievances.

John George, who possessed the only army of any size in northern Germany, had refused to go to the aid of Magdeburg or to ally himself with the Swedish King; George William of Brandenburg was not made of such stern stuff. Even before the fall of Magdeburg he had allowed the Swedes to encamp on his territory and had permitted them to use the fortress of Spandau. Now, within a month of the sack of Magdeburg, he submitted to a series of ultimatums from his brother-in-law, Gustavus Adolphus. On June 11, he signed a treaty placing the resources of Brandenburg and the fortresses of Spandau and Küstrin at the disposal of the Swedes.

Throughout the war in Germany the position of Saxony was of decisive importance. If Gustavus Adolphus could persuade John George to abandon his idea of becoming a third force, all the Protestants would enroll themselves in the Swedish camp. Gustavus Adolphus realized that in order to make the right impression and efface the memory of Magdeburg he must now move forward from his base and seek a victory. On June 24, he decided to advance from Spandau toward the Elbe. Pappenheim had 13,000 men at Magdeburg, but the Swedish army had been substantially reinforced. Gustavus Adolphus crossed the Elbe some fifty miles north of Magdeburg and took the town of Tangermünde; he then withdrew north along the Elbe, since he was not yet prepared to fight Tilly. A clash between the two armies took place in the neighborhood of Werben (north of Tangermünde) at the end of July. After the two sides had engaged in a cannon duel, Tilly drew off. The Swedes had won a moral victory, and several more German Protestant princes hastened to ally themselves with the invader.

The victory at Werben left John George, the great

French government had agreed to subsidize the Swedish army; in return, Gustavus Adolphus promised to respect freedom of worship for Roman Catholics in Germany.

Meanwhile, the King—part dreamer, part astute statesman—was making up his mind about future policy. He aimed to create a league of German princes who would be politically and militarily subordinate to him. As the head of such a league he could dominate northern Germany and humiliate the Emperor. The immediate question, however, was how to deal with the recalcitrant northern electors.

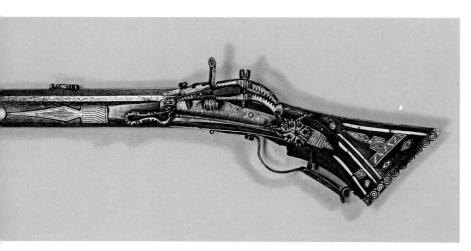

neutral, even more isolated, his electorate threatened by warring armies on two sides. In the middle of August Tilly sent the Elector an ultimatum ordering him to join the imperial army with his troops. Refusing those demands, John George reluctantly turned to Gustavus Adolphus for help, and on September 3, an alliance was signed. The Elector of Saxony promised to join Gustavus Adolphus on the Elbe, to provide food and quarters for the Swedish army in his territory, and to make no separate peace without him. The treaty was a compromise, for John George retained his political independence and promised to submit his army to the orders of the Swedish King only as long as the emergency continued. But whatever the reservations, the Saxon-Swedish alliance was decisive for the future of the war.

Two days after the signing of that treaty Tilly stormed Leipzig, the Saxon capital. Twenty-five miles to the north the armies of Gustavus Adolphus and John George joined forces for the march south, and on Wednesday, September 8, their troops engaged the imperial army in the Battle of Breitenfeld. After two hours of thunderous struggle, the Saxons retreated, but the imperialists were annihilated by the Swedes. Nearly 20,000 of Tilly's men were killed or taken prisoner, and the Empire never recovered.

The destruction of Magdeburg was, therefore, a "milestone" in what modern historians call the Thirty Years War. That war had begun in 1618 as a revolt of Protestant nobles in Bohemia against the Hapsburg crown; Ferdinand II had been ordered deposed, and Frederick V, the Elector Palatine, had been called to the throne of Bohemia. The Bohemians took this revolutionary step because they considered that their liberties—and in particular the freedom of the Protestant churches inside the kingdom—had been menaced. The Emperor Ferdinand II, who had been brought up by Jesuits and was determined to extend the influence of his Church throughout Germany, was undeterred. He expelled the Elector Palatine from Bohemia and deprived him of his hereditary lands, which were ultimately transferred to the Duke of Bavaria, the leader of the German Roman Catholics. Kings James I and Charles I of England and the King of Denmark were eventually dragged into the contest, but up to 1630 the struggle in Germany remained primarily a civil war. And by 1630 Ferdinand appeared to be winning. It seemed likely that a new Counter-Reformation, supported by the secular arm of the Holy Roman Emperor, would spread throughout Germany.

At this point, however, other European states became directly or indirectly involved. For over sixty years the United Netherlands had been struggling to secure its independence and religious freedom from the formerly formidable empire of the Spanish Hapsburgs, who were considered the senior branch of the Hapsburg family. Because Spain now reckoned that she was owed a debt by Ferdinand II, she pressed for German intervention on her behalf in northern Europe. If peace prevailed inside Germany, the Emperor's powerful army could strike northward

The Thirty Years War

1618-29

Frederick, the Elector Palatine and leader of the Protestant Union, was defeated by Bavaria and Austria in 1620 at the Battle of the White Mountain, having had no help from other Protestant states. The Bavarian army, under Tilly, and the Hapsburg army, under Wallenstein, were then supreme in northern Germany.

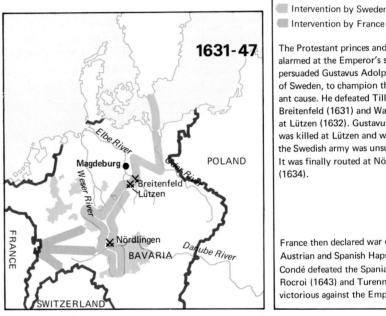

- ◯ Protestant Union of 1608
- ◯ Catholic League of 1609
- ◯ Hapsburg Territories
- — Boundary of Holy Roman Empire
- ▨ Intervention by Sweden
- ▨ Intervention by France

1631-47

The Protestant princes and France, alarmed at the Emperor's successes, persuaded Gustavus Adolphus, King of Sweden, to champion the Protestant cause. He defeated Tilly at Breitenfeld (1631) and Wallenstein at Lützen (1632). Gustavus Adolphus was killed at Lützen and without him the Swedish army was unsuccessful. It was finally routed at Nördlingen (1634).

France then declared war on the Austrian and Spanish Hapsburgs. Condé defeated the Spaniards at Rocroi (1643) and Turenne was victorious against the Emperor.

Treaty of Münster 1648

Germany was by now in ruins, with two-thirds of her population dead, and peace was finally made. The Treaty of Westphalia or Münster (1648) gave Eastern Pomerania, Minden and Magdeburg to Brandenburg; Western Pomerania to Sweden; the bishoprics of Metz, Toul and Verdun and parts of Alsace to France; and Bavaria gained the Upper Palatinate. The Holy Roman Empire was forced to acknowledge the independence of the United Provinces and Switzerland.

- ◯ Gained by Brandenburg
- ◯ Gained by Sweden
- ◯ Gained by France
- ◯ Gained by Bavaria
- ◯ Gained by Saxony

Magdeburg under siege. The fall of the town heralded the great international wars that were to rend Europe and its colonies apart.

The rewards of the defeated, from *Les Malheurs de la Guerre*.

and give his Spanish cousins the aid they needed.

After Christian William fled from Germany to seek succor from Stockholm, Sweden and France entered the scene. King Gustavus Adolphus had long contemplated intervention in Germany, although whether he was essentially a Protestant crusader or merely an ambitious king has been disputed by historians. Whatever his motives, he capitalized on the religious ardor kindled at Magdeburg.

As for France, for some thirty years—ever since the Bourbon Henry IV had succeeded to the throne

of France—a tremendous struggle for power had been waged in Europe between the Bourbons and the Hapsburgs. Henry IV had been determined to end the stranglehold that the two Hapsburg dynasties had exerted over the French kingdom. His successor, King Louis XIII, sustained by his great minister, Cardinal Richelieu, had pursued this policy by every means at his disposal. But Louis was a Roman Catholic, and it was difficult to justify intervention against fellow Roman Catholics in Germany when they were being confronted by Protestant

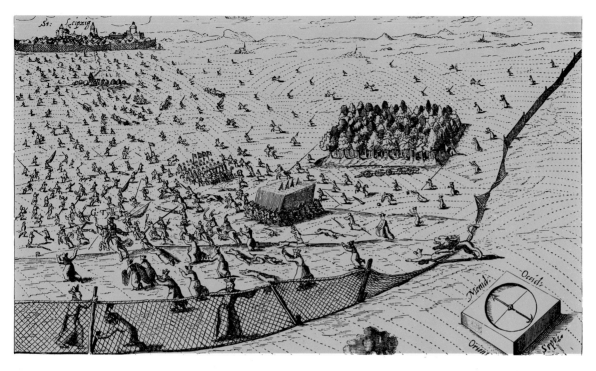

revolts. Richelieu attempted to bribe the Duke of Bavaria, head of the Catholic League in Germany, to fight against his Emperor, for the Bavarian dynasty had always been rivals of the Hapsburgs. But the Duke and his general, Count Tilly, had thrown in their lot with the Emperor and had been promised rich rewards, so Cardinal Richelieu reluctantly turned to the Lion of the North, the Protestant hero Gustavus Adolphus.

Gustavus Adolphus was no man's fool. He was not going to be Richelieu's pawn to humiliate the Holy Roman Emperor. He insisted that the Franco-Swedish treaty (signed at Bärwalde in January,

1631) should be an open treaty; the French were thus obliged to commit themselves in Germany. By the terms of the treaty they agreed only to become the paymaster of the Swedish armies, but after Gustavus Adolphus perished at the Battle of Lützen the French were obliged to send an army into Germany.

The period that followed the fall of Magdeburg heralded the beginning of great international wars. At the same time the fall enflamed religious antagonisms in Germany. The signal humiliation of the German Protestants by Count Tilly rallied all the Protestants of northern and central Germany against their Emperor, enabled Gustavus Adolphus to claim to be their rescuer, and gave him the opportunity to advance from the Oder to the Elbe and to destroy the imperial cause at Breitenfeld and Lützen. Thus, the fall of Magdeburg created the conditions that led to a Protestant resurgence and ensured the division of Germany for many years to come. Protestant Brandenburg, the reluctant ally of the Swedes, was in fact to be the focus of a Lutheran-dominated German empire.

The siege of Magdeburg was significant because it helped bring Europe into Germany. In the end the Calvinists as well as the Lutherans achieved religious equality in those parts of Germany where they predominated. The prospect of a wider and fuller Counter-Reformation was brought to an end. Sweden and her paymaster, France, emerged victorious from the war, having inflicted terrible punishments upon the German people. Revolutions took place in England, France and Spain partly as the consequences of this long, expensive and grueling war. Franco-German enmity was ensured for hundreds of years, and the face of Europe was changed, with the center of power shifting to the west.

MAURICE ASHLEY

A cavalryman of the seventeenth century, from a series of prints on equestrian exercises.

Above left A cartoon showing the Lion of the North scattering Tilly's "Jesuits" at the Battle of Leipzig, 1632.

61

The conflict between the Stuart kings and

Problems in England

England had become involved in the Thirty Years War in 1615 when Frederick v, the Elector Palatine, in defiance of the Emperor, rashly accepted the crown of Bohemia from the Protestant rebels in Prague. The English people's sympathy was aroused for Frederick and his wife Elizabeth, James I's daughter, aggravating James' difficulties both at home and abroad.

Demands for action on behalf

James I welcomes his son Charles home after his visit to Spain.

of the Palatinate's misused champion of Protestantism, Frederick, and his unfortunate young wife grew increasingly clamorous in England. There were demonstrations in favor of Elizabeth and against the Hapsburgs, crowds marched through the streets calling for war against Emperor Ferdinand II and a popular play, Middleton's *A Game at Chesse*, had to be banned because it insulted the Spanish ambassador. Parliament—when it was summoned in 1621 to provide funds for the government's foreign policy —urged a declaration of war against Spain, whose troops had joined forces with the Austrians.

Ignoring the saber rattling of Parliament and the warlike temper of his people, the English King— who had always turned in horror from the thought of war—persuaded himself that he could better serve his son-in-law by coming to terms with Spain. James was sure that he could restore order in Europe by marrying his son Charles to the Infanta, Doña Maria of Spain, and by inducing her brother Philip IV

(1605—65) to use his influence to restore Frederick and Elizabeth to their palace at Heidelberg. The King's policy, unrealistic as it was and fruitless as it proved to be, was abhorrent to Parliament. The members wanted an alliance with Protestants, not Roman Catholics, a war against Spain and an immediate end to the marriage negotiations.

James, who had already dissolved a difficult Parliament in 1614—remarking as he did so that he was surprised that his "ancestors should have permitted such an institution to come into existence"—thus came into direct conflict with the House of Commons once again. He refused to acknowledge their right to question his policy or to interfere with his inherited prerogative powers. "The state of monarchy," he told them, "is the supremest thing upon earth; for Kings are not only God's lieutenants upon earth, but even by God himself they are called gods. . . . Kings are justly called gods for that they exercise a manner or resemblance of divine power upon earth. . . . So it is sedition in subjects to dispute what a King may do in the height of his power."

In James' opinion, it was indeed seditious for Parliament to meddle in matters of state; foreign policy was the King's affair and upon the King's grace did Parliament depend. When the members entered in their journal a protest that their privileges did not depend on the King but were the "ancient and undoubted birthright of the subjects of England," James was so angry that he tore the protest from the book with

his own hand, dissolved Parliament and ordered the arrest of those members whom he took to be the chief troublemakers. The long contest between the Stuart kings and their parliaments had begun.

Buckingham

The failure of the negotiations for the Spanish match delighted the English people, and on the return of Prince Charles and his friend the Duke of Buckingham from the fiasco of their courtship of the Infanta in Madrid, the two young men found themselves suddenly and intoxicatingly popular. To consolidate his triumph the Duke of Buckingham urged the King to call a parliament to impeach the unpopular Earl of Middlesex, who, as Lord Treasurer, was the most influential of Buckingham's critics and one of the leaders of the pro-Spanish party in the country.

"My God, Steenie, you are a fool, and will shortly repent this folly." James told Buckingham, using a special nickname, and added prophetically, "You are making a rod with which you will be scourged yourself." But James was old and ill, helplessly in love with Buckingham and so delighted to have him back that he gave way. A parliament was called; Middlesex was swept from power; the entire foreign policy of the country was reversed; and the principle that Parliament had no right to discuss foreign affairs—a principle that the King had vehemently defended three years before—was abandoned. The advice of the Commons was sought on whether to break off diplomatic relations with Madrid.

With Buckingham, Prince Charles, Parliament and the country all demanding war, the King could no longer resist, and in

Ships of Buckingham's fleet, 1627.

preparation for the forthcoming war, alliances were negotiated with the Dutch and the French. (The young French Princess Henrietta Maria, daughter of Henry IV, now became Prince Charles' bride.) But, although the Commons declared themselves in favor of a campaign in Europe, they refused to vote the money necessary for its proper prosecution. Consequently the Spanish war— which dragged on for four years and was waged by English rogues, vagabonds, drunkards and cripples—was a tragic disaster. By the time it was over, James was dead and his son Charles was showing himself to be a monarch ill-suited to meet the challenge that faced the royal house.

Charles I

Exasperated by Charles' refusal to explain what his foreign policy was intended to achieve or how the money he demanded would be used, the Commons allowed the new King only a fraction of the funds he needed. To make matters even worse, Parliament refused to grant the King the lifetime right to collect customs duties. Charles' predecessors had been granted that right for life; he was obliged to reapply annually. The most formidable orator in Parliament, an emotional, excitable, vehement West Country squire, Sir John Eliot, protested in his loud, harsh voice that he and his fellow members were not creatures of the King, elected merely to grant him money and to approve his policies, but men with individual consciences and a duty to act in accordance with what they knew to be right. He condemned the government's policies —and above all he condemned the Duke of Buckingham who, as Lord High Admiral, had sailed across the Channel in 1627 in command of a disastrous expedition intended to support the Huguenots of La Rochelle in their rebellion against the French King.

Eliot demanded Buckingham's impeachment, just as Buckingham himself had demanded the impeachment of the Earl of Middlesex—and Charles panicked. He ordered Eliot arrested and imprisoned in the Tower, but when the unintimidated Commons refused to do any further business until their champion was released,

their parliaments begins

The Duke of Buckingham with his family.

the King capitulated. Eliot returned to the attack with increased invective, and in an attempt to spare his friend further humiliation, Charles dissolved Parliament. The impetuous young monarch decided to raise the money he so desperately needed without Parliament's help, to collect the customs duties previously denied him and to impose a capital levy. Those who refused to pay that levy were imprisoned.

The Petition of Right

Yet for all his determination to govern without Parliament, Charles found it impossible to do so. The extraordinary expense of the war against France obliged him to summon Parliament once more. The King hoped the recalled Commons would prove more tractable; they proved even less so. Led by Sir John Eliot, they strongly condemned taxation without parliamentary consent and imprisonment without due cause. In 1628 they set out their grievances in a Petition of Right, and they refused to discuss the matter of supplies until the Petition had achieved royal assent.

The period that followed the King's acceptance of the Petition of Right was but a truce in a continuing duel. In January, 1629, a new House of Commons changed the direction of its attack. The archenemy, Buckingham, had been removed by an assassin's knife at Portsmouth a few months before, but Eliot saw that the general principle of the Commons'

right to criticize the King's ministers might be gained if demands for political changes were allied to the growing force of Puritan enthusiasm in the country. He and his supporters therefore launched an attack on the King for having appointed various High Church clergymen to important livings, chaplaincies and bishoprics, and they refused to grant Charles his traditional customs duties until they had debated a resolution that "the affairs of the King of Earth must give way to the affairs of the King of Heaven." Parliament's move was too much for Charles, who was devoted to the Church of England and firmly convinced that the administration of its affairs had nothing to do with Parliament. He sent orders to the Speaker of the House of Commons, commanding him to tell the Commons to adjourn, but its militant members refused to do so. Shouting "No! No!" in the Speaker's face, they passed resolu-

Sir John Eliot, first leader of the parliamentary opposition to King Charles.

tions against both the payment of the customs duties and the religious policy of the government.

Charles was appalled. Bursting out in indignation against the "undutiful and seditious" behavior of the Commons and those "vipers" chiefly responsible, he once again ordered Eliot's arrest. And this time he refused to release him. Even when Eliot became fatally ill, the King continued steadfast in his refusal, and upon the "viper's" death at the age of forty, Charles turned down Eliot's son's request that the corpse be laid to rest in the Cornish courtyard where his family and ancestors lay saying, "Let Sir John Eliot be buried in that

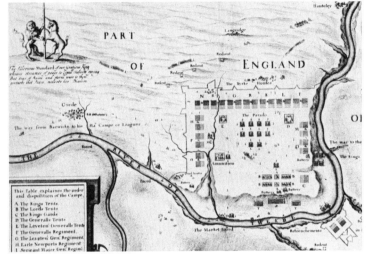

Map of Charles I's camp during the First Bishops War.

parish wherein he died,"

For eight years after Eliot's death, Charles contrived to pay his way without calling a parliament by resorting to a number of devices for raising money—some of doubtful legality, all of them unpopular. Effective control of the government lay in the hands of Thomas Wentworth (1593–1641), Earl of Strafford, and William Laud (1573–1645), Archbishop of Canterbury, both of whom were capable but unpopular.

Troubles in Scotland

It was Scotland that proved to be the cause of Charles' undoing and Scotland remained an important factor in English politics until Cromwell's power was well established. The problems of the crown were partly religious and partly constitutional. Most of the Scottish people were Presbyterian in

sympathy and had little love for bishops, whether Anglican or Roman Catholic. James I had succeeded in reintroducing episcopacy to Scotland in 1610, and the power of the bishops, who were a major force in politics, added to their unpopularity. Charles attempted to make the Scottish Church conform more closely to the English model by introducing a prayer book based closely on the English Book of Common Prayer in 1637. The congregation in St. Giles, Edinburgh's cathedral, rioted when an elderly spinster called Jenny Geddes threw a stool at the bishop. In the following year a Scottish national covenant opposing religious innovations

from England was signed, and attempts were made to abolish episcopacy. In 1639 the people of Scotland took up arms in defense of their Church. In order to raise money to fight the First Bishops' War, Charles was forced to recall Parliament. That Parliament proved no more willing to grant the King money for his war against the Scottish rebels than its predecessor had been to vote money for the war against France. Its members declined to vote any supplies until the country's complaints had been satisfied.

Charles responded, as he had done in the past, by dissolving Parliament—but the humiliating outcome of an attempt to subdue the Scots with an underpaid and ill-supplied army led to the assembly of yet another Paliament. That Parliament, the last of his reign, was to force the King to accept an act prohibiting its dissolution without its own consent.

The Meeting of the Long Parliament

After suffering two defeats by rebellious Scots, whose army then occupied northern England, Charles I was forced to give over his eleven-year attempt at personal rule and call Parliament. Divided roughly between the Court faction and a larger, more amorphous group known as the Country, Parliament sparred with the King for power. Slowly the King was stripped of many of his traditional prerogatives and the stage was set for the truly revolutionary events that would transpire nine years later.

John Pym, the parliamentary tactician who headed the majority Country faction against King Charles.

Opposite Parliament assembles at Westminster on April 13, 1640, after eleven years of personal rule by the King. Known as the Short Parliament it was immediately dissolved. The King's financial straits, however, obliged him to call another, the Long Parliament, six months later.

England was tensely expectant when the Long Parliament assembled on November 3, 1640, for King Charles I could not reject its demands, dissolve it, and attempt to revert to personal government without any parliament, as he had done with the Short Parliament six months earlier. Since then he had not merely failed a second time to beat the rebel Scots—they had routed his own raw troops, and on English soil too, forcing him to a humiliating armistice. Their army was to remain in occupation of northern England at a charge to England of £860 a day until a peace treaty was concluded to the satisfaction of the parliaments of both kingdoms. Their presence was a better pledge than Charles' word for the survival of the Long Parliament, which also had to provide the pay of the English forces which still faced them.

This Parliament had leadership and purpose, even though parliamentary experience had lapsed for the eleven years from 1629–40 in which Charles had wielded personal power. The pacemakers in both houses had been held together not only by ties of friendship and kinship, but to a striking extent by common membership in a Puritan colonizing venture called the Providence Company. John Pym was its secretary and chief manager, Oliver St. John its solicitor, and it met at the London houses of Lord Brooke or the Earl of Warwick. It had not been successful in its original objects of emplanting three rather unhealthy Caribbean islands with godly Puritan communities, which were at the same time to prey on Spanish shipping and return a profit to their promoters; but the political dividends that it yielded were incalculable.

These leaders' political aims naturally had to take account of the state of feeling in the country and the manner in which Parliament reflected it. For twenty years and more the men of property who counted in national and local politics had

been polarized between two broad groups—better described as interests rather than by the too precise name of parties—known as the Court and the Country. The Court centered upon those who made a career in the King's service, whether in his household or in the government. It extended to many country gentlemen who looked to great courtiers or ministers as their patrons, and to many rich merchants who enjoyed lucrative commercial privileges in return for services rendered.

The Country interest was a looser but larger body. Its adherents were bound to the Court by no ties of obligation and had grown increasingly hostile to it, though whether mainly for political, religious, economic, intellectual, moral or purely personal reasons varied much from individual to individual. It was broadly united, however, in disliking the whole tone of the Court, the kind of patronage that won men places there, the dubious financial exactions that kept it afloat, the anti-Puritan doctrines known as "Arminianism" imposed on the English Church by Archbishop Laud, the Roman Catholics in high places and the pro-Spanish foreign policy of the 1630s.

But while the term "Country" implied a claim to speak for the nation's true interests against a corrupt Court, it also bore the meaning of "county." When a member of Parliament talked of his country, he commonly meant Wiltshire or Yorkshire or whatever other shire he hailed from, rather than England. Each county, with its Lord Lieutenant, Deputy Lieutenant, justices of the peace and other officials, was a close-knit political and social community. It was dominated by its leading landowners; and landowners overwhelmingly dominated the seventeenth-century House of Commons. The crisis of 1640–41 was in a very real sense a crucial confrontation between the county communities, which really ruled rural England, and the King's government.

Of God,　Of Man,　Of the Divell.

The English Gentleman

Although it was still novel and rare for elections to be fought on political issues, the Court clearly took a beating when the Long Parliament was chosen. Fewer than fifty royal officials and courtiers obtained seats—less than the number of merchants, in a House of just over five hundred members. The Country gentry and their lawyer allies constituted a huge majority.

John Pym, the great tactician, could count on their support for his three immediate aims: to bring down the ministers who had sustained Charles' nonparliamentary rule, to pass acts which would make such rule impossible ever to repeat and to reverse Laud's Arminian policies in the Church. These were limited objectives; they had to be, for the Country interest was mainly conservative in temper. Most members believed that England was blessed with a constitution as ancient as the nation itself, whose unwritten "fundamental laws" needed only to be reaffirmed with a few new safeguards for all to be well. Over religion they were more divided, but they could agree that in both Church and State it was Charles and Laud and their lieutenants who were the dangerous innovators. The problem will be to explain how so predominantly conservative a body of men ever engaged their King in civil war.

The first and easiest objective was to knock away the props of the "eleven years' tyranny." Only eight days after Parliament met, Pym led the Commons in impeaching the Earl of Strafford, Charles' most feared and hated minister, for high treason. The charge was a capital one, and had to be tried before the whole House of Lords. Then in December, Laud too was impeached, and several other senior ministers fled abroad to escape the same fate. Within weeks, the essential agents of Charles' personal rule were broken and scattered.

The story of how Strafford was hounded to the scaffold in May, 1642, and Laud in 1645, is a long and tragic one. Two features of Strafford's fate, however, are specially significant. One is the part that an ominous new force played in clinching it: the pressure of the London mob. The other is that the parliamentary leaders, by driving Charles to the shame and agony of breaking his promise to save Strafford's life, may have destroyed whatever chance remained of gaining his sincere acceptance of the broader constitutional reforms on which they had embarked.

These reforms had already begun with the Triennial Act, whereby Parliament must assemble every three years at the least, whether the King desired it or not. Later, two acts abolished his most famous "prerogative courts." One, the Star Chamber, had been a wholesome and indeed popular institution until the 1630s, when it had been abused to punish savagely some critics of the Court and the bishops whom the Privy Councillors (who sat as judges in Star Chamber) feared would be too popular to be convicted by a jury. The other, the Court of High Commission, was specially hated for enforcing Laud's ecclesiastical

policies and the licensing laws which muzzled the press. A series of further acts made tonnage and poundage impositions (special tariffs on imports and exports) and every kind of tax firmly subject to Parliament's consent, and outlawed all Charles' various dubious financial expedients.

This great body of statutes, passed between February and August 1641, constituted the Long Parliament's most enduring work. Carrying as they did the King's reluctant assent, only a Parliament could repeal them; they were still in force when Charles II was restored. They altered the whole balance of government, and ran completely against the tide of absolutism that had long been flowing in continental Europe. Their effect was that the King must by law meet Parliament at frequent intervals and depend on it for most of his revenue. No special tribunal would henceforth judge cases involving "matters of state"; the same common law would determine the claims of the crown and the rights of the subject.

Yet their authors did not see these as revolutionary measures. For each there were precedents (of a kind) to be cited, or legal arguments that they were merely clearing the ancient constitution of excrescences or abuses. And most of the Lords and Commons (though not Pym or the more radical men) thought they went far enough.

Far enough in the State, that is; there was still Laud's work in the Church to undo. Members differed more widely over religion. Should they restore the Elizabethan *status quo* or institute a more drastic and Puritan reformation? The example of the Scots, who had lately abolished their own bishops and prayer book, was making many English Puritans raise their sights. In May, 1641, the Commons began long debates on a bill to abolish episcopacy "root and branch." But they went so far mainly out of pique, because the Lords had rejected a more moderate bill which would have excluded the bishops from the upper House. The Root and Branch Bill went further than most members yet wanted, and it was allowed to die quietly.

There were compromises over religion in the air that would probably have satisfied the majority, if the political situation could have been stabilized. Of this the chances looked good by the late summer of 1641. The Country had secured most of what it wanted and the fears of force were receding. The Scottish army had withdrawn, and the English army was being disbanded; so too were the troops that Strafford had raised in Ireland.

What then, against all expectation, led England within a year into civil war? On the one hand there were determined men who wanted to clip the King's wings further. On the other, Charles created suspicion of himself by visiting Scotland from August to November, with the plain purpose of raising a party among the Scottish nobility. But these clouds were as nothing to the black storm that broke over Ulster in October, when the native Irish rose and massacred the Protestant settlers on their land. Rebellion spread rapidly through the rest of Ireland, until England's hold was reduced to a strip of the eastern seaboard.

Some might argue that the basis for mutual confidence between King and Parliament was already so far eroded that a final breach was only a matter of time, but this is highly questionable. What is beyond question is that from the Ulster tragedy onward the summer's détente gave way to an escalation of tension that culminated in civil war. It was made worse by the exhibition of a forged commission purporting to give Charles' own sanction to the Ulster rising, and by wild reports that magnified the number of Protestant victims from thousands into tens and even hundreds of thousands. England's chronic fear of popery took one of its periodic flights into hysteria.

It was clearly necessary, however, to raise a new army. But could Charles be trusted with one? No one could yet utter the thought that he could not; their distrust, however, was such that he must be controlled, and the way to control him must be through his ministers. So Pym exploited the situation to get a momentous demand through Parliament on November 8, that Charles should "employ only such councillors and ministers as shall be approved by his Parliament." Otherwise it would take its own steps to subdue Ireland. The King's right to choose his servants was almost his most basic prerogative, but within a month Parliament was challenging another, even more fundamental: his right to dispose of the nation's militia.

Now, for Parliament to claim control over the state's ultimate sanction, its armed forces, as well as over the highest offices in government, was revolutionary in a sense that its previous acts were not. These new demands could invoke no plausible precedents, no basis in the "fundamental laws." They shocked many old supporters of the Country interest. Coupled with the mounting attacks on episcopacy and the prayer book in pulpit and press, they were creating a new political alignment.

This could be seen during November in the debates on the Grand Remonstrance. Though framed as a remonstrance to the King, this was planned and written as a manifesto to the nation. It attributed all the evils of the reign to "a malignant and pernicious design of subverting the

Charles I received by the Lord Mayor of London upon his return from Scotland in November, 1641. During his absence Parliament learned of the massacre of Protestants in Ulster and debated the Grand Remonstrance. A woodcut from *England's Comfort and London's Joy*, 1641.

Opposite above The "Triple Episcopacie"—a satire of the Puritan party on Archbishop William Laud and the court bishops. Pym led the House in impeaching Laud and reversing his Arminian policies in the Church.

Opposite below The English Gentleman, engraved by Robert Vaughan, 1630. The landed gentry, in defense of their traditional way of life, played the main part in launching the Great Rebellion.

67

King Charles and his court in Greenwich Park, by Belcamp and Stalbempt.

fundamental laws and principles of government," carried on by a coalition of "Jesuited papists," Arminian bishops and clergy, and courtiers working in the interests of the Catholic powers. Although it did not mention the militia and implied that a moderate episcopacy would be preserved, it divided the Commons deeply by its inflammatory partisanship and its offensiveness to the King. Finally it was passed late at night by a bare eleven votes, in an atmosphere so tense that fighting almost broke out in the House itself.

This tiny majority, compared with the vast ones that had carried the acts of February-August, showed that the old Country interest was dividing. Some felt like Pym that Charles was utterly untrustworthy, and that their hard-won reforms would not be safe unless they shackled his ministers and took the sword from his hand. Others saw greater danger, as well as wrong, in departing from the ancient bounds of law. They feared too that by weakening monarchy too far they would shake the whole social edifice that gave nobles, knights and gentry their appointed places; and further that if the radicals had their way they could say farewell to the Church of England as they knew it. Upon such considerations new Royalist and Parliamentarian parties were taking shape, cutting right across the old dividing lines between Court and Country. Among the Country members who rallied to the King were Lord Falkland, whom he made Secretary of State, and Edward Hyde, the future Earl of Clarendon.

Dramatic events widened the gap during the last winter of peace. The Corporation of London, hitherto a bastion of support for Charles in a hostile capital, was lost to him in the City elections of December. Then on January 4, 1642, he made his desperate attempt to arrest five members of Parliament and one peer by going to the House of Commons in person, with a large armed retinue behind him. The five fled to the City of London, and for a brief while thereafter, the City became a refuge for the Commons themselves.

This fearful blunder brought civil war very near, but did not yet make it inevitable. It might still have been averted if Charles had really meant what he said in the public declarations, influenced if not drafted by Hyde, which he issued around this time. He promised to honor the concessions he had made, and offered more; he claimed to stand for the laws of the land, the true Protestant religion, the rightful privileges of Parliament and the liberty of the subject. But, his actions had belied his words and shown time and again that if a chance were offered of worsting his opponents by armed force, he would seize it.

No wonder the militia now became the central issue. Should Parliament nominate and instruct its commanders, or the King? Parliament finally assumed the power in March through the Militia Ordinance, for which it claimed the force of law even though the King had refused his assent. This was a blatant seizure of sovereignty, and if there was one point at which civil war became inevitable, this was it. Yet Parliament would not have pressed Charles so far if he had given it cause to trust him. Now, however, he was on his way to York, against all pleas to return to his capital. As more and more Royalist peers and members of Parliament left Westminster to join him, Parliament's temper became more radical. Its Nineteen Propositions of June 1 would have reduced him to a cipher, and threatened drastic changes to his beloved Church. Soon both sides were raising armed forces, and on August 22, Charles gave the formal signal for war by raising his standard at Nottingham.

The two sides that now opposed each other were not so different as their propagandists made out or as historians used to suppose. The stereotypes of romantic, blue-blooded Loyalists ranged against coarse-grained Puritan fanatics relate only to extreme minorities. The typical men on both sides, at the level of local leadership, were troubled country squires, deeply attached to their country's laws and way of life, and differing mainly as to whether they thought them more endangered by King Charles or "King" Pym.

Predictably, rather more of the nobility were for King Charles, but the Parliamentarian peers were a formidable minority. Equally predictably, most of the mercantile and manufacturing folk were for Parliament, with Puritanism adding its weight to their grievances against Stuart ineptitude in economic matters. Yet it is striking that in a fair number of towns the ruling corporation, generally containing the leading local capitalists, tended to be Royalist.

But it was neither the nobility nor the bourgeoisie who played the main part in launching the Great Rebellion. It was the landed gentry, and the gentry, in the country as in Parliament, were pretty evenly divided. Perhaps, in England as a whole, slightly more of the great county families were for the King, but there were many exceptions.

Textbook maps which show a Parliamentarian south and east confronting a Royalist north and west obscure the facts that every county was divided, and that the motives which swayed the choice of sides could vary much, even between neighboring shires. Local allegiance might be strongly influenced by rival patronage groups in the county communities or by all kinds of in-fighting in the urban oligarchies.

Yet, though material interests could work upon loyalties in various ways, Englishmen in 1642 were essentially making judgments upon great national issues—issues that were not primarily economic or social, but political and religious. There was little to suggest that the way they were settled would effect a transfer of power from one social order to another. The line of division—a blurred line, since so many men remained neutral —ran vertically through every social layer of the political nation.

As yet, the quarrel hardly looked beyond the concerns of the traditional governing class. Parliament trumpeted its claim to represent the people, but said nothing about broadening the franchise, or reallocating constituencies so as to relate them to population, or putting the common law more within reach of the common man, or making education available to all, or remedying gross inequities in the system of land tenure. Such aims were even further from its intentions than the abolition of monarchy. As for religious toleration, the Grand Remonstrance had expressly condemned it.

But all these aims would be powerfully advocated within the next half-dozen years—long before the execution of the King. Thus the issues and the shape of parties changed between 1640 and 1642. They would change again even more profoundly before 1649.   AUSTIN WOOLRYCH

Terracotta bust of Oliver Cromwell, leader of the parliamentary forces who as Lord Protector was to fall out with Parliament in much the same manner as Charles I.

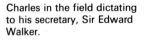

Charles in the field dictating to his secretary, Sir Edward Walker.

Sweden enters the Thirty Years War

When the Long Parliament met, it still seemed likely that England's problems would be resolved without recourse to war. Neither Parliament nor King wanted war, with the example of Germany before them.

The situation in the Thirty Years War had changed largely as a result of the interference of Sweden. Since the reign of Gustavus I, a century before, Sweden, although able to hold its own internationally, had been internally weak. It was largely due to Gustavus Adolphus (1594–1632) that Sweden became politically strong. Determined to make his kingdom into one of Europe's great powers, he expanded Sweden's territory at the eastern end of the Baltic—preventing Russian access to the sea—and pushed into Poland. He also saw Germany as a source of plunder and military glory.

While Gustavus Adolphus sought glory on the battlefield, domestic affairs were left in the hands of his able minister, Count Axel Oxenstierna (1583–1654), who was appointed Chancellor in 1612. Oxenstierna was responsible for carrying out substantial internal reforms during Gustavus Adolphus' reign. The King's death at the Battle of Lützen in 1632, and the succession of his young daughter Christina (1626–89) left the Chancellor in almost complete control of the government. He continued the Swedish presence in Germany.

Under Oxenstierna, Sweden even began to look overseas and financed a joint expedition to North America with the Dutch. This expedition was unsuccessful, and later efforts did not lead to any Swedish settlement.

Gustavus Adolphus' army caricatured.

Russia

After the death of Boris Godunov in 1605, Russia had been plunged into a time of troubles, with rival claimants, some of them imposters, fighting for the throne. The time of troubles ended in 1613, when the sixteen-year-old Michael Romanov, son of the Patriarch of Moscow, was elected Tsar. His empire was in a poor state; as a result of the civil war the crown was virtually bankrupt, and many of Russia's cities had been destroyed. Both Sweden and Poland had taken advantage of the civil war to push into Russian territory.

Michael managed to restore order. The roaming groups of Cossacks, who had done so much damage over the preceding years, were persuaded to join an army to fight the Swedes, but the country was unable to afford continued war either with Sweden or Poland and peace was soon made. Unlike his predecessors, Michael chose to concentrate on the development of his shattered empire, rather than on attempts to push the country's borders forward; even when offered the Black Sea port of Azov—a prize that Ivan the Terrible would have been proud to win—he refused it in order to avoid war with the Turks. But, despite Michael's efforts, the finances of Russia remained precarious for the whole of his reign.

The problem of financial security led to several rebellions in the reign of Michael's son, Alexis (1629—76). In order to increase his income, Alexis sought to raise the tax on salt and to sell tobacco by a government monopoly. The former measure was unpopular with the

Alexis, Tsar of a troubled Russia.

people, the latter with the Church, and both led to risings in 1648. In 1656, Alexis allowed the coinage to be debased, which caused inflation and widespread rioting over the following years. Still more serious was the rebellion of the Cossack Stenka Razin in 1670. This took on many of the characteristics of a popular rising and was only put down with difficulty.

Under Alexis, Russian expansion, halted during the time of troubles and Michael's reign, began once again. The Ukraine, under Polish government had degenerated into social and religious disorder. The formation of a Uniate Church (Orthodox in practice but recognizing the claims of Rome) had split the people. A minority favored the Uniate Church, which was supported by the government, but the majority remained Orthodox. Rebellions became more and more frequent, and the Ukrainians regarded the Tsar as their protector against the tyranny of the Polish government. In 1654, the Ukrainians acknowledged Russian sovereignty. This led to war with Poland which ended in 1667 with Poland's partial defeat. The area to the west of the Dnieper River remained Polish for another fifty years, but even there Russian influence was strong, and the whole of the eastern bank came under Russian rule.

Religious disagreements extended to Russia, and the last few years of Alexis' reign were clouded by them. In large measure the disputes were due to the tactlessness of the Patriarch of Moscow, Nikon (1605–81), whose claims that the Church was independent of the State forced Alexis to depose him in 1667. However, the important liturgical reforms for which Nikon had been responsible remained. These brought Russian religious practice more into conformity with the Greek Church. A minority refused to accept them and formed a new religious body, the Church of the Old Believers.

Spain

During the first half of the seventeenth century, the Spanish economy, already in difficulties during the sixteenth century, deteriorated rapidly. This was partly due to the underlying economic problems of the country and partly to the Duke of Lerma's inept handling of the government. Lerma's fall from power in 1618 had not improved matters, as his son, his successor as royal favorite, was no more capable.

The death of Philip III in 1621 brought about a change of favorite. Philip IV (1605–65), who had little interest in politics, left affairs of state in the hands of the Count-Duke of Olivares (1587–1645), a man as incorruptible as Lerma had been corrupt. Olivares at once set about tightening the lax administrative arrangements that Lerma had encouraged. He made use of small juntas of officials who were devoted to him, rather than working through the large formal councils with their strong vested interests.

But Spain's problems were too deep-seated even for a man of Olivares' energy. The various Spanish provinces all felt aggrieved—Castile because of the heavy taxation imposed on it, and the rest because of the predominant position of Castilians in the royal administration and because the King scarcely ever left Castile. In 1640, there was a revolt in Catalonia, as a result of Olivares' steadily more desperate efforts to raise taxation. A series of bad harvests during the 1620s and the capture of the treasure fleet from America by the Dutch in 1628 exacerbated Spain's financial problems. Even by demanding special taxes from the traditionally exempt classes, Olivares found it difficult to finance the royal expenditure.

Throughout the seventeenth century, as the influence of Spain declined, that of France grew. During the wars between the Hapsburgs and the Valois in the sixteenth century, Spain had

Gaspar de Guzmán, Count-Duke of Olivares, by Velásquez.

almost always been the victor; now it was France's turn. From 1622, when an Italian quarrel led to war, Spain, already embroiled in the Netherlands, was hard pressed militarily. The French aided the Catalan rebels and recognized the province as an independent republic. Even the Treaty of Westphalia in 1648, which ended the Thirty Years War, did not end the war between France and Spain. Unfairly, Olivares was regarded as responsible for the country's economic difficulties, for the revolts of Catalonia and Portugal and for the military defeats by the French, and was dismissed in 1643.

The Revolt of Portugal

Under Hapsburg dominion, the Portuguese believed that they were being deprived of their independence and were becoming another province of Spain. Most of the senior government officials, both in Portugal itself and in its colonies, were Spaniards. The revolt in the Netherlands had laid open the Portuguese colonies, particularly in the Far East, to the threat of attack from the Dutch, a threat that was more and more often realized as Dutch seapower grew. After their early colonial efforts in North America—a trading post had been established

John IV of Portugal, founder of the Braganza dynasty.

in Manhatten in 1613, and the island itself was purchased in 1626—the Dutch began to see that it might be more profitable to take over Portuguese possessions in the Far East, and Dutch settlements were even made in Brazil.

The revolt in Catalonia in 1640 gave the Portuguese the oppor-

tunity that they had been waiting for. Already in 1634 there had been unsuccessful armed attempts to throw off Spanish dominion, but in 1640 the Spanish were too busy elsewhere to suppress rebellion.

A group of conspirators carried out a coup d'état and set John, Duke of Braganza, a legitimate descendant of the former kings, on the throne. Although France and Holland quickly recognized the new regime, there remained a danger of Spanish invasion. It was only the weakness of Spanish government in the period after Olivares' fall that prevented any serious attempt to recover Portugal. The new Portuguese government was so weak that reconquest would have been easy. Abroad, too, Portuguese weakness was clear, at least to the Dutch, who made energetic attempts to continue the expansion of their own empire at Portugal's expense.

Persia

The late sixteenth and early seventeenth centuries saw a revival of the fortunes of the Persian Empire. After the death of the weak Tahmasp in 1576 there was a brief period of civil war, from which in 1586 Tahmasp's grandson, Abbas 1, emerged as Shah. His reign began badly. Encouraged by the state of anarchy, the Turks invaded the country, and in 1590, Abbas was forced to recognize the Turkish conquest of western Persia. The rest of his reign was more successful. During the following years the Shah built up his army, and in 1604 he drove the Turks out of Tabriz and Erivan. Georgia, Azerbaijan and Baghdad were also later taken from the Turks. In the east, too, Abbas was militarily successful, and he was able to drive the Moguls out of Kandahar. He was friendly toward the Europeans, with the exception of the Portuguese, whom he saw as a threat. In 1622, with the help of an English fleet, he drove the Portuguese out of Ormuz.

Abbas was not merely concerned with the expansion of his empire, but sought also, with European assistance, to modernize it. He made Isfahan his capital in 1599 and for the rest of his reign spent much energy in beautifying it—an early attempt at town planning. The religious establish-

Abbas I. All whom the despot suspected of treason would be executed, even his children.

ment was reformed and simplified. But modernization was not allowed to interfere with royal power. Even Abbas' children were in danger when he thought them guilty of treason. He had his eldest son murdered, his two other sons were blinded, and his grandson Safy, who was nominated as his successor, was kept dosed with opium to keep him under control.

Despite all Shah Abbas' talents, his attacks on his family left the government seriously weakened after his death in 1628. Safy, his brain befuddled by opium, showed little of his grandfather's military ability. He followed a despotic home policy, imprisoning all who opposed his whims. He lost Kandahar to the Moguls and eastern Iraq to the Turks, and in 1639 was forced by a treaty with the Ottoman Sultan, Murad IV,

to withdraw all claims to Iraq. The rest of the century saw a steady decline in the power of the Safavid dynasty. Abbas II (1632–67) was able to recapture Kandahar in 1648, but this was due more to Mogul weakness than to Persian strength.

While Persian arms expanded her empire, farther east, in China, the ruling Ming dynasty was faced by intractable problems; and in 1636 the Manchu Ch'ing dynasty claimed rulership of China. It is ironical that the fall of the Ming may have been due in part to the Russian expansion in Asia; in the vast wastelands of Asia, unable at that time to support a large population, the Russian presence was one factor in encouraging the nomadic groups to attack the ancient civilization to their south and east.

Foundation of the Ch'ing Dynasty

1644

As the last of the Ming emperors allowed their inheritance to degenerate into moral and financial bankruptcy, two candidates to replace them put themselves forward. One was Li Tzu-ch'eng, a native bandit leader. The other was the leader of a newly united people from the northeast, from lands beyond the Great Wall, who had taken the name of Manchus. The struggle was won by the Manchus, whose ruler, Fu-lin, took the reign-title of Shun-chih and established a dynasty that would last until 1912.

In the turbulent history of imperial China one pattern of events occurs over and over again. As a ruling dynasty declines, it is replaced by another which rises to power during internal rebellion or invasion from outside. Thus the "Mandate of Heaven," by which each successive dynasty was believed rightfully to sit upon the dragon throne of Peking, was transferred sometimes to a peasant leader (such as the founder of the Ming dynasty), sometimes to a mighty foreign warrior (such as Genghis Khan, who established the Mongol Yuan dynasty in China). But the circumstances which led to the emergence of China's last imperial house, the Ch'ing, were unusual in that they combined both of these familiar elements—internal revolt and invasion by an alien power—and after a while it was the invading force, the Manchus, that effectively ousted China's last native dynasty and established a hold over the Chinese Empire that was to last for almost three hundred years.

The Manchus were a group of tribes inhabiting lands to the northeast of China proper, beyond the coastal pass of Shanhaikuan, where the Great Wall meets the sea. The Western term, "Manchuria," has no Chinese equivalent, since there is no actual country with defined boundaries in which the Manchus lived; similarly, "Manchu" does not refer to any single race, but included the various peoples who united under that name a few years before their invasion of China. The name is of uncertain origin, but may be derived either from a word meaning "chief" or perhaps from Manjusri, an ancestor of their leader, Nurhaci. The Manchus included then, as now, tribes of the Jurchen group of the same Tungus stock which had provided a former Chinese dynasty, the Chin (1122–1234), and which remained under Chinese domination and, in part, occupation, as a tributary state.

Outside the Chinese-influenced core area, which had developed agriculture and walled towns not unlike those of North China, lay arid steppe lands to the west and northwest inhabited by nomads of Mongol origin, following their herds of cattle, sheep and camels from pasture to pasture. To the north and east were Tungusic nomads with a hunting and fishing economy who used reindeer and dogsleds in the harsh winter conditions. The central zone—the Chinese-Manchurian basin—was the most affected by Chinese culture and had, during centuries of contact with its Chinese overlords, absorbed in addition to a Chinese-oriented agricultural and urban economy, many words, art forms and particularly an appreciation of the traditional Chinese administrative system based upon ancient Confucian state philosophy.

At the end of the sixteenth century the inhabitants of this area represented no more than an insignificant group of what the Chinese regarded as "barbarians." Although skilled horsemen and warriors, they were largely primitive and illiterate and lacked any sort of political cohesion which might otherwise have made them a threat to their Chinese masters. Then, in the 1580s, there arose a tribal leader called Nurhaci who was destined to change this situation, to unite these warring tribes into one powerful nation and to set them upon the road which would lead to their conquest of the Chinese Empire.

Born in 1559, Nurhaci rose to power as chief of a minor Jurchen tribe and gained a reputation as a great warrior. It is worth noting that while his biographers assign to him such traditionally warlike features as "the face of a dragon, the eyes of a phoenix," they also remark on his long, drooping ears—features which the Chinese associated with intellectual ability. At this time, and throughout most of the Ming period (1368–1644), the Chinese attempted to subdue the tribes of the Chinese-Manchurian basin by organizing them into *wei*, or military units, the leadership of which

A portrait of Shun-chih (Fu-lin), grandson of Nurhaci, first official Emperor of the Manchu Ch'ing dynasty.

Opposite Illustrations from an early Ch'ing manuscript of a Manchu emperor, a general, a soldier with a gun and an empress.

73

Festival on the river; a watercolor of the Ch'ing period. By embracing Chinese culture and admitting native Chinese to official positions, the Manchus won the confidence of the landed gentry who had lost faith in the imperial leadership of the late Ming period.

(in contrast to the traditional hereditary system) was ratified by Peking only if the incumbent proved loyal to them. It was in one of these *wei*, based on the Chien-chou tribe, that Nurhaci gained in rank and importance. Succeeding his murdered father in 1583, he rose against a rival chieftain to avenge the deaths of his father and grandfather, and was victorious. Like Genghis Khan, Nurhaci used the family feud as the basis of his rise to power, and having wiped out his enemy, furthered his position by making a number of diplomatically important marriages. As a result of his ability in controlling neighboring tribes he became the ostensible ally of the Ming, who in consequence awarded him the title (1595) of "General of the Dragon and Tiger." He also gained in prestige among his own people, becoming known as *Sure Beile*, or "Wise Prince." In particular, under Chinese protection, he became extremely wealthy, securing treaties which gave him a monopoly of mining and trading rights over such commodities as pearls, furs and the valuable root ginseng (used medicinally by the Chinese, especially in rejuvenating elixirs).

Nurhaci also became relatively Sinicized during his contacts with the Chinese, learning much of their way of life and form of government on his tribute missions to Peking. As his power increased, he built a castle on the northeast border of Liao-tung and there developed a city-state based on trade and industry, attracting blacksmiths and armorers, and even Chinese military advisers, and built storehouses to provide for his ever-growing army. The Chinese, naïvely continuing to regard him as their ally, permitted him to expand his military strength until he was ready to organize his people into a new army-based administrative structure.

Starting with company units, or *niru*, of some 300 warriors, Nurhaci arranged them in four divisions symbolized by banners (*ch'i* in Chinese) colored white, blue, red and yellow. When in 1615 a further four banners were added, they took the same colors but added red borders, except the red which adopted a white border. As the banner system took into account the families of the warriors, it was a system which could be used equally in peace or war. The banner divisions dealt with such matters as conscription and taxation, and a bureaucracy of clerks was employed to keep accounts. Hereditary chiefs were replaced by appointed officers, although the senior command remained under the control of Nurhaci's descendants, who eventually constituted the imperial clan. The banner organization grew rapidly, eventually acquiring a further eight Chinese and eight Mongol banners. (By 1644, by absorbing neighboring tribes and disenchanted Chinese, there were 278 Manchu *niru*, 165 Chinese and 120 Mongol. At about 300 men to a company, we can thus estimate the strength of the standing army at almost 170,000.) The banners did not fight as units, but sent representatives to join task forces for particular missions; for example, on a campaign in Inner Mongolia in 1634 each *niru* provided twenty-eight cavalrymen and eight

74

guards, making a total force of 11,000. Unlike the Ming *wei* system from which it was derived, the bannermen were not assigned lands in any one place, and thus had no affiliation with a given territory.

As Nurhaci's war machine expanded, he became openly hostile to the Ming, ceased to acknowledge their suzerainty and after 1609 cut off tribute payments to Peking. Simultaneously he began to develop a system of government as if in anticipation of the forthcoming success of his people and in the awareness of the truth of the advice once given to Genghis Khan—that an empire won from the saddle could not be ruled from it. Accordingly, in 1599, he had a system devised to produce a written form of the Jurchen language, which then enabled him to have translated and disseminated important Chinese legal works and books on Confucian state philosophy. The administrative system which he set up was in every aspect closely modeled on the time-honored Chinese form of government.

By 1616, Nurhaci's power was so great that he was able to take the title of Emperor T'ien-ming ("Heaven-ordered"—but with a full title which meant "Brilliant Emperor who Benefits all Nations") and proclaim the refounding of the Chin dynasty of his ancestors (though twenty years later, possibly in deference to his Mongol allies, whose enemy the Chin had been, the name was dropped). In 1618 Nurhaci drew up a list of seven major grievances against the Ming, regarding their increasing support for his rivals, the Yehe, and other disputes, and in a ceremony to symbolize his communion with the ancestral spirits of his tribe— and as an act of defiance against the Ming— burned it. This rite marked his declaration of war on the Chinese Empire. With an outnumbered force of 10,000, Nurhaci attacked a vast Ming army, defeated it, and took the town of Fushun and part of the province of Liaotung, capturing the learned Chinese official, Fan Wen-ch'eng, who became an important adviser to the Manchus. Other Chinese inhabitants of the frontier zone also joined the ascendant Manchu side, shaving their heads and adopting the queue, or pigtail, and Manchu costume as signs of their allegiance.

Gradually Nurhaci conquered most of the Chinese frontier states, the last to fall being Yehe in 1619. (The last Yehe prince, as he died in his blazing castle, is said to have hurled down a curse on the Manchus, declaring that they would be destroyed by a woman of Yehe. As a result, no Yehe females were allowed into the Manchu harem until the Empress Tzu-hsi—whose reactionary policies certainly contributed to the ultimate downfall of the dynasty.)

In 1621 Nurhaci took Liaoyang and then the important town of Mukden, taking first one and then the other as his capital, Mukden remaining his capital and that of his successors from 1625 to 1644. He allied with the Mongol tribes to the west, thus securing his right flank. In many confrontations between the Manchus and Ming during the early 1620s the Manchu archers often found themselves facing artillery, the use of which the Chinese had learned from Jesuit missionaries from Europe. But despite the threat of this firepower (and perhaps because the novice Chinese gunners frequently ran out of gunpowder) the Manchus were almost invariably victorious.

By the mid-1620s, the Manchu confederation under Nurhaci had become such a threat to the Chinese that the decision was taken to withdraw Ming forces from the Chinese-Manchurian basin to behind the fortified Great Wall, leaving the heavily guarded pass of Shanhaikuan as the only feasible lowland entry point for would-be Manchu invaders. The frontier town of Ning-yuan, under the governor Yuan Ch'ung-huan, continued to defy the advancing Manchus. This last stronghold of Chinese power inside Manchu territory actually managed to hold Nurhaci at bay. Though only

A portrait of Nurhaci, chief of the Mongol Jurchen tribe who built up the powerful Manchu confederation that overthrew the Ming. For his role in founding Manchu power he was canonized as T'ai Tsu, or "Great Ancestor."

A carved wood chest of the early Ch'ing period showing Manchus and Chinese joined in battle.

Opposite A woven silk tapestry of the late sixteenth or early seventeenth century with phoenixes amid peonies. The phoenix symbolizes the Empress and peonies, the spring.

slightly wounded in the fighting, he was now aged sixty-eight and this major setback hastened his end. He died in 1626. Later, he was canonized by the Manchus as T'ai Tsu, or "Great Ancestor," for his role as the founder of Manchu power.

Nurhaci was succeeded by his eighth son, Abahai (1592–1643). While apparently conducting negotiations for a treaty with the recalcitrant governor Yuan—on absurd terms, for the negotiations were clearly no more than a delaying tactic —Abahai's army attacked and temporarily subjugated Korea, partly to acquire money, since currency supplies had been cut off when tribute and trading relations with China had ended, and food supplies, but also to secure his eastern flank. Abahai then attacked Yuan a second time (1627), but was again repulsed. Turning his attention away from the Chinese-held frontier, he led his army along the Mongol-controlled route through the Jehol mountains and made several raiding missions into North China in 1629–30. However, lack of communication in this difficult region meant that, despite acquisitions of loot, territorial gains were short-lived. The only practical route to Peking remained that which the Chinese held at Shanhaikuan. During these incursions, Yuan was apparently accused by Peking of treason and was publicly cut to pieces. These charges were probably unfounded sedition spread by Abahai's agents. Now the strongest border opponent of Manchu advance was gone.

In the 1630s, more brief sorties were made into North China by the mountain route, and the remainder of the region now called Manchuria fell into Abahai's hands. By 1635 he abandoned the names Jurchen and Chien-chou, the origins of which carried with them notions of long-established subservience to China, and began to call his people Manchus. The following year he was declared Emperor and proclaimed the founding of the Ch'ing dynasty. After gaining control of the Amur region, which he added to his now huge dominion,

Abahai made further successful raids into North China, returning to Mukden in 1643 with a vast booty after (again temporarily) taking sixty-seven cities and routing the Ming army thirty-seven times. In that year, when Abahai died, Manchu territory extended right up to the strategic Shanhaikuan pass, and his vast army lay poised on the very doorstep of the Chinese Empire.

Meanwhile, in Peking during the early seventeenth century the once great Ming dynasty was clearly waning. A succession of degenerate emperors, particularly Shen-tsung, had by their extravagance and submission to the power of the court eunuchs—always a sinister element in Chinese imperial life—brought financial ruin and loss of prestige to the ruling house. Especially guilty also—through neglect rather than willful corruption—was Shen-tsung's grandson the young Emperor Chu Yu-chiao (1605–27) whose obsessive interest in his hobby of carpentry and total lack of concern for affairs of state permitted the rise of Wei Chung-hsien.

Wei, literally a self-made eunuch (there being an ancient law which made the imperial court responsible for the welfare of eunuchs, he had castrated himself to avoid paying his gambling debts), had inveigled himself into a position in the catering division of the boy-emperor's household, gained the favor of his scheming wetnurse, K'o, and eventually, having eliminated all his rivals, rose to a position of supremacy at court. Under his virtual rule temples were erected and vast sums of money spent on ceremonies in his honor, and to testify to his virtue, the rumor was circulated that a sacred unicorn had been seen in Shantung. Wei's high-handed behavior and the factionalism he had promoted among the gentry, who in consequence refused to pay their taxes, lost the dynasty the confidence of the people, a process which was slowed, but not halted, by his suicide on the death of the Emperor and the succession of Chu Yu-chien (1611–44).

A Manchu soldier, from an early Ch'ing manuscript.

his home region of Shensi in 1628 had made numerous raids in that province with up to 200,000 peasant-bandits under his command. By the late 1630s, Li had emerged as the leader of this potent military force, especially after the death of Kao, and was beginning to take small towns such as Fengyang by 1635. In this powerful role he had under him a band which, though ill-trained and poorly disciplined was, by sheer weight of numbers, a match for the weakening Ming army. In 1642 Li succeeded in capturing the major town of K'ai-feng by breaking a dike in order to flood the city—and after losing an eye in the struggle. As the Ming forces managed to crush minor rebels, their followers tended to turn to Li, so that on New Year's Day, 1644, in complete control of Shensi province, he was sufficiently strong to proclaim himself Emperor of the Great Shun ("Harmonious") dynasty, issuing his own coinage to commemorate the event. He then marched on the capital, Peking.

The situation at court was one of terror. Lack of cash to pay the imperial guard had demoralized the defending troops, and the predictions of court astrologers of the imminent collapse of the Ming dynasty added to the prevailing atmosphere of despair. Emperor Chu Yu-chien was urged to send for his ablest general, Wu San-kuei (1612–78) who was then holding the border against the Manchu threat, but, typically, he procrastinated and left his decision until it was too late. As the eunuch garrison commanders and court officials fled for their lives, Li's advance was barely resisted, and a eunuch guard opened the gates of Peking to, apparently, China's next bandit-emperor.

Inside the imperial palace the Empress bade farewell to her children and hanged herself. Sending his three sons into hiding, Chu killed several of his favorite concubines rather than let the one-eyed bandit, Li, seize them. He tried to kill his own daughter, but, hiding his face with his robe as he brought his sword down, succeeded only in lopping off her arm. With a eunuch companion, he tried to leave the city in disguise, but found his way barred. He returned to the palace and rang a bell to summon his advisers; it remained unanswered. Finally accepting Li's victory, he ascended Coal Hill which overlooks the city and there, on April 25, 1644, in a pavilion on its summit, hanged himself. His suicide note, written on the lapel of his coat, reads:

I, poor in virtue and of contemptible personality, have incurred the wrath of God on high. My ministers have deceived me. I am ashamed to meet my ancestors; and therefore I myself take off my crown, and with my hair covering my face, await dismemberment at the hands of the rebels. Do not hurt a single one of my people!

Though a few unsuccessful pretenders later emerged, the formerly magnificent Ming dynasty was finished.

Down in the city, Li had taken the father and other members of the border general Wu's family,

Under Chu's grossly inefficient rule, the government fell into a state of chaos. The usually stable presidency of the administrative bodies, the Six Ministries, changed hands 116 times from 1621 to 1644 and was symptomatic of his vacillating policies. His reign was further characterized by an inadequate appraisal of the potential danger of the situation at the Manchu front, but in this and in most areas of his domestic policy the Emperor was powerless to act, the moral poverty of his court being matched by the bankrupt state of his finances. The generally unstable rural situation was worsened by the response of the landowners who, left to their own devices, exempted themselves from taxation while imposing an extra heavy burden on their tenants. Piracy along the southeast coast and disastrous famines and floods in the 1620s resulted, as always in Chinese history, in large numbers of peasants, out of sheer necessity, turning toward secret societies or joining groups of marauding bandits. Again a pattern familiar in China's past was repeated: one brigand rose to a position of preeminence.

He was Li Tzu-ch'eng (c. 1605–45), a former member of the great imperial postal service who had been made redundant when the service was disbanded—a further feature of the decline of the Ming administrative system. He joined his bandit uncle, Kao Ying-hsiang, known popularly as the "Dashing King," who after a terrible famine in

78

as well as his favorite concubine, Ch'en Yuan, as hostages, sending messages to him demanding an alliance to defeat the Manchu army which waited menacingly just beyond the Great Wall. Wu, however, probably had aspirations to the dragon throne himself, and despite the threat to the lives of his family was not prepared to join forces with a rebel and a brigand in whose uncertain company his own life and position might be jeopardized. Shaving his head to mark his loyalty to the Manchus, Wu met them on May 27 and opened the vital pass of Shanhaikuan to the mighty force under Prince Dorgon, regent of the new Manchu boy-emperor, Abahai's son, Fu-lin.

On the advice of his trusted Chinese adviser, Fan Wen-ch'eng, Dorgon now entered China to contend with Li for the imperial throne. Li's army advanced against the Manchus and was decisively defeated. Returning hastily to Peking, Li murdered the captured Ming princes and the family of Wu—though taking Ch'en Yuan for himself. He melted down all the silver in the palace which he then destroyed along with nine city gate towers and many other fine buildings, and on June 4 left the blazing city and fled westward. Two days later, Wu and the Manchus entered Peking as liberators,

Wu perhaps ingenuously believing them to be his partners in raising himself to the throne.

It was therefore to Wu's surprise that the Manchus, once installed in the remaining palace buildings, showed no signs of leaving. He was duty bound to avenge the deaths of his father and family and, chasing Li across China, regained his concubine and drove the rebel into the hands of a group of peasants who slew him. Wu then half-heartedly returned to Peking to acknowledge the Manchus' success, and on October 19, 1644, the young Manchu Emperor, Fu-lin, entered the city. Eleven days later, declaring that the "wheel of the world" had turned and that the Ming had relinquished the heavenly mandate to the Manchus, Fu-lin was proclaimed the first Ch'ing Emperor of China, with the reign-title, Shun-chih, the first of the house which was to rule China until the twentieth century.

The Ch'ing conquerors immediately took the reins of government in a firm grip. They continued to utilize the banner system to control certain areas of the country, although appropriation of lands for bannermen's families led to much discontent (and by the nineteenth century the banner organization became unwieldy and cripplingly expensive). Among the early statutes enacted by the Ch'ing were some racially biased laws to prohibit Chinese from entering the imperial harem, enforcing Manchu styles of dress and banning the Chinese practice of foot-binding, but most later lapsed or were withdrawn. In fact the main cause of the Manchu success and the explanation of how a minor tribal group came to dominate China for nearly three centuries—longer than any other frontier invader—lies in their acceptance of the Chinese in official positions (up to eighty or ninety per cent of the lesser positions). Although at the time of the Manchu invasion many local officials committed suicide, most collaborated and were ready to work with a dynasty which aimed to perpetuate the traditional elements of Chinese government. In doing so, the Manchu gained the confidence of the gentry who had lost faith in imperial leadership during the late Ming period. The bandit, Li, had he remained in power, would not have won them over because his avowed aim and that of his followers was one of self-gain, totally lacking in direction or political credibility. In the early years of the Ch'ing, tighter control limited corruption and the power of the eunuchs and guarded against a repetition of the situation which had weakened and impoverished the Ming emperors.

Within two years of their entry into China, the Manchus were virtual masters of the entire country. A feeble Ming revival in 1648 and the rebellion, thirty years later, of their ever-reluctant ally, Wu, were quickly crushed, and the dynasty firmly set on a course which led within a few decades to a period, under Emperor Ch'ien-lung, which stands out as the pinnacle of Chinese civilization.

RUSSELL ASH

Chu Yu-chien, last of the Ming emperors who hanged himself when a bandit, Li Tzu-ch'eng, seized Peking.

Economic difficulties

While dynasties changed in China, Europe had difficulties of its own. The first half of the seventeenth century was a time of real and continuing crisis in European history. The upheaval of the Thirty Years War in Germany, the wars of religion and the Fronde in France, the constitutional problems and the civil wars in England and the rapid decline of Spanish power, are all aspects of a more general crisis, which was mainly economic in character, although it had widespread social, political and religious implications. The rapid economic growth of the sixteenth century, which was largely made possible by the development of trade and mining beyond Europe's borders, and by rapid population growth, continued, but at a far lower rate. Population, which had grown so rapidly in the sixteenth century, grew far more slowly in the seventeenth. The violence of the seventeenth-century wars, death by famine and illness and emigration to colonies overseas meant that in many regions population was lower at the end of the century than at the beginning.

Even more important than changes that affected Europe as a whole was the relative shift between different areas. Spain's economic dominance, which was in any case insecurely based, gave way to that of Holland, France and England. The economic rela-

tionship between different classes was also changing rapidly. In general, the European aristocracy gained at the expense of the lower classes. In some countries— most notably in England—where rents were usually fixed for long periods, the smaller gentry and the farmers gained at the expense of the larger landlords, while in Holland the effect of the growth in trade was felt by almost every economic group. In part, the success of England, Holland and France must have been connected with the growth in population in those countries, which stand in marked contrast to Spain, Germany and Italy, all of which had declining populations.

It is fairly easy to see the basic economic trends of the century: continuing price rises until about 1650, a movement away from agriculture toward trade, industry and manufacture. But the period is confused by conflicting signs of improvement and deterioration, and there were many contradictions within the broad trends.

The end of the Thirty Years War

The siege of Magdeburg in 1631 did not by any means end the Thirty Years War; it merely marked the beginning of a new phase. Nor did the death of the leading generals on both sides prove effective as a means of getting peace: Tilly was killed at the Lech in 1632 and Gustavus Adolphus at Lützen in the same

The Battle of Regensburg.

year, and Wallenstein was murdered in 1634, but the war continued. A new generation of generals replaced the old.

Swedish armies, most notably under Johan Banér (1596-1641), continued to be successful despite the death of Gustavus Adolphus— the Lion of the North—and the increasing interest of the French in the struggle further aided the Protestants. In 1634, France began subsidizing the Swedish campaign.

In 1635, the whole pattern of the war changed again. By the Treaty of Prague in that year the Emperor Ferdinand made peace with one of his leading German antagonists, the Elector John George of Saxony. Ferdinand agreed to withdraw the 1629 Edict of Restitution, to recognize Lutheranism and to hand over some disputed territories to Saxony. Other Protestant princes including the Elector of Brandenburg soon saw the advantages of accepting this treaty. As a result, the religious character of the war became less important, and the war became more a revival of the old struggle over Hapsburg dominance in Europe. But now the Hapsburgs were in a weak position. Instead of increasing their power at the expense of the weak states around them as they had done for much of the sixteenth century, they were under attack from two strong and hostile neighbors. Military success had never come easily to the Hapsburgs; their most brilliant achievements had all resulted from dynastic marriages. Their greatest talents had been apparent in diplomacy and the bedchamber rather than on the battlefield.

During the next few years, the Hapsburgs, despite the aid of those Protestant princes who were

prepared to help the Emperor in return for substantial modification of his claims, were under relentless pressure. In 1641, Swedish General Johan Banér attacked Regensburg and almost succeeded in capturing Ferdinand III, who had become Emperor on the death of his father in 1637. The deaths of Richelieu and Louis XIII led to a slight modification of French policy in Germany. Mazarin and Louis XIV showed an early interest in the peace talks at Münster in 1644, as Mazarin preferred to establish his position in France firmly than to pursue conquest abroad. This did not prevent the French from throwing their finest general, the Viscount of Turenne (1611-75), who had previously been fighting in Spain, into the struggle. The Emperor, the Lutheran princes and France now all wanted peace. Even the Swedes, who had just completed a highly advantageous peace treaty with the Danes, were now beginning to see that peace might bring more benefits than war.

The Peace of Westphalia

By 1647, it was clear that all the combatants wanted peace. The French and the Swedes, who were poised to capture Bavaria, agreed by the Treaty of Ulm not to do so. In return, the Elector of Bavaria and his brother, the Elector of Cologne, the two leading non-Hapsburg Roman Catholic princes, promised to remain neutral for the rest of the war. Other German princes followed suit, and although the Elector of Bavaria broke the treaty, he was quickly beaten by Turenne.

Two important treaties were signed in 1648. On October 24,

A German merchants' warehouse in Venice.

Years War to a close

the Treaty of Westphalia formally brought the Thirty Years War to an end. Most of the concessions were made by the Emperor, while most of the benefits went to Sweden and France. Sweden made substantial territorial gains in the north, which brought control of the mouths of the Elbe, Weser and Oder Rivers. French sovereignty over Alsace and the Lorraine bishoprics was acknowleged. The Edict of Restitution was canceled. The right of the princes to direct their own foreign policy was recognized. However the original issues, long since forgotten, were

The ratification of the Treaty of Münster painting by Geraert Ter Borch

decided in favor of the Roman Catholics: Bohemia was retained by the Emperor and the Upper Palatine by Bavaria (although Charles Louis, son of Frederick V, "the Winter King," was allowed to keep the rump of his principality).

Connected with the Peace of Westphalia, although it did not form part of it, was the Treaty of Münster, signed nine months earlier. The Spanish, hard-pressed by both the French and the Dutch, at last formally recognized that they had no hope of reconquering the north, and acknowleged Dutch sovereignty. Although this represented a serious defeat for Spanish hopes, it had long been clear that there could be no other outcome to the Dutch War of Independence. By recognizing this, the Spanish reduced the danger of a further loss of territory in the Spanish Netherlands.

The year 1648 marked the formal end of Hapsburg domina-

tion of Europe. The Spanish Hapsburgs abandoned their claim to their richest European territory, the United Provinces, while their Austrian cousins were reduced to a purely formal leadership of the Holy Roman Empire. The Hapsburg threat was rapidly replaced by another, which the princes of Europe found little less serious. Fifty years of strong rule by French monarchs and their able servants had increased Bourbon rule dramatically.

The Emperor Ferdinand III saw that one of the reasons for the defeat of Hapsburg hopes in the Thirty Years War was the lack of an effective army. In 1649, a standing army was introduced. Ferdinand saw the need for a strong central authority in Germany, but Hapsburg power had been too far reduced for him to have any real effect on German politics. The future of Germany lay with individual principalities, and with one in particular— Brandenburg. The future of Austrian Hapsburg rule lay largely along and beyond the eastern borders of the Holy Roman Empire. As the seventeenth and eighteenth centuries continued, the power of Brandenburg grew, while Austria became less and less a significant factor in European politics—although it remained powerful in eastern Europe and Italy. The Peace of Westphalia was a major factor in bringing about these changes to the balance of power, and its importance is easily underrated.

Brandenburg

The dynasty that ruled the territory that had formerly belonged to the Knights of the Teutonic Order was that of Hohenzollern, the family of the last Grand Master of the Knights. As a result of the dismemberment of the Palatinate during the Thirty Years War, Brandenburg was the only important Calvinist principality left in Germany. The growth in Brandenburg's importance was largely due to Frederick William, who became Prince in 1640. His ability was recognized both by later historians and by his subjects, who called him the Great Elector.

The principality to which Frederick William succeeded was divided. Brandenburg itself was the largest and richest region, but he was also Duke of Prussia, an enclave in Poland, for which he had to do homage to the King of Poland, and the ruler of the Duchy of Cleves and the counties of Mark and Ravensburg. Frederick William saw the need for an efficient army and formed a professional force of about 8,000 men during the first year of his rule. Although his army was fairly small, at least in comparison with the forces available to Sweden and the Emperor's supporters, it was large enough to make Brandenburg a useful ally in a divided Germany, and as a result Frederick William's support was sought by both sides. At the Peace of Westphalia, Brandenburg was

Frederick William, the Great Elector of Prussia.

given Further Pomerania and the bishoprics of Magdeburg, Minden and Halberstadt—gains quite out of proportion to the small part that Brandenburg had played during the war.

Internally, Frederick William's policy was no less successful. He pushed up taxation to a high level in order to pay for his expensive foreign policy, which involved an attempt to play off his principal neighbors, Sweden and Poland, against each other, and for the upkeep of his army, which he made no attempt to disband after 1648. As a result of his efforts, Brandenburg had become by the time of his death in 1688, a major factor in German politics.

The arrest of the five members

In his anger and alarm at the loss of his most devoted servants, Strafford and Laud, Charles I of England—who had previously attempted to stem the tide of Parliament's demands by promises and prevarications, by standing his ground for as long as he could and then gracelessly giving way, and by alternating between compromise and fitful moods of determination—made a rash and disastrous move. On January 4, 1642, he marched to the Commons with a squad of soldiers, intending to arrest five of its leading members. Those members, warned in time of his approach, escaped by boat down the Thames from Westminster to the City, London's trading district. The King, whose personal courage was never in doubt, followed them there and demanded that they surrender to him. When they refused, he returned to his palace at Whitehall through streets filled with crowds shouting, "Privileges of Parliament! Privileges of Parliament!"

A few days later the five members came out of hiding and proceeded in triumph up river to Westminster, where they were met by cheering citizens and beating drums. There were shouts for war against the King and his supporters, and as the placard-bearing crowds passed the royal palace of Whitehall they pointed with excitement and satisfaction to its curtained windows. The palace was empty; the King had fled from London the day before. When he returned, it was to his death.

"A Cruel Necessity"

On January 27, 1649, "Charles Stuart, Tyrant, Traitor, Murderer and Public Enemy" was condemned to death by England's highest court. Oliver Cromwell, leader of the Puritan Revolution, labeled the execution of Charles I "a cruel necessity." Cruel it certainly was—but there were many who doubted its necessity. The King's death effectively terminated a long and bitter struggle between Cromwell and the crown, but it did not solve the Protector's problems. In the decades before his trial, Charles had dissolved four Parliaments for refusing to grant him his legal revenues—and each time he had been forced to recall the Members. After eliminating the King, whom he called a meddlesome "Man of Blood," Cromwell discovered that Parliament could no more exist without the King than the King without Parliament. A decade after Charles' execution, his fugitive son returned to England to reclaim the throne.

"I fear not death," said Charles I, King of England, as he dressed on the morning of the day on which he was to die. "Death is not terrible to me. I bless my God I am prepared."

Throughout his trial, Charles' courage and his spirit had impressed all who had seen him. His sunken cheeks, shadowed eyes and gray hair had made the forty-eight-year-old monarch look tired, old and worn, but he had walked briskly into Westminster Hall, had sat quietly before the president of the court, and had gazed calmly, almost aloofly, at the judges in front of him and at the spectators behind him as counsel for the prosecution read out the crimes with which he stood charged. When instructed to answer the charges, he spoke with clarity and confidence—and quite without the stammer that normally hampered his tongue—insisting in his Scottish accent that the court had no right to try him. Neither on that day nor on the two following days of the trial could he be induced, by any manner of persuasion, to betray the trust committed to him by God—and "by old and lawful descent"—to make answer to this "unlawful authority."

He was their "*lawful* King" he reminded his judges, and he demanded that they show him a "legal Authority warranted by the Word of God, the Scriptures, or warranted by the constitution of the Kingdom." Since they had no such legal authority, he could not and would not answer them. And he still had not answered them when, on January 27, 1649, as "Charles Stuart, Tyrant, Traitor, Murderer and Public Enemy," he was condemned to be put to death "by the severing of his head from his body."

Shocked by the abrupt ending of the trial, Charles called out, "Will you hear me a word, Sir?"

"You are not to be heard after the sentence," the president of the court insisted.

"No, Sir?"

"No, Sir, by your favor, Sir. Guard, withdraw your prisoner."

"I may speak after the sentence—by your favor, Sir, I may speak after the sentence. By your favor, hold! The sentence, Sir—I say, Sir, I do—"

For the first time in the trial he was incoherent; but as the soldiers closed around him to withdraw him from the court, he regained his former composure. "I am not suffered for to speak," he said with resignation. "Expect what justice other people will have."

Only once during the few days he had left to live did Charles again seem on the verge of losing control of his emotions. That moment came when the doomed King said good-bye to the two of his children who still remained in England. Having blessed them both, he walked quickly away to his bedchamber and with trembling legs fell down upon his bed.

On his last morning he was tranquil, almost serene, assuring the attendant who brushed his hair and fixed the pearl earrings in his ears that this was his second marriage day, that by nightfall he would be espoused to his blessed Jesus. When an army officer came to inform the King that it was time for him to leave, he knelt for a few moments in prayer and then, taking the hand of Bishop Juxon, who had been allowed to stay with him to the end, Charles said in a firm voice, "Come, let us go." As he walked out of Whitehall Palace toward the Banqueting House, his faithful dog Rogue gamboled after him.

The scaffold had been draped in black, and on it, surrounded by lines of helmeted soldiers with pikes and halberds, stood two army colonels, a group of reporters and the executioner and his assistant, both of them masked and disguised with false hair and beards. The King spoke to them all briefly. Then, tucking his long hair up into his white satin nightcap so that it would not deflect the edge of the executioner's blade, he looked up at the sky, said his last prayers, and lay down with his neck on the block.

The axe fell; the head was severed in a single stroke; and "at the instant whereof," said a young spectator, "I remember well there was such a grone by the Thousands then present as I never heard

Charles I's wife, the French princess, Henrietta Maria, whose Catholicism made her unpopular in England.

Opposite The execution of Charles I. Although Charles was not a popular king, most of his subjects were saddened by his death.

The execution on Tower Hill, London, in 1643 of William Laud, Archbishop of Canterbury, the King's most able supporter.

Charles I's family, with the future Charles II in the center.

before and desire I may never hear again."

Curiously enough, there were no disturbances. The execution had taken place outside the Banqueting House instead of on Tower Hill, for the square in front of Inigo Jones' imposing building was small and easily guarded. But the guards were scarcely needed, and although there was a scramble around the scaffold as men and women ran forward to dip handkerchiefs in the spilled blood, the square was soon cleared by mounted troops and London fell into silence.

To Oliver Cromwell, an East Anglian farmer of modest estate who had become the most influential man in England in the years following the civil war, the execution of Charles I in January, 1649, was a cruel necessity. Cromwell had been a member of Parliament during much of the long conflict between that body and the King that is known as the Puritan Revolution. Although it derived its name from the fact that the King and his followers supported the

Church of England while his opponents were on the whole Puritan, the Revolution involved much more than religion. Part of the conflict was constitutional—a dispute between a King who believed in his divine right to rule and a Parliament that wanted a constitutional monarchy. There were also economic issues, for the middle-class gentry and merchants who made up the bulk of the Parliamentarian party were fighting for a greater role in determining financial and commercial policies.

The struggle intensified as Parliament sought to find new ways to limit the King's power. In retaliation, Charles tried to rule without a Parliament, but he found that he could not raise money by himself, and financial pressures forced him to reconvene Parliament several times. In 1640 the so-called Long Parliament began its session. Its demands, and the King's rejection of them, ultimately led to civil war.

When the final breach with the King came in 1642, Cromwell, who had been active in the Puritan cause, rushed home from Westminster. Out of his slender resources he equipped and paid a troop of horsemen to fight for the "preservation of the true religion, the laws, liberty and peace of the Kingdom." After the Battle of Edgehill—in which Parliament's cavalry were driven from the field by Prince Rupert's Cavaliers (as the King's supporters were called)—Cromwell raised and trained a far larger force of cavalry. His new troops scattered the Royalists on Marston Moor "like a little dust," securing the north for the Roundheads (the name given the supporters of Parliament). At Naseby, Cromwell's cavalry, which formed part of Parliament's professional, regularly paid and well-disciplined New Model Army, once again proved its sterling quality. And at Stow-on-the-Wold, on March 21, 1646, Charles' last army in the field was defeated.

Parliament and the army soon fell out among themselves, however, and in their quarrel the captured King sought and failed to find his own salvation. The quarrel began in a religious dispute. Cromwell had urged Parliament, after both Marston

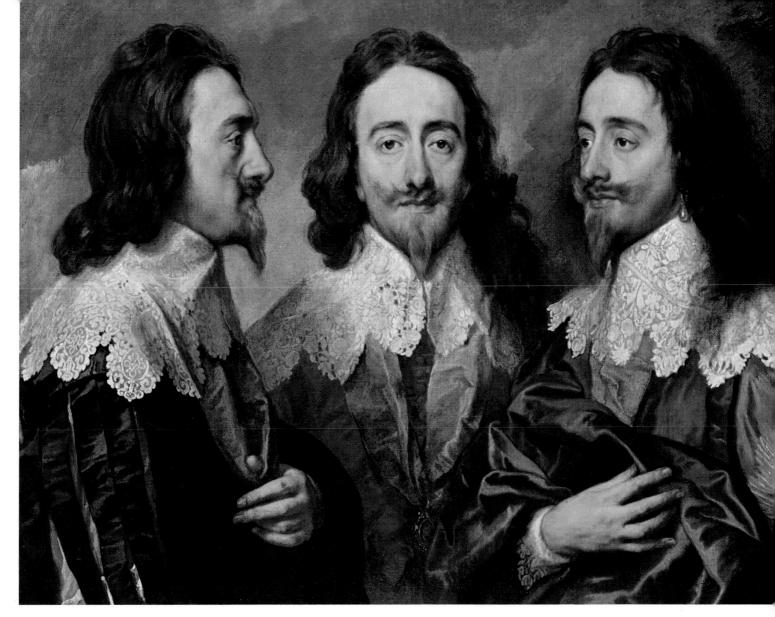

Moor and Naseby, to remember that the soldiers had risked their lives not only for the political liberty of their country but for religious toleration as well. The one cause was, after all, just as fundamental to the issues over which the civil war had been fought as the other. But the Presbyterians in Parliament, rigid in their orthodoxy and not content with persecuting those who, like the King, were devout members of the established Church of England, were insisting that Baptists should be subjected to life imprisonment, that laymen should be prohibited from preaching in public, and that all Independents should be dismissed from the New Model Army. Further, they attempted to disband the army without back pay.

Cromwell attempted to act as mediator in the increasingly bitter quarrel between Parliament and the army. He urged Parliament to be more tolerant and attempted to dissuade the army from falling under the influence of those wilder spirits who were preaching universal suffrage and radical reform. Cromwell himself was far from being a radical. He had nothing against the monarchy as an institution and earnestly desired to come to terms with the King. With the idea of a settlement in mind, he begged Charles to consider the "Heads of the Proposals," a moderate offer based on wide toleration.

Van Dyck's triple portrait of Charles I, designed to help the Italian sculptor Bernini execute a bust of the King. On seeing the portrait Bernini said that the features were those of a doomed man.

Prince Rupert of the Rhine, a brilliant but erratic general, whose undisciplined enthusiasm cost the King dear.

85

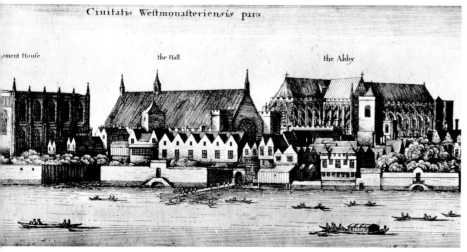

ment House   the Hall   the Abby

The proposals envisaged the use of the English Book of Common Prayer for those who wanted it, a limited form of episcopacy, and an end to Parliament's sequestration of the estates of Cavaliers—a punitive measure that eventually caused the Royalist squires to develop an irreconcilable hatred of Puritanism.

There was nothing in these proposals that Charles could not in all honor have accepted, and his more sensible advisers strongly urged him to agree to them. "A crown so near lost was never recovered so easily as this would be," one of them informed him. But Charles believed that by playing off one side against the other he could solve all his difficulties and return to Whitehall in triumph. And thus he preferred to dissemble, prevaricate and intrigue. Although he was a man of high moral character, Charles had no

A view of Westminster in the mid-seventeenth century, by Wenceslas Hollar. One of the centers of opposition to the royal government was the House of Commons.

Below A playing card attacking the Rump Parliament, a small group of militant members of the House of Commons who refused to allow Parliament to be dissolved.

Right Oliver Cromwell, the Lord Protector, as the Savior of England.

political scruples—and although he was in some respects a learned man, he was not an intelligent one. He was a fine judge of art and horses, but he had little understanding of the human character. He tried to deceive the army, he intrigued with Parliament, and he came to a secret understanding with the Scots that led to a brief new outbreak of the war.

By this time Cromwell had completely reversed his attitude toward the King. He had become convinced that Charles Stuart must be regarded as "a Man of Blood," and that the only hope for peace and order in the country was to bring the King to that justice which his underhanded and traitorous dealings so richly deserved. "I tell you," Cromwell cried out to the hesitant commissioners appointed to try the King, "I tell you, we will cut off the King's head with the crown on it."

Cromwell, his clever, earnest son-in-law, Henry Ireton, and those other regicides whose actions were not prompted by malice or desire for personal gain were all sincerely convinced that the execution of the King could alone prevent the country from falling into anarchy. So long as Charles lived, it was impossible to carry on government by consent; with his death it would become possible to rule by force. And by force they had to rule, or they too would perish.

Although there had been no disturbances in London after the execution, the mood of the country at large was alarming. To many Englishmen, the killing of the King was a sacrilege that God would surely punish, and republicanism was an evil system of government that would arouse His deepest wrath. To others, the new leaders of the country were as unworthy of trust and respect as the dead King himself had been—"silken gentlemen" who would soon prove their fundamentally conservative, not to say reactionary, nature.

Royalists who had fought for the King and Presbyterians who had fought against him joined in condemning the new government. The domestic situation deteriorated rapidly, as economic distress and social unrest were added to political uproar and religious dissent. Beggars roamed the streets; highwaymen by the hundreds infested the roads; the navy, grown mutinous, abandoned the control of the seas to Royalist privateers under the direction of Prince Rupert; Scotland and Ireland looked eagerly to the day when Prince Charles would return in triumph to his father's throne; and the monarchies of the Continent looked upon England as a country beyond the pale—convicted and doomed.

Yet the rulers of the country were at first inspired rather than intimidated by the problems that beset them on every hand. Once the new republic, known as the Commonwealth, was established in 1649, they acted quickly to abolish both the office of King and the House of Lords, thus giving to the House of Commons the supreme legislative and executive power in the state. Very soon afterward they set up a council of state of forty-one members whose duty it was to administer the country's affairs.

Within four years of its establishment, this council

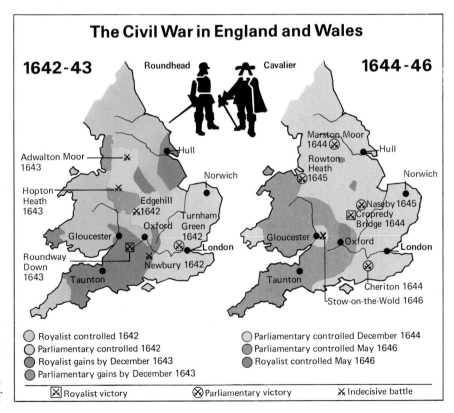

The Civil War in England and Wales

1642-43   Roundhead   Cavalier   **1644-46**

1642-43 map labels:
Hull
Adwalton Moor 1643
Norwich
Hopton Heath 1643
Edgehill 1642
Turnham Green 1642
Oxford
Gloucester
London
Roundway Down 1643
Newbury 1642
Taunton

1644-46 map labels:
Marston Moor 1644
Hull
Rowton Heath 1645
Norwich
Naseby 1645
Cropredy Bridge 1644
Gloucester
Oxford
London
Taunton
Cheriton 1644
Stow-on-the-Wold 1646

○ Royalist controlled 1642
○ Parliamentary controlled 1642
● Royalist gains by December 1643
● Parliamentary gains by December 1643

○ Parliamentary controlled December 1644
● Parliamentary controlled May 1646
● Royalist controlled May 1646

⊠ Royalist victory   ⊗ Parliamentary victory   ✕ Indecisive battle

had overwhelmed its enemies. Ireland was subjugated with exceptional ferocity—the garrisons of Drogheda and Wexford were slaughtered without mercy at Cromwell's orders—and two-thirds of the Irish lands were transferred to English ownership.

The council next turned its attention to Scotland. On September 3, 1650, Cromwell destroyed a Scottish army at Dunbar, and thus united Scotland to England in a single British Commonwealth.

Overseas, an overhauled, strong and efficient navy and the talents of Admiral Robert Blake, a seaman of genius, combined to make England the greatest naval power in the world. Prince Rupert's privateers and the Barbary pirates of the Mediterranean were attacked and defeated; war was waged against England's leading commercial and naval rivals; Jamaica was captured; and the Spanish fleet was crippled at Tenerife.

The cost of those wars led to heavier and heavier taxation and to the disruption of trade, and consequently to the increased unpopularity of Cromwell's government. Despite the benefits that its advocates prophesied, the kind of republicanism that

Cromwell's council imposed upon the nation did not recommend itself to the people; the majority of them were pleased when, in 1653, Cromwell forcibly dissolved the Rump Parliament (a group composed of those who had survived Colonel Thomas Pride's 1648 purge of unsympathetic, anti-military members). The members of the Rump Parliament had shown themselves jealous of their powers, addicted to interminable debate, and capable of enacting a statute that made adultery punishable by death. But the Nominated Parliament that followed it—and that in turn persuaded Cromwell to assume the title of Lord Protector—was no more capable of winning the people's trust than its predecessor had been.

The division of the country into eleven districts, each commanded by a major-general, contributed more than any other factor to the disesteem in which the people held Cromwell's government, for these major-generals were required to assume the duties of guardians of public morality as well as those of tax collectors and policemen. They suppressed horse races and cock fights, prohibited the performance of plays, closed brothels and gambling dens, enforced

The Royal Martyr; the frontispiece of *Eikon Basilike* (*Image of a King*). Charles' ineptitude as a ruler was only equaled by his piety as a man.

The execution of the King; an imaginary reconstruction.

the laws against drunkenness and blasphemy and closed down numerous alehouses.

Aware that the only hope for the future lay in a return to the constitutional rule that he had unwillingly abandoned and to the civil legality that had been suppressed, Cromwell turned to the constitutionalists and legalists in an attempt to release himself from his dependence upon the army. Some of his advisers suggested that he take up the crown of England and restore to the country the benefits of monarchy. Although at first inclined to do so, Cromwell ultimately rejected the suggestion in deference to the views of those Puritans he most admired. But by the time of Cromwell's death in September, 1658, there was no doubt that most Englishmen longed for a return to the traditions of monarchy—and so it was that, eighteen months later, the return of Charles' son as King Charles II was achieved not merely without bloodshed but with acclamation.

The Great Rebellion had not, however, been in vain. The period of the Commonwealth and of the Protectorate (the years from 1653 to 1659 when England was ruled by a Lord Protector), though rich in political debate and constitutional experiment, has been described as "an interlude in the domestic history of the British people." But it was more than that. It is true that most of what was achieved in the interregnum did not survive the Restoration, and it is true that Cromwell was unable to rule either with parliaments or without them, being compelled by the force of events to carry on a military government that flouted the sentiments of the British people as well as his own conservative instincts and preferences for constitutional rule. Yet it is also true that the experiences that the English people underwent in that era confirmed their hatred of military rule and of the kind of stark Puritanism with which it was associated. In the next decades Parliament suppressed Puritanism with vigor.

For the future, the English monarchy was to develop along peaceful and constitutional lines. In 1688, Charles II's brother and successor, the Roman Catholic James II, attempted to coerce the nation and he was replaced by his Protestant nephew, Prince William III of Orange, in a Glorious Revolution that was bloodless and quick. The power of Parliament, asserted by the execution of Charles I, was finally confirmed.

Henceforward, the English were to experience nothing to correspond with the absolutism prevalent on the Continent in the eighteenth century. Having undergone their Reformation in the sixteenth century and their Revolution in the seventeenth, the English were finished with much of the work that elsewhere remained to be done.

Nevertheless there was still a great deal to do in England: despite local regulation and private philanthropy, social conditions in many areas were appalling; the penal code was ferocious; nonconformists were discriminated against—although not so fiercely that they lived without hope of amelioration or that they emigrated to America in the numbers that had left under the persecution of the High-Church Archbishop Laud in the 1620s and 1630s—and Roman Catholics were subjected to unjust discrimination. Nonetheless, foreigners felt that the English were the most enviable of people and that their government and institutions were worthy of the highest praise and the closest imitation. Montesquieu pointed to their system of government as a model; and in his *Philosophical Letters* Voltaire expressed a widespread opinion when he wrote, "The English nation is the only one on earth which has succeeded in regulating the power of its kings by resisting them; and which after repeated efforts has established that wise government under which the prince, all powerful for good, is restrained from doing ill."

CHRISTOPHER HIBBERT

The Juxon Medal, the gold medal that Charles gave Bishop Juxon (later Archbishop of Canterbury), just before his execution.

89

French cultural life blossoms while

The classic age of French drama

Before Charles' death Henrietta Maria fled to France. The almost continuous wars at the time did not prevent the age from being one of unparalleled advancement in the development of art and in the improvement of standards of living. And although most of the countries of Europe had, at one time or another, been ranged in conflict against France, French culture had not suffered in the esteem of the civilized world.

The genius of the French dramatists of the seventeenth century was indeed undeniable. Pierre Corneille (1606–84), a former lawyer whose early comedy *Mélite* was enthusiastically received in Paris in 1629, produced a succession of plays that included *Le Cid* (1637), a masterly piece that marks the beginning of the greatest period of French drama, and *Le Menteur*, a comedy of remarkable originality. The enormous success of his plays was in some measure due to the characterization, and in large measure to the concentration on *la gloire* (glory) which appealed to a wide public in the reigns of Louis XIII and Louis XIV, when France was expressing its European supremacy in so many ways.

For a time, Corneille was one of Richelieu's "five poets" and was obliged to produce plays on themes suggested to him by the Cardinal. Corneille, awkward and independent, was quite unsuited to such profitable but restricting work, and soon angered Richelieu by declining to follow his master's schemes. Jean de Rotrou, the only one of the five poets worthy of comparison with Corneille, died of the plague at the age of forty—but by then he had produced an extraordinary number of plays, of which four (*La Véritable Saint Genest, Don Bertrand de Cabrère, Venceslas* and *Cosroès*) are acknowledged masterpieces.

While *Cosroès* was being performed in Paris, a popular theatrical company was touring the provinces. One of its number was Jean Baptiste Poquelin (1622–73), whose stage name was Molière. Molière had already proved his gifts as a comic writer, but it was not until his *Précieuses Ridicules* was published in 1659 that he achieved his first real success.

Molière, by Mignard.

Kindly, overworked, anxious and painstaking, Molière was an authentic genius. A most fertile and inventive comic dramatist, he was an inspiration to successive generations of writers for the theater, none of whom were able to match his mastery as a creator of artificial comedy and of scintillating dialogue. Although suffering from serious lung disease, Molière insisted on playing the title role in *Le Malade Imaginaire* (*The Hypochondriac*), in the seventh presentation of his play.

The later years of Corneille were shadowed by the rise of a still greater dramatist, Jean Racine (1639–99). Ironically Racine, who was to become France's greatest tragic poet, was associated, like Pascal, with the convent of Port Royal, which strongly disapproved of the theater. Racine's earliest play, *La Thébaïde ou les Frères ennemis*, was performed by Molière's company at the Palais-Royal in 1664. His great series of classical dramas, which included *Andromaque* (1667) and *Bérénice* (1670), reached its peak in the final play, *Phèdre* (1677). His portrayal of the struggle of the passions for good and evil, morality and vice was probably due to the conflict that he felt between the teachings of Port Royal and his own sexual desires and needs—he was even accused of having poisoned a woman who had probably been his mistress. After 1677, in which year he was fully reconciled with Port Royal, Racine wrote nothing for the stage apart from two religious pieces for Madame de Maintenon's schoolgirls at Saint-Cyr.

Mazarin in power

Once his power was firmly established, Mazarin continued Richelieu's policies with skill and determination. He maintained the campaign against Austria and guided France expertly through the Thirty Years War, avoiding its worst dangers and profiting by the opportunities it presented. And when the war ended in 1648 he was able to negotiate a settlement that could scarcely have been more favorable to French aspirations in Europe.

Yet Mazarin was distrusted and hated in France, where he was vilified as a foreigner, condemned as a profligate and a gambler, censured as the new and evil power-behind-the-throne (his influence over the unpopular Queen Anne was purportedly due to his gratification of her unnatural physical passions), detested by the nobles—who could gain places at court only through his influence—and, above all, execrated by every class as the man responsible for insupportable war taxes. When the Thirty Years War drew to an end, France was on the verge of revolution—and in their universal condemnation of Mazarin's financial policies, the nobles, the people and the *Parlement* of Paris united in an attempt to overthrow the Cardinal and destroy his autocratic power.

Mazarin provoked the outburst by levying a tax on the judicial officers of the *Parlement* of Paris. When his demand was met by blank refusal—and by counterdemands for constitutional reforms—he ordered the arrest of the leaders of the *Parlement*. Parisians rushed out into the streets, built barricades, and—by slinging stones through the windows of known supporters of Mazarin—gave the incipient civil war its name, the *Fronde* (the sling).

Condé and the court

These events took place in August, 1648. The Treaty of Westphalia had not been signed, and the government's troops, commanded by the Prince of Condé, had not yet returned home from their recent victory at Lens. The court was therefore powerless to meet the threat of the *frondeurs*. Releasing prisoners and promising reforms, Mazarin and the Queen fled from the capital. Two months later, Condé's troops were released from further foreign obligations by the signing of the treaty. They promptly marched home and laid siege to Paris—and on March 11, 1649, they imposed the Treaty of Rueil on the rebels.

Although he had saved the court, Condé soon became estranged from it. Condé—a man of enormous wealth and proved military ability, the acknowledged head of the French nobility and the owner of vast estates—was at the same time utterly unlikable and intolerably arrogant. He showed an equal contempt toward the Queen and toward the low-born Mazarin, who deeply regretted the necessity of having to call upon the Prince for help against his enemies.

The second Fronde

In an action that was every bit as daring, as sudden and as provocative as his arrest of the leaders of the *Parlement* of Paris, Mazarin ordered the arrest of the proud and famous Prince and his leading supporters (who included the Prince's brother, Conti, and his brother-in-law, the Duke of Longueville). The country was immediately plunged into the second Fronde, a period of tumult,

Part of a satirical series attacking Mazarin.

civil war rages

discreditable intrigues and disgraceful humiliations. The Prince's supporters attempted to release the captives from their prison at Le Havre; the Duchess of Longueville entered into negotiations for military help from Spain; and Marshal Turenne, whose successes in the recent war had rivaled those of Condé himself, invaded Picardy at the head of a Spanish army—a move prompted by the Marshal's love for the Duchess of Longueville as much as by support for the rebellion.

The history of the second Fronde was one of plots and counterplots, deceptions, conspiracies and betrayals. It was at once a tragedy and a farce, for there were no heroes, merely characters who did not understand the succession of events in which they had become involved. For a time it appeared that the rabble-rousing priest Jean de Gondi would overthrow the government but he was won over by the promise of a red hat and became the Cardinal de Retz. Marshal Turenne's invading army was defeated at Rethel, but Turenne also succumbed to a bribe (and emerged at the head of the government forces a few months later). Cardinal Mazarin, living in exile at Brühl, appeared at one point to have lost his influence—but by January of 1652 he was back at court, his power confirmed and his confidence increased.

When Mazarin returned to court, his enemy Condé was still rampaging about the countryside with a motley band of disaffected nobles and an army of recruits, half of whom were French and half Spanish. In July, 1652, the Prince reappeared at the gates of Paris, and once again Mazarin wisely withdrew into exile for a short time.

Although Condé entered Paris in triumph, Mazarin knew that the victory was really his, for the people were exasperated by the antics of the rebellious nobles, by the continual disruptions of trade and by Condé's effrontery in having brought in Spanish troops to patrol the streets of Paris. Realizing that the tide of public opinion was running against him, Condé withdrew from Paris at the end of that summer and accepted a high command in the Spanish army.

A new enemy

The second Fronde was over and Mazarin could now concentrate on the defeat of Spain and the destruction of Condé. Like his mentor Richelieu, who had been willing to accept allies wherever allies could be found, Mazarin joined forces with Cromwell's republic against their common enemy, Spain. In 1658 an English army landed in Normandy to fight alongside the French, led by Turenne, against the Spanish, who were led by Condé. Turenne soon developed a deep respect for the discipline and bearing of the

Prince of Condé: his arrogance and mannerlessness matched his ability as a military leader.

English troops, and he reassured Mazarin that they were "the finest soldiers possible." The Marshal was confident of victory and his confidence was not misplaced. At the Battle of the Dunes in July, 1658, the Spaniards were soundly beaten. And by the Peace of the Pyrenees in November, 1659, they were obliged to abandon Dunkerque to the English, and large tracts of land in the southeast and along the Netherlands frontier to the French.

Condé, no longer a threat to the French government, was granted an amnesty and withdrew into a quiet retirement that lasted for the rest of the Cardinal's lifetime.

Mazarin concentrated his remaining energies upon winning the Spanish Netherlands for France and by arranging a marriage between Maria Teresa, the eldest daughter of Philip IV, and her cousin Louis XIV, who was twenty-one in 1659.

Louis XIV

Louis married Maria Teresa in June, 1660, and made his state entry into Paris at the end of August. As he rode past the balcony where Cardinal Mazarin stood watching the procession with the Queen Mother, he raised his white plumed hat and bowed low in the saddle to them. But Mazarin, although only in his fifties, was a dying man. In constant pain from gout and gallstones, he existed on a diet of milk, broth, game and opium. He had hoped to succeed Alexander VII as pope, but it was too late for that ultimate ambition to be fulfilled. He was obliged to be content with having completed Richelieu's work, with having brought peace to France, with having accumulated both art and jewel collections of surpassing beauty and an immense fortune.

During his last illness he urgently advised the King: "Govern. . . . Let the politician be a servant, never a master. . . . If you take the government into your own hands you will do more than a minister cleverer than I could do in six months." It was advice that Louis was to follow.

An allegory of the Fronde; Mazarin is struck down by "Mademoiselle," the amazonian sister of Louis XIV.

Louis XIV and Philip of Spain meeting to discuss the former's betrothal to Philip's daughter Maria Teresa. The marriage was to lead to the succession of the Bourbons in Spain.

"L'état c'est moi"

With the death of Cardinal Mazarin—who was officially the godfather of Louis XIV and actually the ruler of France during the Sun King's minority—the full power of the state passed to the untested twenty-two-year-old monarch. Acting with astonishing self-assurance, Louis ordered his court into full mourning for the Cardinal, summoned a meeting of his highest ministers—and bluntly informed them that he wanted the benefit of their advice only when he asked for it. Mazarin's pupil had learned his lessons well: the country, threatened by internal rebellion and foreign intrigues, needed an absolute ruler and the young King was determined to be precisely that. Insisting that he was the state, Louis XIV lifted France to the apogee of her glory and stamped his name on an age.

In early February, 1661, an outbreak of fire at the Louvre Palace forced the seriously ill Cardinal Mazarin to leave for Vincennes. There he continued to meet frequently with his godson and disciple, Louis XIV, the young King of France. On March 3, the First Minister's condition grew more grave, and the disconsolate young monarch was seen weeping as he left Mazarin's room. That evening Louis convened the Council for the first time since the Cardinal's illness, but he hardly spoke during the meeting.

On March 8 it was clear that the Cardinal was dying, and that night a watch was kept over him by Pierrette Dufour, Louis' former nurse. Early the next morning Pierrette informed Louis that Mazarin had died sometime between two and three o'clock.

Louis ordered the court to go into full mourning, an honor usually reserved only for members of the royal family. (Some historians claim that Louis' action was proof of a secret marriage between Mazarin and the Queen Mother. It seems more likely, however, that the contrary was the case; if a marriage had taken place, the King certainly would not have advertised it in this way.)

On the following day, March 10, at seven o'clock in the morning, Chancellor Séguier, the ministers and the secretaries of state assembled in the Louvre Palace. The eight politicians gathered dutifully around the King, and with a mixture of fear and curiosity they studied the face of that twenty-two-year-old man whose expression reflected his cold, enigmatic and determined personality.

The King addressed the Chancellor in the tone of a man who was "master of himself and of the universe"—a manner he was to maintain throughout his life:

Sir, ... up to the present time, I have been content to leave the governing of my affairs in the hands of the late Cardinal Mazarin. However, the time has now come for me to take over the reins of government myself. You will kindly assist me by giving me the benefit of your advice *when I ask you for it.* . . . From now on, Mr. Chancellor, you will not make any decision or sign any paper except on

my orders and not before having discussed the matter with me, unless, of course, you are brought these orders directly from me by one of my secretaries of state. As for you, sirs, as my secretaries of state, I forbid you to sign anything at all, not even a safe-conduct pass or a passport, without my prior approval.

Louis' words were received in stunned silence. Yet even those seasoned politicians did not realize that the King's speech ushered in a new and revolutionary phase in the history of France and of the world.

What led this seemingly timid, inexperienced young man to make such a momentous decision—a decision that amounted to a coup d'état? Fortunately, Louis' *Mémoires* provide much of the answer: Mazarin had advised him "not to appoint a First Minister," and Louis had decided to follow his advice "since nothing is more shameful than to see all the functions of the state collected together on the one side while, on the other, there is only the title of king." Louis was devoured by a passion for glory: "In my heart, I desire, more than anything else, more than life itself, an illustrious reputation. . . . The one emotion which overpowers all others in the minds of kings is the sense of their own greatness and glory."

France in 1661 required strong leadership. The country was exhausted by the excesses of the Fronde, the armed rebellion of the nobility that had lasted from 1648 to 1653. Louis recognized that fifty years of civil and foreign wars, financial chaos and court intrigue had left France in a deplorably weakened state. He was conscious of the weight of his new responsibility, for "when one holds such a high rank, the slightest error of judgment can lead to the most unfortunate consequences." Yet an unshakable belief in his own divine authority gave him complete self-assurance. That belief was to be the cornerstone of his government: "When God appointed kings to rule over men, He expected them, as His lieutenants, to be shown the respect due to them. Only He has the right to question the conduct of kings."

It was only after 1789 that revolutions were

Cardinal Mazarin, who built up the power of the throne which Louis XIV inherited.

Opposite Louis XIV, the Sun King: he said, "L'état c'est moi."

Louis XIV visiting the tapestry factory of Les Gobelins. Louis was a patron of the arts.

associated with movements whose aim, at least in theory, was to further the interests of the masses. Therefore, the sudden change in government that Louis XIV inaugurated after the death of Mazarin was not fully appreciated by his contemporaries. A conventional monarch who respected ancient traditions would not have behaved as Louis did. He was acting on his own initiative, in the style of a Julius Caesar. Although his conception of kingship had its roots in Mazarin's theories, Louis himself developed it into a new and original philosophy. According to his view, a monarch should possess virtually dictatorial powers, the like of which had never previously been seen in France.

Unlike a twentieth-century dictator, who has to maintain his position of power through frequent, spectacular achievements, an absolute ruler such as Louis had nothing to fear from the fickleness of public opinion. Therefore he could rule with the serene self-assurance of one who knows that he is part of a divine, eternal pattern of life.

Like Napoleon, Louis XIV tried to impose his will not only on the French government but on every aspect of national life. He controlled everything—from the order of precedence at court to troop movements and theological controversies. Nothing—from an important marriage to the building of a road—could be arranged without his approval. King and country eventually became synonymous, and it was no longer possible for Frenchmen to imagine the separation of the two without a sense of anguish and

disorientation. In fact, it was unthinkable that anyone should dare to replace Louis—the divine king who had been empowered by God to rule over his people. Louis created an excellent intelligence service and founded the modern police force, but his authority was never based on a system of police terror. He succeeded in stifling the various factions, destroying the parties and wiping out ideological divisions with the general approval of the people and without resorting to violence.

The France of Louis' time, like the France of today, was a mass of contradictions. Theoretically, there were no limits to Louis' authority, but in practice he was continually confounded by traditional customs and franchises. Feudalism survived in many forms throughout the country, and the *parlements* still claimed to be the arbiters of power. Although individual liberty was unknown, various groups possessed collective liberties and privileges that obstructed the work of the central government. Even civil servants were not directly answerable to the state—having purchased their positions, they were immune from transfer or dismissal. The King had no control over education, and the economy was in a complete state of chaos, hemmed in by a mass of restrictions and anomalies.

Louis set out to correct these deficiencies with a tenacious will and determination. The people were clamoring for law and order, and he intended to give it to them. But he had something even more precious to offer them: he was the personification of a nation

at the height of its powers, overflowing with vitality and health, a nation that longed for magnificence.

Louis XIII, an austere, reserved monarch, had been respected from a distance by his subjects, while they had loathed Richelieu and despised Mazarin. Their joy and relief were unbounded when they discovered that their new King was a proud, handsome young man, as yet untarnished by corruption and dishonesty. France was soon infatuated with Louis. The nobles, fresh from their rebellion, and the masses, including the forerunners of the angry revolutionaries of 1789, did not submit passively to absolute rule—they were carried away on a wave of enthusiasm for and devotion to Louis. Their obedience was not forced on them but grew out of their state of mind and the particular needs of the moment.

Voltaire commented thàt during the first half of Louis XIV's reign, he had proved "that when an absolute monarch wants to do good, he can achieve anything he sets out to do." Indeed, with the support of both nobles and commoners, Louis' untried government was able to transform the country in an astonishingly short space of time.

Jean Baptiste Colbert, Louis' Finance Minister, embarked on a systematic economic policy of mercantilism with the object of promoting France's industrial and commercial prosperity. He created new manufactures, encouraged a higher birth rate and methodically set about mobilizing the labor force. During his ten-year term of office, he supervised a major reorganization of the economy: new

roads were built, canals dug and abandoned ports reconstructed. Colbert created a merchant marine and increased the number of warships from a mere twenty to three hundred. The army was modernized, while the administration was streamlined and carried on with a high degree of efficiency.

Culturally, Louis' reign marked a new high for France. Paris was transformed and monuments were built in every major city. The Louvre, the Tuileries and Saint-Germain were given a new look, and masterpieces of architecture were created: Versailles, the Trianon, Marly. The French genius was at the peak of its brilliance.

Louis XIV cannot be personally credited with these extraordinary achievements. Yet he did preside over a galaxy of talented men—statesmen, generals, engineers, artists, writers, preachers and philosophers, who were the envy of Europe—like an orchestra conductor, carefully controlling them, maintaining harmonious relations among them and, when necessary, manipulating them to serve his own ends.

At the end of twenty years, France, the absolute monarchy, and Louis XIV himself were at the height of their glory. The palace of Versailles epitomized the splendor of France and served as a magnificent setting for a king who was universally acclaimed as the greatest monarch of the day and who fully justified the title "The Sun King." No European state dared to fire a gun or make a move without first

consulting Louis. Virtually singlehandedly, France under Louis' rule had held the powerful coalition of European powers that opposed her in check, had been victorious on both sea and land, had annexed Flanders, Franche Comté and Strasbourg, occupied Lorraine and dictated terms to her defeated enemies. Overseas, the French flag was flying in Africa and America.

Other monarchs were quick to appreciate and profit from Louis' example. Since the Renaissance and the Reformation, two distinct currents of political thought had developed in Europe. Catholicism and autocratic centralized monarchy had prospered in the Mediterranean countries. (Long before the accession of Louis xiv, Philip ii ruled as absolute monarch over Spain's vast empire.) The political life of the northern regions, on the other hand, had moved in various directions: in England, a constitutional monarchy had been established; in the Netherlands, democracy. Germany, in a state of anarchy, was broken up into a number of small states. Some of these states were ruled by an autocratic monarch, notably the newly created state of Prussia which the Hohenzollerns governed despotically. In the same way, in Russia, Peter the Great had established an autocracy after crushing the boyars, while Catholic Austria was ruled by the Hapsburg dynasty.

A similar situation might easily have arisen in Great Britain, for the Stuarts were only too eager to rule as absolute monarchs in spite of the unfortunate fate of their predecessor, Charles i. The Stuarts' designs were thwarted by the simultaneous growth of commercial capitalism and utilitarian individualism, which eliminated governmental control over private property—a control that was considered a natural and essential function of absolute monarchy. When William of Orange landed in Great Britain in 1688, he brought with him not only 15,000 soldiers— symbolizing protesting, Protestant Europe—but also the English philosopher John Locke, who had been in exile in the Netherlands. Locke believed that absolute power was incompatible with civil society. "The law of nature," wrote that philosopher of the new thinking, "has instituted political law in order to prevent the natural rights of man from being threatened in the course of his daily life." Locke's political theories triumphed in 1697: Louis xiv was forced to recognize William as King of England and, for the first time, "divine right" gave way to the "natural rights of the people." Divine right was again discredited in 1713 after the War of the

Opposite above A symbolic drawing showing how heretics will be driven from France by the Sun King.

Opposite below Louis XIV establishing the Academy of Sciences.

Left Versailles under construction.

97

Spanish Succession, when Philip v was forced to relinquish all rights to the French throne.

Meanwhile, the absolutist system had already revealed some grave weaknesses. The most serious—the fundamental mistake of Louis XIV—was the expectation that an absolute monarch could successfully shoulder responsibilities beyond the capacity and endurance of a single individual. By vesting all the powers of the state within himself, Louis had exposed absolutist monarchy to the frailties of nature. As he grew older and his faculties began to fail him, so France gradually and simultaneously declined.

The successors of the Sun King were not equal to the task he left them. Louis XV, contrary to general belief, was an extremely lucid, intelligent and hardworking man, and would have probably made an excellent constitutional monarch. Because of his timidity and lack of decisiveness, however, two opposing protest movements developed during his reign, both in revolt against the concept of absolutism: the popular movement, based on the ideas of the *philosophes*, and the revolt of the privileged classes, which, from generation to generation, fundamentally opposed the power of the monarchy. The clash of these two revolutionary movements eventually produced the final explosion that became the French Revolution.

Louis XVI, on the other hand, committed a fatal error of judgment when he tried to extricate himself from chaos and confusion by attempting to preserve an obsolete system. He was a scrupulous and virtuous man, but he totally lacked the qualities of leadership. It is said that when he succeeded to the throne, he cried out in desperation: "What a responsibility! I have the feeling that the whole world is going to topple over on top of me!" These prophetic words were to come true in 1789.

Before the final collapse of the absolute monarchy, however—while it was being attacked on all sides, by the *philosophes*, by the *parlements* and by a large

number of the aristocrats—France enjoyed an un-paralleled success in Europe. Paradoxically, the European nations that had been at loggerheads with Louis XIV during his lifetime began to emulate him after his death. Now that he could no longer dictate to and control them, the European monarchs began to adopt the French way of life with mounting enthu-siasm. Every king and prince had to have his own palace of Versailles and his own court etiquette modeled after that of the Sun King. French became the language of diplomacy and was adopted by the world of culture. Thus, absolutist monarchy had not only transformed France into a modern, prosperous country but had also served as a model for Western civilization.

Louis XVI supported the American colonists in their fight for independence, and in so doing, he bankrupted the French treasury. Thus, ironically, the American colonists may be held largely respon-sible for the downfall of the monarchy in France and for the preservation of the monarchy in England. If the Americans had lost the war, the trend toward

authoritarianism in England would inevitably have been accelerated and the English would most likely have reacted violently against it, as they did at the time of the Stuarts. Because George III was defeated, however, he had no choice but to revert to consti-tutional and parliamentary rule.

The Revolution of 1789 swept away the absolutist monarchy in France, but it was a long time before absolutism disappeared from the rest of Europe. In Austria, Germany and Spain, the ruling monarchs reluctantly accepted constitutions, although the rulers managed to retain quite a large share of power —the power that had formerly been theirs by "Divine Right."

Up to 1914, Kaiser Wilhelm II of Germany, Franz Josef of Austria and Tsar Nicholas I of Russia ruled over their empires despotically. It was the disruptions of World War I and the revolutionary movements that developed out of it that finally put an end to the system of absolute monarchy conceived by the young King Louis XIV at the deathbed of Mazarin. PHILIPPE ERLANGER

Louis XIV and his family : the King's ambitions for his relations were the cause of struggles that involved most of the countries of Europe.

Opposite above A corner of the Throne Room at Versailles, Louis' great palace fifteen miles from Paris.

Opposite below The Battle of Rocroi, 1643, at which the Duke of Enghein, who was to be better known later as the Prince of Condé, won a great victory over the Spanish army.

99

A rich and colorful new style of art

Baroque art

Seventeenth-century art, although it lacked the classical perfection of the Renaissance, had a greatness of a different kind. Richness of color, a real sense of perspective and an almost architectural feeling of depth characterize Baroque art. Like their Mannerist predecessors, Baroque painters were concerned primarily with effect, and were prepared to distort their figures in order to achieve the effect that they wanted. The change between Mannerism and Baroque is perhaps best illustrated in the work of Michelangelo Merisi da Caravaggio (*c.* 1565–1609), much of whose early work was rejected as coarse, vulgar and indecent. This was largely due to his attempt to give his figures reality. His most characteristic technique as a painter, the use of *chiaroscuro*—heightened light and shade—was strongly criticized by conservative contemporaries, although it added to the vividness and directness of his work. Both the violence—he was involved in several duels and tavern brawls—and the sensuality—one of his love

The Ecstasy of St. Teresa, by Bernini.

affairs led to a fight with a jealous rival—that formed such a large part of his life were reflected in his paintings.

It was the attempt to portray life and, even more important, nature realistically, as opposed to the desire for simple effect that typified the Mannerist approach, that characterized Baroque art. But it remained a highly architectural style and it is not surprising that the greatest Italian exponent of the Baroque, Gian Lorenzo Bernini (1598–1680), was

a sculptor and architect rather than a painter. The Rome of the mid-seventeenth century was largely his creation. St. Peter's in its final form with its two great colonnades was his work, as was much else in the Vatican and other parts of the city. His sculptures, such as the *Ecstasy of St. Teresa,* his tomb of Alexander VII and his huge altar canopy in St. Peter's, brought him an immense popularity throughout Europe and won him commissions from Louis XIV of France and Charles I of England. The interiors of the churches that he built and rebuilt provided painters with an immense opportunity, and Baroque art in its purest form was Roman and was largely inspired by Bernini.

Spanish Baroque

In Spain, Baroque art, largely under the influence of Domenikos Theotokopoulos (*c.* 1541–1614), better known as El Greco because he was born in Crete, took a slightly different form. El Greco went to Spain in about 1575. Influenced by the Italian artistic ideal and by his almost-mystical imagination, he used color to give life even to inanimate objects. Although Spanish Baroque artists such as Francisco de Zurbaran (1598–1664) and Bartolomé Esteban Murillo (*c.* 1617–82) were not consciously influenced by El Greco, something of the feeling of his paintings can be found in theirs. Others, like Francisco Ribalta (1555–1628) and Jusepe Ribera (1588–1652) show a more conscious dependence on El Greco. The writings of the two great sixteenth-century Spanish mystics, Teresa of Avila (1515–82) and John of the Cross (1542–91), were another important influence on Spanish artistic development.

It was, however, the aristocratic Diego Rodruigez de Silva y Velásquez (1599–1660) who most perfectly fulfilled the Baroque ideal of realism. He became court painter to Philip IV, and his portraits of individuals and groups had an immense popularity.

Both in Spain and to an even greater extent in its colonial empire huge Baroque churches celebrate the close relationship between Church and State. Some of the finest examples of Baroque architecture, often filled with

The Water-seller of Seville, by Velásquez.

pictures by Spanish masters, are to be found hidden in South American jungles or surrounded by Indian hovels.

Art in the Netherlands

In Spain's European colony, the Spanish Netherlands, Baroque painting reached its peak. This was largely due to Peter Paul Rubens (1577–1640), whose immense output was eagerly snapped up by collectors. Despite his use of dozens, if not hundreds, of assistants, he was never able to satisfy the demand for his work. He completed several large commissions, such as the interior of the Jesuit church in Antwerp and the ceiling of the Banqueting Hall of the palace of Whitehall in London, where he had been sent on a diplomatic mission, but these did not prevent him from producing a quantity of portraits and historical and religious paintings. His rather substantial women may not appeal to twentieth-century taste, but they seem to have expressed a love of life that had an irresistable appeal in the troubled times in which he lived.

Many of Rubens' pupils rose to eminence in their own right. Anthony van Dyck (1599–1641), for example, became a portrait painter of great distinction, and Frans Snyders (1579–1657) came to be regarded as the leading painter of still-lifes of his generation, but none of them had Rubens' wide range of talents.

Although Baroque was the characteristic style of the Roman Catholic world during the seventeenth century, the close links between the Spanish Netherlands

and the United Provinces gave Dutch art a chance to develop a similar style. Frans Hals (1581–1666), although born in Antwerp, spent most of his life in Haarlem, and played an important part in introducing Rubens' ideas to the Dutch art world. Jacob van Ruisdael (1628–82) had an enormous influence on later landscape painting and Jan Vermeer's (1632–75) interiors were much copied.

But the greatest figure in Dutch painting was Rembrandt van Rijn (1606–69) whose portraits and self-portraits had a revolutionary effect on the genre.

Baroque in France

As elsewhere, Baroque art in France took on certain national characteristics. This was largely due to the influence of Georges de La Tour (1593–1652) and Nicholas Poussin (1594–1665). De La Tour introduced a modified form of Caravaggio's painting, characterized by the use of indirect lighting, and Poussin, by the use of soft colors, modified the often rather harsh impact of Italian Baroque.

In architecture, too, France adopted a national style. It was one that was to be taken up throughout Europe, as princes had their palaces modeled on the finest archievement of French Baroque architecture, the palace of Versailles of Louis XIV.

German Baroque was largely an architectural style; its finest achievements, the churches of Balthasar Neumann (1687–1753), such as his magnificent pilgrimage church of the Vierzehnheiligen (fourteen saints) in northern Bavaria, were begun later than those of the rest of Europe, in the eighteenth century rather than the seventeenth.

England under the Commonwealth

The proclamation of Charles II as King of England after his father's execution was largely ignored in England. The role of the army in political life and the attitude of the government toward the more radical political groups in the country were more important issues. Parliament acted quickly after the death of Charles I to declare the country to be a

flourishes on the Continent of Europe

A Bacchanalian revel, by Poussin.

commonwealth and to abolish the House of Lords. A council of state, under Cromwell's chairmanship, was set up to carry on the actual government. The radicals could see little difference between the old government and the new. A Leveler pamphleteer wrote: "We were before ruled by King, Lords and Commons, now by a General, a Court Martial and a House of Commons. And we pray you, what is the difference?" Beyond the Levelers, who sought to widen the electorate substantially, were other far more extreme groups, such as the Diggers, who attacked property rights. Cromwell was determined to suppress all the minority groups, as he thought that their views represented a serious challenge to the firm government that he so loved.

The Scots, furious that Charles I had been executed, tried once again to intervene in English affairs, but they were defeated at Dunbar in 1650. In Ireland, too, there was widespread monarchist feeling, but a rebellion under the Earl of Ormonde was quickly crushed, and during the Commonwealth period thousands of English settlers were encouraged to emigrate to Ireland—a major factor in creating the difficulties that were to beset Ireland as much as three centuries later.

By 1652 Charles II's supporters had been defeated and Charles, who had landed in Scotland, was forced to take refuge in France. The Rump Parliament, which Cromwell regarded as unrepresentative, refused to dissolve itself, but instead dragged the country into war with the Dutch. It was only after Cromwell had expelled the members from the House and elected a new body, the "Barebones" Parliament, that he was able to make peace with the Dutch. But the relationship between the all-powerful army and the elected Parliament remained a problem. The Barebones Parliament started attacking certain property rights, and to avoid this, Cromwell dissolved it.

In 1653 Cromwell became Lord Protector, but any hopes that this would help to solve the disputes between the army and Parliament were soon shown to be false. In 1656, following in Charles I's footsteps, he decided to rule without Parliament. The country was divided up into eleven districts, each of which was governed by a major-general. The outbreak of war with Spain, which wanted to put Charles II on the throne, forced Cromwell to summon a new parliament. Some of the members were excluded by the army, but the remainder were very conservative and offered Cromwell the crown—an offer that he declined. It was now obvious that England's constitutional problems could not be solved by a conservative military dictatorship.

It became clear that either there would have to be a far-reaching revolution, to which the army would have been opposed, or a return to the old system with slight modifications. After Cromwell's death in 1658, his son Richard succeeded him as Protector. But he had little liking or ability for the problems of government, and soon resigned. The army, too, showed little taste for the thankless job of governing the country. Since many members had refused to accept Cromwell's forcible suppression of the Rump of the Long Parliament, it was regarded as the only legitimate authority in the country. Its remaining members were recalled, but disagreement between army and Parliament soon broke out again, and the commander-in-chief of the army in Scotland, George Monck (1608–70), started negotiating with Charles II. On May 29, 1660, Charles II entered London. A significant shift in the balance of power between King and Parliament occurred as a result of the Commonwealth, but the decisive constitutional battles were still to come.

The Restoration

The Restoration did little to solve the political and constitutional problems that had led to the civil wars. The monarchy and the House of Lords were restored, although the prerogative courts and the rest of the extraparliamentary machinery by which Charles I had attempted to rule were not. The Church of England was reestablished, and new bishops, many of them Laudian in attitude, if more liberal in politics, were appointed. Despite a promise made by Charles, Parliament passed acts discriminating against nonconformists. Crown and Church lands were returned, although many Royalist families returning from exile found themselves dispossessed.

The main instrument of the Restoration Settlement was the "Cavalier Parliament," which was dominated by Royalist interests. It was also, however, determined to defend its own rights. The taxation that it granted to Charles was scarcely adequate for his current needs and took no account of the substantial royal debts. Tension quickly arose over Charles' refusal to disband the army; like so many other monarchs of his time, Charles was determined to have a standing army. While England remained at peace, Charles was able, with difficulty, to make ends meet, but from the beginning of his reign it was obvious that the Restoration Settlement could only be a temporary one.

Charles was, however, a patron of artists and scientists, and it was no coincidence that England produced the finest scientific mind of the age, Isaac Newton.

A contemporary Dutch print of Cromwell dismissing the Rump Parliament in 1652.

Cambridge's Young Genius

In the same year—1665—that Isaac Newton graduated without distinction from Trinity College, Cambridge, the Great Plague struck England. The colleges at Cambridge closed, both scholars and faculty dispersed, and Newton went home to Woolsthorpe. Two years later, mathematician Isaac Barrow's shy and unpromising protégé returned to Trinity—where he promptly astounded his master with the results of his independent experiments. In two short years, Newton had laid the groundwork for discoveries in the fields of geometry, optics and planetary motion that were to revolutionize those disciplines and radically alter man's conception of his universe. Indeed, Newton's studies of motion and gravitation—summarized in his monumental 1687 work, Principia Mathematica—*and his experiments with light and color—detailed in* Opticks, *which Newton published some seventeen years later—are the basis for modern physics.*

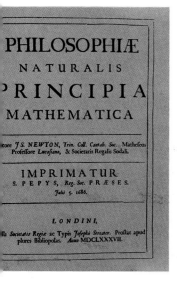

The title-page of the first edition of Newton's revolutionary work, *Principia Mathematica*, with Pepys' *imprimatur* on behalf of the Royal Society. The *Principia* explained Newton's ideas about gravity.

Opposite Newton's reflecting telescope; until the development of radio astronomy in the mid-twentieth century, the reflecting telescope remained the usual design for large telescopes, such as that at Mount Palomar, in California.

Isaac Newton, perhaps the greatest intellectual giant among scientific men, is remembered primarily for his theory of universal gravitation, which was published in 1687 and which opened a new chapter in the scientific revolution. Newton demonstrated that the force of gravity could account precisely for the motions of bodies on earth and in space—motions that had previously been considered essentially different, and that had defied mathematical analysis. Newton also developed novel mathematical techniques—particularly the calculus—discovered the nature of white light and colors and designed and built the first practical reflecting telescope.

Newton was born at the small manor house in the village of Woolsthorpe in Lincolnshire on Christmas Day, 1642. Although sickly as an infant, Isaac grew sturdier each year. He was enrolled at a local grammar school to prepare him to manage the small family estate, but Newton was no farmer. He was more interested in making model waterwheels than in minding sheep, and his mother was persuaded by the headmaster of the grammar school to allow her son to attend a university. Newton went to Cambridge in June, 1661. The family finances were limited, however, and he entered Trinity College as a subsizar—which meant that he would pay his own way by waiting on his tutor and doing other tasks.

Neither at grammar school nor at the university did Newton show any particular intellectual brilliance, but in 1663 he came under the influence of the remarkable scholar and mathematician, Isaac Barrow. Barrow recognized something of Newton's abilities, although when he examined the young man in 1664 he found that his young protégé's knowledge of geometry—in those days one of the most important of mathematical studies—was poor. Under Barrow's guidance Newton began to develop and to take an increasing interest in light and the behavior of lenses. When he took his B.A. in 1665, however, he passed without any distinction.

The year 1665 saw the advent of the Great Plague,

first in London and then, less virulently, at Cambridge. The university closed and the scholars dispersed to their homes. Newton returned to Woolsthorpe, and there, in the quiet and isolation of his home, he began to make the first attacks on the problems that he was later to solve so brilliantly. He developed his mathematical skills and began to lay the foundations of a method for calculating quantities that depend upon one another in ways that are never the same from one moment to the next—what has since become known as the calculus. His optical work was concerned first with grinding glass lenses and experimenting with them to try to improve the telescope, and second with investigating the way in which sunlight ("white" light) is broken up into colors by a prism. The latter led him to devise crucial experiments which showed that while white light could be dispersed into colors by one prism, a second prism would disperse each color no further but, if turned upside down, could cause the colors to recombine to form white light. Newton therefore decided that white light was really a mixture of the light of all colors, a view different from those then in general currency, which supposed each color to be a mixture of white light and darkness in different proportions.

The idea of gravity—the attractive power of the earth on objects—was much discussed at this time, and also the behavior of the planets as they orbited the sun. Newton was naturally intrigued by these problems. (His niece, Catherine Barton, first recounted the well-known story of how an apple fell at Newton's feet while he was sitting under a tree at Woolsthorpe, causing him to question whether the earth's gravity, which had pulled the apple downward, extended out as far as the moon.) Newton felt that without gravitational pull, there was nothing to keep the moon from moving straight out into space, and that only a "fall" toward the earth could change a straight path into a curved one centered on the earth. But although Newton at this point made some

A meeting of the Royal Society, with Newton in the chair.

Working at the Royal Mint. Newton became Warden of the Mint in 1696 and Master in 1699.

calculations—and although he said as an old man that they answered the facts "pretty nearly"—recent scholarship indicates that he was still very far from his final theory when he was at Woolsthorpe.

Using the extremely accurate observations of planetary positions made by the Danish nobleman Tycho Brahe between 1576 and 1597, the German astronomer Johannes Kepler had analyzed planetary motions and come to the conclusion that the planets orbited the sun in elliptical paths, not in circular orbits as hitherto believed. Kepler also found that the time taken to complete an orbit depended on a planet's average distance from the sun, and that the motion of a planet was not uniform, but accelerated as the body approached the sun.

These three "laws" of planetary motion had been published between 1609 and 1621; there is evidence, however, that Newton did not know of the law of changing planetary velocities when he was at Woolsthorpe or, indeed, for some years later.

In addition to accepting Kepler's teaching on planetary motion, the scientific world of the 1660s much favored the general picture of the universe that René Descartes had published in 1644. This was particularly so at Cambridge, and there is no doubt that Newton was familiar with every detail of Descartes' theory; it seems certain that Descartes' ideas also exerted considerable influence on Newton during his first years of research. Descartes thought that the universe was completely filled with material that was collected together into giant vortexes. At the center of each vortex lay a star, and around it orbited planets carried by the whirling material of the vortex. The theory concerned itself too with the nature of matter and of other physical aspects of the universe, including light. It was broad in scope and exercised immense influence for a time, and when Newton was at Woolsthorpe turning the question of gravity over in his mind, it is almost certain that he was doing so within the context of Descartes' theory.

That context is especially significant, because although Newton later claimed that he reached his main conclusions about gravitation while at Woolsthorpe, he made no announcement of what he thought until almost twenty years later. It is usually accepted that during his Woolsthorpe years Newton did not know the size of the earth—and thus the moon's distance—with sufficient accuracy, nor could he prove that the earth attracted bodies in space as if its power of gravitation were concentrated

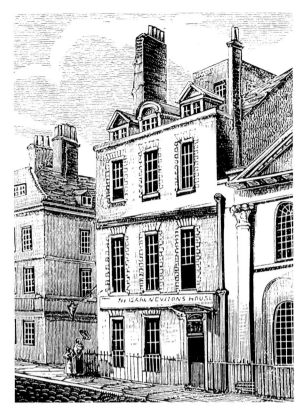

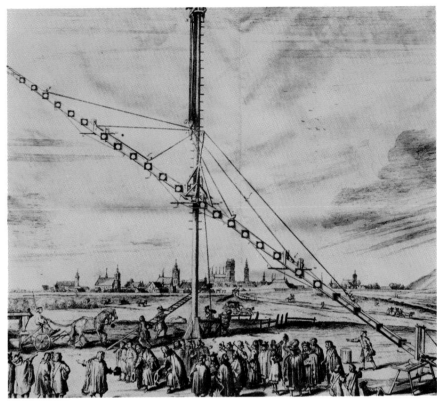

at its center. Scholars have always felt that neither of these difficulties would have prevented Newton from bringing his ideas to a reasonable state of completion. It seems highly probable, however, that Newton's acceptance of Descartes' idea of vortexes prevented him from being able to calculate his answers with complete precision.

Newton returned to Cambridge late in March, 1667, and received his M.A. a year later. He worked with Barrow, helping him to compile a book on optics, but made no reference to his own experiments at Woolsthorpe. Because Newton was shy and feared controversy, he never went out of his way to publicize his achievements. Indeed, Barrow might never have known of his pupil's independent work had he not mentioned Nicholas Mercator's success in calculating the area under a hyperbola. Newton replied that he himself had already done that, and he showed Barrow his notes. It was clear that he had indeed done so—and before Mercator. Barrow soon made Newton's mathematical genius known, and in 1669 he resigned his chair at Trinity in favor of his protégé.

In the seventeenth century a professor of mathematics included in his purview such physical subjects as light and optics, and Newton frequently lectured on those topics. The lectures appear to have created no great stir, but Newton also spent some time constructing a reflecting telescope, and rumors about his work in that area did move outside his immediate circle. Contemporary telescopes were of one type: refracting instruments that consisted of a large lens at the front and a small eye lens at the rear. Such telescopes had several notable defects: they displayed colored fringes around objects and they had a very small area of sharp focus. To obtain even

limited results, telescopes had to be as much as 150 to 200 feet in length. Newton's Woolsthorpe experiments had convinced him that a refractor could never be cleared of its colored fringe images. In this he was wrong, but the mistake led him to consider the construction of reflectors, in which a curved mirror at the back replaced the lens at the front. James Gregory, a Scottish mathematician, had published a design for a reflecting telescope in 1663, but no one had constructed the instrument, which Newton felt had many faults. He therefore designed his own instrument and built a small model, which, although no more than six-and-one-quarter inches long, was as good as any refractor a dozen times larger.

For some years Newton remained at Cambridge, but in 1677 Robert Hooke—one of his sternest critics—became an honorary secretary of the Royal Society and wrote to try to mollify Newton. After Newton agreed to discuss scientific matters again, Hooke began trying to draw him out on the still unsolved question of planetary motions.

Hooke was not alone in trying to find a solution to the movements of the planets. In London Sir Christopher Wren, architect and onetime astronomer, and the astronomer Edmund Halley also discussed the question with Hooke. But although they were all convinced that the planets kept in their paths because the sun attracted them, and that the force of this attraction became less with distance in a particular way, they could not prove their point. The mathematics defeated them. Halley decided to consult Newton and in August, 1684, visited him at Cambridge. Newton agreed that Hooke, Halley and Wren were correct in their surmise about the law of

A refractor telescope made by Hevelius in 1673. Newton's invention of a reflector telescope meant that more satisfactory results could be obtained from a far smaller telescope than was previously possible.

Above left Newton's house in London, off Leicester Square.

John Flamsteed, Astronomer Royal. Newton's insistence that Flamsteed should publish the results of his work as soon as possible led to a quarrel between the two men.

Newton by Kneller, painted in 1702.

of two printers to overcome any delay, and it was published in London in 1687, with the title *Philosophiae Naturalis Principia Mathematica* (*The Mathematical Principles of Natural Philosophy*). Known ever since as the *Principia*, it ran to three editions in Newton's lifetime and brought its author undying fame.

The book is amazingly comprehensive. It deals first with the motions of bodies, both on the earth and in space. Both are controlled, Newton shows, by the three laws of motion: first, a body is either at rest or moves forever in a straight line unless acted upon by external forces; second, the change in such motion is proportional to the external force and the direction in which it is applied; third, to every action there is always an equal and opposite reaction. Newton extends and develops these laws into a whole theory of planetary motion. He then considers the difficult problem of the motion of bodies in a resisting medium such as air or water. Finally he moves on to practical applications of his theoretical assertions.

Revolutionary though the *Principia* was, and widely read as it was, it took time before the teachings it contained were fully accepted. This was true especially in France, where it was primarily due to the efforts of Voltaire that opinion turned in favor of Newton's theory of universal gravitation. Further, writing the book had cost Newton much mental strain. After it was finished, he turned more to other interests, in particular to his studies in chemistry and alchemy. He also turned to theology, for Newton was a Unitarian who spent a great deal of effort on biblical exegesis to support his views.

In 1693, the strain told: Newton suffered a nervous breakdown. After his recovery he spent very little time and concentrated effort on science, and when recoinage of the currency was agreed on by Parliament, Newton's friend and supporter Charles Montagu obtained the post of Warden of the Mint for him. Newton held the position from 1696 until he was appointed Master of the Mint three years later. During the recoinage the work of Warden was arduous.

In 1701 Newton resigned his chair at Cambridge.

attraction, because he had proved it. But he could not find his proof and promised to rework the mathematics and send the results to Halley. When Newton's proof arrived, Halley realized that the significance of what had been achieved was much broader than mere planetary motion. He therefore persuaded Newton to summarize his ideas of motion and gravitation in the form of a book and he obtained the Royal Society's agreement to act as publisher. As it turned out, the Society was unable to meet the publishing costs and Halley defrayed these out of his own pocket.

Halley had more than costs to worry about in getting the book published, for when Hooke raised a question of acknowledgment while Newton was writing, Newton decided to write no more. It took all Halley's powers of persuasion to make him continue. Halley nursed the volume through the hands

Right The Manor at Woolsthorpe where Newton was born.

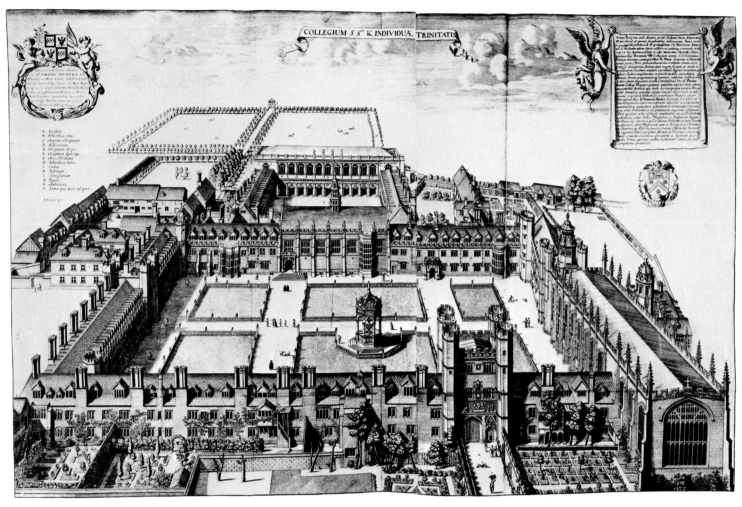

Two years later he was elected president of the Royal Society, an honorary position that he held for the rest of his life. It is unfortunate to record that during his presidency, Newton was the center of two bitter controversies, one with the first Astronomer Royal, John Flamsteed, the other with the German mathematician Gottfried Leibnitz. The trouble with Flamsteed arose because, although he had been appointed Astronomer Royal in 1675, he had not published any observations. Since he had to supply his own observing instruments, Flamsteed claimed that the observations were his own property and that he would publish when he had them as correct as he could make them. Newton and many others disagreed, and in the end Newton obtained a royal grant for publication and placed Halley in charge of the material that Flamsteed deposited—under duress—with the Royal Society. In 1712 the results came out. Flamsteed had unquestionably been uncooperative and stubborn, but Newton himself behaved in a high-handed way throughout.

But if Newton had personal failings, his scientific contributions make these pale to insignificance. In 1704, after the death of Hooke, he allowed his book *Opticks* to be published. In it he set down not only his theory of colors, but also his view that light was caused by minute particles, a view that allowed him to explain all optical phenomena then known. In 1705 he received the first knighthood to be awarded for science. So immense was his reputation that when he died he was buried in Westminster Abbey.

Newton's greatest monument is his work. Vindicated time and again after his death, first by Halley and then by others, his theory of universal gravitation has acted as a foundation for vast areas of scientific development. It lies behind present space technology and has acted as a beacon to those who have followed his voyages into what he once called "the great ocean of truth."   COLIN RONAN

Above Trinity College, Cambridge. Newton's rooms are between the Chapel and the Gate; the Library is in the rear.

Below left Isaac Barrow, Master of Trinity, who gave up his professorship so that Newton could succeed him, and who persuaded Wren (*below*) to design the Library without charge.

107

Science and philosophy scrutinize all

Descartes

Isaac Newton was the greatest among the many contemporary scientists who were making large contributions to knowledge. As the seventeenth century progressed, the implications of the Copernican revolution came gradually to win acceptance, despite the efforts of the papacy. Newton himself was able to benefit from the work of Copernicans from Johannes Kepler to René Descartes (1596–1650). Descartes can be seen as the first modern scientist. His refusal to accept anything as true if there was the slightest possibility of disproof introduced a new skeptical note into scientific research that had been almost totally lacking before. Descartes' *Discours de la méthode*, published anonymously in 1637, marked the beginning of a new approach to science by laying the foundations of a scientific methodology. Descartes wanted to see scientific problems broken up into their constituent parts. Simple problems were to be solved first

René Descartes, "the father of modern philosophy."

in order to facilitate the solution of more difficult ones. Strangely enough, this was in many ways a rather medieval approach to knowledge; scholastic theologians always saw the division of the problem as the first step toward its solution. But Descartes was the first to apply the full rigor of scholasticism to scientific problems.

As a philosopher as well as a methodologist of science Descartes was of revolutionary importance. He applied his reasoning to the question "Does God exist?" It had normally been taken as axiomatic

by medieval philosophers that God did exist (and sixteenth- and seventeenth-century theologians had been more interested in religious controversy than in theological speculation), and they had been more interested in the question "Why must God exist?" To Descartes the question of the existence of God was subordinated to that of the existence of the individual. He "proved" his own existence by his doubts about his existence—"I think, therefore I am"—and went on to prove God's existence from his own. But the Cartesian God was little more than a creator who had ceased to have any impact on the world that he had made. The material universe was subject to natural, definable laws, which could be discovered by scientific research.

The close link between philosophy and science—most scientists described themselves as natural philosophers—continued throughout the century. Both Pascal and the German philosopher Gottfried Leibnitz (1646–1716) were interested in calculating machines, and Leibnitz's calculus, which was based on differentials, went a step beyond Newton's. The introduction of logarithms in 1614 by the Scottish mathematician, John Napier (1550–1617), was another significant advance. No less important was the work done on probability theory and the study of infinity.

England

The center of scientific advance had shifted northward as the century advanced, and while France produced the greatest philosophers and mathematicians of the seventeenth century, English scientists were without equal. The Royal Society, founded by Charles II in 1662, provided a focus for scientific study, and the publication of its *Philosophical Transactions*—the world's first scientific journal—from 1665 made it possible for the scientific community to communicate quickly and without difficulty. Robert Hooke (1635–1703) and John Ray (1627–1705), both of whom were fellows of the Royal Society, were among those men making spectacular discoveries in the natural sciences during the second half of the seventeenth century.

Fame crowning the bust of Charles II: the founding of the Royal Society.

But, apart from Newton, the most important scientist of his generation was Robert Boyle (1627–91), the inventor of the first effective pneumatic pump, which enabled him to undertake important experiments on respiration and vacuums. He was able to show that animals need air to breathe—the basis of all later study on respiration. Boyle's importance went far beyond this. He was the first to define a chemical element as a substance incapable of being further decomposed; he proved that the pressure and volume of gases are inversely proportional (Boyle's Law); and he destroyed contemporary notions of the composition of matter.

Political philosophy

The great English scientific advances were not equaled by technological progress, although a primitive steam engine was produced in 1698 by Thomas Savery (c. 1650–1715). The development of political ideas on the other hand advanced rapidly in the seventeenth century, most notably in England. Two outstanding seventeenth-century theorists, Hobbes and Locke, show how rapidly ideas were changing as the century wore on. Thomas Hobbes (1588–1679) expressed his mature ideas in *Leviathan* (1651). He held that sovereignty lay originally in the people, but that it had been transferred by them to the government, whether the form of the government was republican or monarchical. Once the sovereignty of the people had been lost they could not reclaim it; the abdication

of sovereignty was absolute. As a result the power of the government was total; the state was "that great Leviathan, or rather to speak more reverently . . . that mortal God to which we owe, under the immortal God, our peace and defence." Hobbes' ideas took Bodin's doctrines to their logical conclusion, making the state into a mortal god—a conclusion that led to the banning of *Leviathan* as atheistical. But in reality Hobbes' ideas probably went no farther than those of Charles I; the only difference was that Hobbes expressed his in a more logical and graceful way.

John Locke (1632–1704) was very different; Hobbes had been tutor to the Royalist Cavendish family, and later to the young Charles II, while Locke was secretary to the leading Whig peer, Lord Shaftesbury. After Shaftesbury's fall, Locke went into exile at the court of William of Orange. He became the philosopher of the rebellion of 1688. His *Letters concerning Toleration* (1689–92) and *Two Treatises of Government* (1690) expressed views very different from Hobbes', and showed

Thomas Hobbes.

a deep concern for the rights of individuals, the right of citizens to depose their ruler and the need for consent to taxation. Locke's ideas were to be an important influence both on the rationalists of the eighteenth century and the American rebels of 1776.

A naval nation

When Louis XIV assumed absolute power in France, William, Prince of Orange, who was to become one of Louis' most formidable enemies, was still a boy at school. Twenty years earlier, William's father, the

established beliefs

Dutch Stadholder, had married Mary, oldest daughter of Charles I of England and Henrietta Maria. The fourteen-year-old bridegroom died ten years later, in 1650; his son Prince William was born a week later.

William grew up in a world that—with the exception of Louis XIV's France—was rapidly coming to be dominated by the rivalry between England and Holland, the two great maritime powers of northern Europe. From the earliest days of the Republic, the energy and expertise of Dutch seamen, shipbuilders and merchants had won the Dutch international renown. In Asia, the successes of Dutch traders and of their East India Company were the envy of the commercial nations of the West; in Australasia Dutch explorers opened up vast tracts for settlement and exploitation; and in Europe, Dutch engineering skills, administration and economy were much admired.

The hustling, aggressive, sometimes ruthless enterprises of the Dutch naturally brought them into competition with England

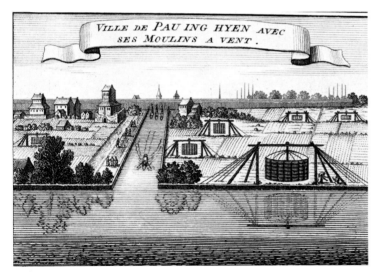

Dutch commercial enterprise in the Far East.

and Spain, and much that happened in Europe before the Dutch economy began to decline can be seen in terms of the conflicts between these great rivals.

There had been a time when their shared Protestantism united the English and Dutch. In 1588, for example, a Dutch fleet lying off Dunkerque had prevented the Duke of Parma from joining the Spanish Armada's final assault on England. Since that time the

Dutch had twice demonstrated their prowess at sea in brilliant style. In the Battle of the Downs, in 1639, Marten Harpertszoon Tromp, a native of Brill, had roundly defeated a strong Spanish fleet under Admiral Oquendo in a naval engagement that confirmed the eclipse of Spanish power in Europe and dealt a blow to the Spanish navy from which it never recovered. And in 1640 at Itamarca (off the coast of Brazil), another Dutch fleet decisively disposed of a Hispano-Portuguese armada that had crossed the Atlantic in a last desperate bid to remove the upstart Protestants from their South American empires.

The Scandal of the Downs

Although they did not regret the collapse of Spanish power, the English viewed the rise of Dutch naval power with concern. The Battle of the Downs had actually been fought in English waters, and Tromp had arrogantly used those waters as his own. As a result,

outraged Britons referred to the sea clash as "the scandal of the Downs." Fortunately for the Dutch, the English, who were on the verge of civil war, were in no state to punish the pretensions of "the damnable Dutchmen." While the impotent English watched, the Dutch pushed their way into overseas markets that had formerly been English preserves.

The end of the civil wars, the execution of King Charles I and

A Dutch flagship by Van de Velde.

the rise to power of Oliver Cromwell opened the way for England's resentment to find expression in war. To British regicides war with the Dutch seemed additionally appropriate, for the young Prince of Orange was the grandson of the monarch they had put to death in 1649.

Anglo-Dutch wars

The opening shots in the Anglo-Dutch wars were fired by the English, whose Navigation Act of 1651 had forbidden the importation of all Asian, African and American goods in non-British ships. (The act also forbade imports from Europe that did not arrive in British ships or in ships belonging to the country of origin.) Since the English did not have enough ships to break the Dutch monopoly themselves, the Navigation Act was more of a petulant challenge to the Dutch than a real threat to their carrying trade. But when the English backed up their challenge by asserting their right to board Dutch ships to search them for French goods, war was inevitable. For fifty years the Dutch had ruled the northern seas, and they could see no reason to observe the outmoded practice of saluting the English flag. They refused to do so, and they opened fire on the English instead.

It was a bitter and costly war in

which first one side and then the other seemed to have the advantage, a war in which the English admiral, Blake, and the Dutch admiral, Tromp, proved themselves to be among the greatest commanders in the history of naval warfare. And when the war ended in 1654, the rivalry was by no means settled; the English continued to regard the Dutch with that mixture of envy, admiration and distaste that they normally reserved for the French.

Open war was touched off again in 1663, when an English squadron sailed to West Africa to help the Royal Africa Company in its quarrel with Dutch West African merchants. The fleet seized various Dutch possessions—all of which the Dutch admiral, Michel de Ruyter, almost immediately recaptured—and the ensuing years of war were as costly and indecisive as those of the 1650s had been. The continuing power of the Dutch navy was forcibly demonstrated in 1666, the year of the Great Fire of London, when Admiral de Ruyter trounced the English in the Channel, inflicting nearly 8,000 casualties. (The corpses of countless English sailors were left floating in the sea.) Even greater triumphs for the Dutch navy were to come in the following year. The year was also to be memorable for the publication of a great epic poem in English, John Milton's *Paradise Lost*.

[Banner in image 2: VILLE DE PAU ING HYEN AVEC SES MOULINS A VENT.]

John Milton Publishes "Paradise Lost"

The Restoration of Charles II sent Milton briefly to jail and then back into private life, after years spent as a civil servant and antiroyalist pamphleteer. It also returned him to his true vocation—poetry. Disillusioned with his fellow men and with the political process, Milton dropped his plan to write a "national" epic and instead took no less than the human condition as his theme. Paradise Lost, *the result, takes an honored place on any list of masterpieces of world literature.*

In August, 1667, when the first edition of *Paradise Lost* was published, John Milton was fifty-eight years old. With his third wife he was living quietly in London, blind, poor, politically disreputable and neglected. At the restoration of Charles II he had gone into hiding, fearing that his support of Charles I's execution and the Cromwell regime would cost him his life. But he had escaped this fate (though he was briefly imprisoned) and now he lived in obscurity, detached from the frenetic world of Restoration politics.

In the same year his friend Andrew Marvell, poet and Member of Parliament, wrote his *Last Instructions to a Painter*, a bitter criticism of Charles II's ministers, his incompetent government, and the deteriorating relations between King and country. Also in 1667 John Dryden, soon to be made Poet Laureate, as a Royalist counter to earlier attacks, published *Annus Mirabilis*, idealizing the behavior of the English navy in the Dutch war, portraying Charles as the savior of his country, and prophesying England's future greatness. In 1660 the English had welcomed Charles back; by 1667 there was widespread disillusion. The diarist Samuel Pepys, who had served under both Cromwell and Charles, was amazed that the King could contrive to lose so much goodwill so quickly: an extravagant court, an inefficient government, a mismanaged war, plague and fire—misfortunes multiplied. The Lord Chancellor Clarendon was exiled to France, a scapegoat for the country's resentment. The King was alternately idolized and attacked.

But Milton did not comment directly on these developments. In the early months of 1660, a lonely prophet among a fervently Royalist people, he had foreseen many of the consequences a return to monarchy would bring. Having given his warning, he withdrew from the depressing day-to-day facts of English politics. He changed his perspective and concentrated on *Paradise Lost*, a history of the human race. In it Milton tried to "justify the ways of God to men," to explain man's essential liberty, his propensity to sin, his tendency to betray his true nature and his capacity for regeneration and the creation of a better earthly society. But because of Milton's disappointing political experience he had come to believe that only a few individuals in any age would be able to use their human capacities to the full. He was forced to qualify the optimism of his youth. Hence some readers have found *Paradise Lost* a pessimistic poem, which it certainly is not. In order to appreciate some of the poem's complexities we need to look briefly at Milton's poetic career, at the part he played in the English revolution, and at the way his ideas developed.

He was born in London in December, 1608, the son of a prosperous scrivener (a kind of lawyer and merchant banker). His father, who was also an amateur musician, wanted his son to have the best possible education, and the career he planned for him was that of a clergyman in the Church of England. Milton went to St. Paul's School (founded by the sixteenth-century humanist John Colet), where he chiefly studied the classics. He was also tutored privately in modern languages, Hebrew, music and mathematics. In 1625 he went up to Christ's College, Cambridge, where he spent the next seven years. But Milton, who was to become one of the most learned men of his day, found the intellectual atmosphere of Cambridge repressive and stifling. He thought the undergraduates wasted their time in futile exercises in logic and the study of Aristotelian metaphysics, whereas they should have been broadening their minds with history, poetry and science. Milton was a true humanist; he believed education should be moral and practical, not abstract and removed from life. He shared Bacon's view that

John Milton. The Puritan poet's disillusionment with political life led him to write his masterpiece *Paradise Lost*.

Opposite Satan arousing the rebel angels, one of William Blake's watercolor illustrations to *Paradise Lost*.

A satirical engraving of
Charles I as the enemy of
religion. Milton was the
greatest propagandist of the
Puritan Revolution.

men, unlike angels, should not be lookers-on.
Later, after some experience as a tutor, he wrote
a short book called *Of Education* (1644), in which he
said: "I call therefore a complete and generous
education that which fits a man to perform justly,
skillfully and magnanimously all the offices both
private and public of peace and war."

Milton received his master's degree in 1632;
his father and friends expected him to proceed to
holy orders. But he himself by now had decided
against a career in the Church, to which he had
earlier felt drawn. While Milton was an under-
graduate, Laud was made Bishop of London; in
1633 he became Archbishop of Canterbury. Laud's
Church policy was to emphasize ritual and ceremony at the expense of preaching, and to suppress
any disagreement over doctrinal or disciplinary
matters. Many Puritans left for New England,
despairing of ever reforming the Church at home.
Milton was horrified at what he regarded as the
corruption of the Church and the clergy; he was
fired by a sense of personal mission, of a great
enterprise that his divine taskmaster expected of
him. On leaving Cambridge he retired to his
father's house and spent the next five years in
private study (chiefly of ecclesiastical and political
history), trying to find his vocation.

The life that gradually emerged was that of poet.
In Milton's day poets (excluding dramatists) were
rarely professionals; they were usually courtiers or
clergymen, whose writing was an adjunct to their
main interests. During his student days, at Cambridge and at home, Milton experimented with
various kinds of poetry. He wrote two masques,
Arcades and *Comus*, for the nobility, as well as short
religious pieces and Latin verse letters. In many
of these poems he seemed to be testing his own
future. In *L'Allegro* and *Il Penseroso*, for example,
he compared the character and the tastes of the
happy to the thoughtful man. Though he did not
as yet commit himself to poetry as a career, he
was beginning to regard the role of poet as akin
to that of priest. The deaths of two young men
helped him crystallize his ideas. Edward King, a
young fellow of Christ's College was drowned in
1637; in *Lycidas*, his elegy of King, Milton ex-
plored the themes of immaturity and fame, and
he examined the roles of priest and poet, and his
obligations to art and to his fellow men. Charles
Diodati, his closest childhood friend, to whom he
had revealed many of his problems, died in 1638.
Milton lamented him in a Latin elegy, *Epitaphium
Damonis*. He must have felt that time was running
out and that he could no longer delay his decision.

In 1638, to complete his education, Milton went
on a continental tour. He was in his thirtieth year.
The effect of this journey on his self-esteem was
enormous. In England he was unknown, a scholar-
recluse. In Italy, where he was befriended by the
Florentine academicians and the Neapolitan
nobleman Manso, one-time patron of the epic
poet Torquato Tasso, he was treated, on the basis
of the work he had so far produced, as an eminent

man of letters. He began to see himself as an epic
poet who would celebrate a glorious episode in
British history; the career of poet he determined
should not be private and aloof but public and
national.

Milton returned home in mid-1639, at a crucial
period in his country's history. Laud's attempt to
impose English Church discipline on the Scots
was being challenged, as was Charles I's personal
rule without Parliament. In 1640 the Scots won
the right to their own Church government; later
that year the Long Parliament met, and immediately impeached Strafford and Laud, the King's
advisers. The Puritans' long-smouldering resentment against the bishops resulted in the Root and
Branch Petition, which demanded their extirpation.

Meanwhile Milton had set up house in London
and was supporting himself by teaching his
nephews and the sons of friends. At the same time
he was feverishly planning literary projects, and
widening his studies even further. He continued
his researches into British history, which were to
culminate in his *History of Britain*, eventually
published in 1670. He also began a systematic
study of Christian theology. In the late 1650s he
was to organize this work into his longest book,
his Latin theological treatise *Christian Doctrine*.

Left A Dutch seventeenth-century illustration of the Ptolemaic system, upon which Milton based the universe of *Paradise Lost*.

Below Doorway of Christ's College, Cambridge. The poet found the intellectual life of Cambridge repressive and stifling.

It is clear that Milton regarded all this intellectual activity as necessary preparation for the great poem he was to write.

But as yet he was not sure of the form this poem would take. His historical researches made the Arthurian epic he had envisaged impossible; what he had regarded as history transpired to be mostly legend and propaganda. Perhaps the Saxons would be more promising material. Then again a tragedy might be more appropriate than an epic. Milton jotted down lists of possible tragic subjects, both historical and biblical. (These lists, together with the manuscripts of the early poems, still exist in the library of Trinity College, Cambridge.) He knew that he was living in a period of great religious and political ferment. He wanted to produce art both worthy of the times and influential. But he did not know where to begin.

All his life Milton had been a powerless intellectual, standing in the wings. He was enthusiastic and naive. He wanted events to move according to his own idealized conceptions. Suddenly he was given the opportunity to take a part, even though in a small way, in public affairs. If he could have foreseen the twenty wearying years of political involvement that lay ahead of him, that were to deflect him from poetry, he might have hesitated. His old tutor Thomas Young was one of a group of Presbyterian ministers calling themselves Smectymnuus (made up from their initials) who in 1641 attacked the bishops of England through pamphlets. The bishops defended themselves, and Milton joined in the attack against them, writing five books in 1641-42, of which *Of Reformation* and *The Reason of Church Government* are the most interesting. The tone of these books is extraordinary; they are at the same time abusive and arrogant, apocalyptic and ecstatic. Milton obviously thought that if only the office of bishop was abolished the long-awaited reformation of the Church would be completed, and Charles' difficult relations with his people resolved. But in 1642 the civil war broke out, and Milton was soon to be disillusioned with his Presbyterian allies.

In 1642, much to everyone's surprise, Milton married Mary Powell, the daughter of a Royalist country gentleman. The marriage was unhappy, and she soon returned home. Milton tried unsuccessfully to get her back. The following year he published *Doctrine and Discipline of Divorce*, in which he evolved a theory of marriage as an intellectual and emotional as well as a physical union which could be dissolved, if unsatisfactory, by mutual consent. The Presbyterians were appalled. He was attacked as a "divorcer"; it was the first time Milton had come to the attention

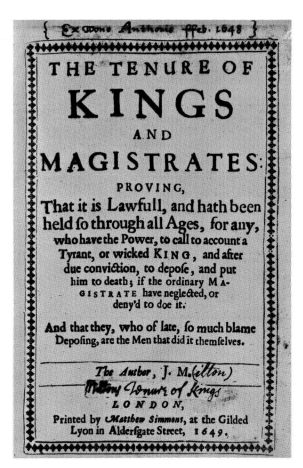

of the English public. He retaliated by publishing three more books on divorce, and also began to reconsider his moral and political ideas.

In 1644 he published *Areopagitica*, his prose work best known today. The book is an interesting combination of Milton's old fervor coupled with a new moral realism. He still hoped that England would become a godly society, but he now saw that this would be far more difficult to achieve than he had thought. In 1643 Parliament set up the Westminster Assembly to settle the question of the Church's role. The Assembly consisted largely of Presbyterians, who in their own way were as intolerant as Laud. Appalled at the activities of the extreme Puritan sects they wanted to suppress them. Parliament similarly feared the outbreak of pamphleteering that the civil war had occasioned, and decided to restrict the freedom of the press, using legislation very like Laud's. *Areopagitica* was not only a plea for the abolition of this legislation; it was also an argument that the good society could only come into being if the individual was allowed to develop his moral self through conflict with evil. "We bring not innocence into the world, we bring impurity much rather: that which purifies us is trial, and trial is by what is contrary." Milton thought that the Presbyterians would only create a nation of sheep.

As the first civil war was followed by the second, and the Presbyterians joined the Royalists against the Independents, Milton became more disillusioned. During these years his wife returned to

him; he became absorbed in family life, worked on history, and watched public affairs from a distance. Like Cromwell, he gradually became convinced that Charles could not be trusted, and that the people must be coerced for their own good by the enlightened (Independent) part of the nation. In 1649, a month after the King's execution, he published *The Tenure of Kings and Magistrates*, defending regicide as the people's right. As a result Cromwell's Council of State appointed him Secretary for Foreign Tongues, a post he held until shortly before the Restoration.

Milton was now a civil servant; his work consisted mainly of writing Latin letters to heads of State. But he was also a sort of propaganda minister; he had to defend the regime against its numerous critics both at home and abroad. In 1649 he wrote *Eikonoklastes* as a counter to *Eikon Basilike*, a very popular account of the King's last years; from 1650 to 1655 he wrote three enormous Latin *Defenses of the English People* (they were also defenses of himself) against Royalist scholars, one of whom, Salmasius, was commissioned by the exiled Charles II. In the course of this labor he went blind. These were difficult years; his wife died in 1652, leaving three small children. He married again in 1656, only to lose his second wife in 1658. But he believed that he had served the government well; his *Defenses* to some extent satisfied his desire to write an English historical epic.

But Milton obviously found the Cromwellian regime a disappointment. He believed in liberty, but he served a military dictator. Cromwell alienated many of his former allies, but Milton did not leave him. Though he had doubts, Milton thought the Protectorate was necessary. He believed that the English would grow in political stature, that they would emulate their enlightened leader, and that coercion would become unnecessary. He was wrong. Given the educational limitations of the time, he both overestimated the capacity of the individual and underestimated the appeal of authority and ancient forms. The Protectorate was a step toward kingship, not toward a Roman republic.

In the confusion following Cromwell's death Milton launched once more into pamphleteering, passionately arguing that the political situation must be stabilized, that the rival army leaders and republicans must come to terms, that anything was better than a return to monarchy, that only a commonwealth could guarantee religious freedom. But the nation had had enough and chose Charles. From Milton's point of view in the *Ready and Easy Way to Establish a Free Commonwealth* (published in two editions in early 1660) this was an absolute betrayal; the Israelites were turning back to Egypt when they were in sight of the promised land.

These years of political experience culminating in the Restoration changed Milton's view of history. In the three great works published at the end of his life, *Paradise Lost*, *Paradise Regained* and *Samson Agonistes*, he concentrated less on the reformation of society and more on the regeneration of the individual. The Jesus of *Paradise Regained* is a private man who resists the temptations of fame, wealth and power in order to be king over himself. But this did not mean that Milton became pessimistic, quietist or self-absorbed in his last years. He now knew more about human nature; he recognized the difficulties that confronted the individual who wanted to be free.

Milton began to write *Paradise Lost* about 1658, though he had earlier sketched it out as a play; he finished it by 1665. He presumably then wrote *Paradise Regained* and *Samson Agonistes*, although their dates are not known for certain. These two poems were published in 1671. Many twentieth-century readers have found Milton's handling of his material difficult. *Paradise Lost* tells the story

of mankind from God's point of view. Milton used a traditional framework, but his understanding of the human condition is timeless. Moreover, though he used epic conventions descending from Homer, he parodied them, and though he based his poem on the outdated Ptolemaic cosmology, he obviously meant it as a metaphor. *Paradise Lost* describes God's elevation of his son, the Messiah, the rebellion and fall of Satan, the creation of Adam and Eve, their temptation by Satan and their fall, their repentance, the promise of the Messiah to redeem them, and their expulsion from Eden to live a life of struggle and hope in the world, free to make of it what they could. Some readers have been put off Milton's portrayal of God, which, while theologically necessary, is a literary failure. Milton wrote his tragedy *Samson Agonistes* from the human point of view, and the argument is easier to follow. The blind Samson, a slave to the Philistines, gathers up his strength to destroy them and himself; it is clear to the reader that if the Israelites do not follow Samson's heroic example his sacrifice will have been in some sense a failure. Using the barbaric Old Testament story, Milton commented on the irresponsible England he lived in. Only free individuals could make a free society; the English had abdicated their individuality.

In spite of the author's politics, the reading public soon recognized his greatness. *Paradise Lost* sold 1,300 copies in two years (a fair number for such a book at such a time); Milton's early works were in demand, and in 1674 he brought out a second edition. He died later the same year. After 1688 his politics seemed less disreputable, and his position as England's great epic poet was established. The Tory and Royalist John Dryden, who did much to advance Milton's reputation, in 1688 added these lines to the fourth edition of *Paradise Lost*, placing Milton above Homer and Virgil:

> Three poets, in three distant ages born,
> Greece, Italy, and England did adorn.
> The first in loftiness of thought surpassed;
> The next in majesty; in both the last.
> The force of nature could no further go:
> To make a third she joined the former two.

ISABEL RIVERS

The concluding lines of the original manuscript of *Lycidas*, Milton's elegy of his friend Edward King.

The Dutch in the Medway

In the summer of 1667, a Dutch fleet climaxed three years of war with England by sailing up the Thames River and into its tributary, the Medway. There they destroyed several ships of the British navy and captured two others, including the **Royal Charles,** *once the pride of the fleet. However, the peace that shortly followed was not so much an outgrowth of this humiliation as it was a realization on the part of both powers that the attempts by Louis XIV of France to expand into Spain posed far more serious perils to them both than either could to the other.*

Admiral Michel de Ruyter, the Dutch naval hero, commander of the fleet that humbled the English.

Opposite The Four Days' Battle, a Dutch victory in one of several engagements between the rival fleets before the English big ships were laid up in March, 1667.

By the summer of 1667 the English and the Dutch had been at war on the seas and in the colonies for almost three years. The naval campaigns had been inconclusive—victories had been won by both sides. Diplomatic negotiations to end the war had opened at Breda in March, but earlier that month Charles II of England made a drastic decision. After consulting his leading ministers and expert advisers, he resolved to lay up all the big ships in his navy and retain only a squadron of frigates to harass and intercept the Dutch merchant marine. His motives were threefold. First, he had little money to pay the sailors or buy the necessary supplies; second, he thought that such tactics might weaken the Dutch, rendering them vulnerable when the big ships, refurbished by a grant promised him by the House of Commons, set out in the coming autumn. Last, Charles was "heartily weary of the war" into which he had been pushed by his Parliament; he was confident that, with the help of the French, peace terms would soon be agreed upon.

But the Dutch saw things in a completely different light. Under the influence of their leading statesman, the Grand Pensionary of Holland, Jan de Witt, and his able brother, Cornelis, who besides being Burgomaster of Dordrecht was an extremely competent sailor, the Republic determined to put a strong fleet to sea, at whatever cost, convinced that an ensuing victory over the English in their home waters, would win them a profitable peace. A fleet of seventy-two men-of-war, a dozen frigates and two dozen fireships (seventeenth-century "torpedo boats") was fitted out and placed under the command of the brave and experienced admiral, Michel de Ruyter. Jan de Witt himself supervised the preparations for an expedition against England while his brother was appointed plenipotentiary of the States-General with the fleet, which virtually put him in control of strategy. The two brothers had worked out a daring plan: a

raid on the Thames River and its tributary, the Medway, with the aim of wrecking the dockyard installations at Chatham and destroying the big English warships known to be laid up in these rivers. Pilots familiar with the navigation of the two rivers notorious for their sandbanks and mudflats were hired from among the English naval prisoners of war.

On May 25, Cornelis de Witt embarked at Texel on de Ruyter's flagship *Zeven Provincien* (named after the seven Dutch provinces). A week later the fleet sailed to the island of Walcheren to take on troops. Only then were de Ruyter and his senior naval commanders informed of the nature of the operation, of which they had been kept in the dark by the States-General. On June 4, the Dutch fleet, over fifty men-of-war with auxiliaries, including fourteen fireships, sailed across the North Sea for the Thames estuary. Off the North Foreland on the Kent coast a gale blew up and dispersed the ships, but they were soon reassembled. On Friday June 7, the Dutch entered the King's Channel, one of the approaches to the Thames, anchored and held a council of war. The decision was taken to send a squadron up the Thames but it was not until two days later that the planned operation took shape.

Meanwhile the English had ample intelligence of the enemy's movements from spies in Holland. The fleet had of course been seen off the North Foreland, and the Dutch squadron's entry into the Thames and subsequent withdrawal were duly reported to Whitehall. Nevertheless the danger of an attack on the Thames was discounted. Besides, it was felt, peace could not be far off. However, it was thought advisable to collect fireships and reinforce the defenses particularly in the Medway below the Chatham dockyards. The King ordered his Captain-General, George Monck, Duke of Albemarle, who had restored him to his throne in

Top A contemporary Dutch print of the burning of the English fort at Sheerness.

Above George Monck, Duke of Albemarle, the English commander, who had helped restore Charles II to the throne.

1660, to take charge at Chatham, while Prince Rupert, another naval and military commander who like Monck had fought in the civil wars, though on the other side, was instructed to organize the defenses of Woolwich arsenal. The militia in Kent were called up and the Secretary of State told the Lords Lieutenant of all the counties that the best way to deal with a Dutch threat of invasion would be with horses not ships.

By Monday June 10, events were moving rapidly. The Dutch bombarded Sheerness fort to the northwest of the island of Sheppey guarding the entrance to the Medway. The sparsely manned guns of the fort were quickly silenced by the Dutch who seized both guns and stores before burning the fort. The main Dutch fleet anchored off Sheerness on the night of June 10, and on the following day a small Dutch reconnaisance force sailed up the Medway. The same day the Duke of Albemarle arrived at Chatham where a number of panic orders, often contradictory, were given to the military and naval forces in the area. Chatham was guarded by Upnor Castle; a few miles below it a chain, submerged nine feet deep, stretched across the river at Gillingham Reach. Albemarle ordered three ships to be towed from the dockyard and sunk near the chain, which was then raised and four warships were moored to guard against a Dutch advance on Chatham. Farther down the river at Mussel Bank, about four miles from Gillingham Reach, no fewer than eight vessels, most of them originally intended for use as fireships, were sunk so as to block the river.

The Dutch reconnaissance force penetrated the Medway as far as the Mussel Bank where it witnessed two English naval commissioners sinking their own ships. This fact was duly reported to Cornelis de Witt at Sheerness; but he was not

deterred. He at once resolved to sail up the Medway. An advance force managed to remove some of the obstacles at the Mussel Bank and clear the way for the main force, which left Sheerness at six o'clock in the morning of June 12, reaching the guarded chain at Gillingham Reach four hours later. The obstructions here, organized by Albemarle, were a much tougher proposition. However, the captain of the *Vrede*, a ship of forty guns, Jan van Brakel, who had been placed under arrest because of his crew's indiscipline, volunteered to sail up to the chain to draw the fire of the English guardships, while fireships were sent in. He did more: he successfully boarded and captured intact one of the guardships, the *Unity* of forty-four guns, a feat for which he was awarded a gold chain and medal while the prize value of the *Unity* was shared with his crew. The second of two Dutch fireships managed to break through. Two other guardships were set on fire and blown up, while the captain of the fourth guardship, which had been moored above the chain, withdrew. Another English warship, the *Royal Charles* (which in Cromwell's day had been known as the *Naseby*), lay in the river, half-rigged and with only thirty-two guns in position, awaiting repair. Once the pride of the navy, it surrendered to the Dutch without a fight.

On the following day (June 13) Dutch warships and fireships moved further up the river to Upnor, intent on inflicting more damage on the English navy. Here they met with an extremely hot reception both from the battery at Upnor Castle and from cannon on the other side of the river, which narrowed at this point. Nevertheless, inspired by Admiral de Ruyter, the Dutch warships engaged both batteries, while fireships set alight three more English warships, which had been withdrawn up the river for safety. Samuel Pepys, then Clerk of the Acts at the Admiralty, received a report from an eye-witness:

The destruction of these three stately and glorious ships of ours was the most dismal spectacle my eyes ever beheld, and it certainly made the heart of every true Englishman bleed . . . .

The battle now saw only one hero on the English side: Captain Archibald Douglas, a Scottish officer aboard the *Royal Oak*. Deserted by his soldiers he stood alone to perish in the flames. Andrew Marvell wrote:

Much him the glories of his ancient race
Inspire, nor could he his own deeds deface,
And secret joy in his calm breast doth rise
That Monck looks on to see how Douglas dies.

Having inflicted so much damage, the Dutch wisely decided to retire. Thanks to the energy of the Duke of Albemarle the safety of the Chatham dockyards was ensured. The river was blocked and reinforcements had at last arrived. Moreover, the Dutch had exhausted their supply of fireships. They withdrew in good order, with the *Unity* and *Royal Charles* in tow. Though they were fired upon from both banks of the river and some of the ships temporarily grounded, losses were minimal. The *London Gazette* put the best face it could upon the event but it was a blow to English pride. Pepys thought that "the whole kingdom is undone." Fearful of invasion, many Londoners tried to take their money out of the banks and make for the country. But by July 1, it was known that the provisional peace terms had been agreed upon at Breda. The final treaty, signed in August, 1667, was undoubtedly hastened by the attack on the Medway.

The success of the raid, which shattered the confidence of the British public, was due to the two de Witts who five years later were murdered by an angry mob in The Hague, and to the Dutch commanders, especially de Ruyter and van Brakel. On the other side the King was principally to blame for the humiliation of his armed forces. Charles II maintained that he had been pushed into the war by the House of Commons and that its members had let him down. English sailors and merchant seamen, as well as the fishermen who resented the huge hauls of fish that were taken every year from British coastal waters, had legitimate grievances against the Dutch. Questions of prestige about who should salute whom in which seas were involved. But the Dutch too had reasonable complaints over the application of English navigation laws and England's right to search neutral vessels for enemy goods. The Dutch had been understandably provoked when, in time of peace, British warships had been sent to the West African coast and to the New Netherlands (the site of modern New York State). Rivalry in Africa had developed over slave-trading and the New Netherlands had been established between

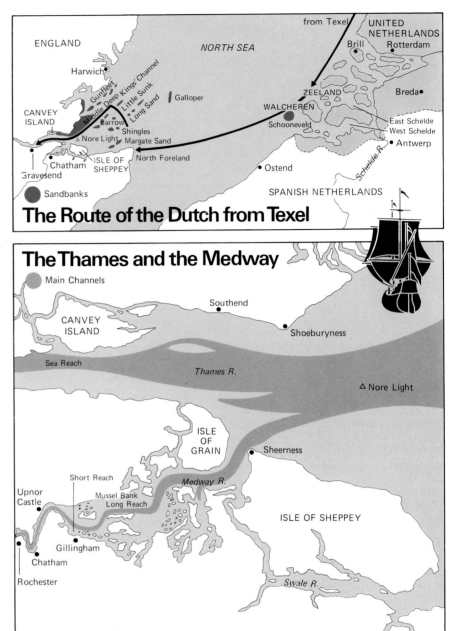

The Route of the Dutch from Texel

The Thames and the Medway

the English settlements in Virginia and New England.

Charles saw the Dutch as the main obstacle to his country's commercial and colonial expansion. To overcome this obstacle he was prepared to resort to extreme provocation, especially as he thought that the Dutch had no wish to be involved in a war in Europe. Before the war broke out he wrote to his sister, Henriette: "The States keep a great bragging and noise but I believe that when it comes to it, they will look twice before they leap." He counted on the French, the allies of the Dutch, to restrain them and not to intervene themselves. He was wrong on all counts. Second, the House of Commons voted him altogether a total of £5,500,000 to pay for the war, which lasted three years. Taking into account that

Charles' annual revenue was only a little over £1,200,000, the amount with which he was furnished was generous. Admittedly, war was always more costly than governments and parliaments realized in the seventeenth century. Moreover, borrowing remained difficult until the foundation of the Bank of England. But the fact remains that contemporaries were convinced that embezzlement and corruption was going on. Lastly, it was the King himself who took the decision to lay up the warships at a time when a summer guard usually put to sea. It was unrealistic to suppose that frigates alone could damage that "mountain of gold," the Dutch mercantile marine, that they could protect the British coasts against invasion and could counter the activities of Dutch warships. No doubt it was hoped that British privateers, licensed pirates, would hamper the Dutch oceanic trade; to some extent they did so. Yet the volume of prizes that had been captured in the previous Anglo-Dutch war had been the direct result of the Commonwealth navy's victories. The evidence (though incomplete) indicates that Charles' three chief naval advisers, the Duke of York, who was the Lord High Admiral, the Duke of Albemarle and Prince Rupert were all opposed to the new strategy. "The King," wrote the Earl of Clarendon, in the continuation of his *History*, "had not himself thought of this defensive way of naval warfare but approved of it very much when he heard it so fully discussed." Pepys believed that the reason Charles was so eager for peace was in order to save money "and thus need the help of no

Right The burning of the English fleet on the Medway, by William Schellinks.

Below The first official English naval ensigns, standardized by Samuel Pepys while he was working at the Navy Office.

more parliaments." But it is fair to add that the English had some bad luck during the war; in 1665 the court and the government had been scattered by the Great Plague, estimated to have killed a hundred thousand people, mostly in London, while the following year the Great Fire of London caused extensive damage and destroyed administrative records. However, the fact remains that the English were beaten and disgraced in a war which they themselves had provoked.

So far as the peace was concerned one must not exaggerate the effect of the raid on the Medway. In fact, what made the two maritime powers reach agreement relatively quickly was not that raid but the known intention of the French to attack the southern or Spanish Netherlands (modern Belgium) about whose security both of them were sensitive. King Philip IV of Spain, whose daughter had married Louis XIV, left as heir on his death in September, 1665, a weakly child, Charles II. Louis at once claimed that so far as the southern Netherlands were concerned his wife, the daughter of a first marriage, had a superior claim to the succession over that of a son by a second marriage. The war, which began in May, 1667, while the Treaty of Breda was being negotiated, was short and sharp. The Spaniards had few defenses, whereas the French armies were the best trained and equipped in Europe. The importance of the French victory in this war,

known in France as that of the Queen's Rights, was that Louis had staked his claim for a share in the booty if the Spanish empire broke up when Charles II died, for he had no obvious Spanish successor except for his sisters and their foreign children. The Anglo-Dutch treaty, which was provisionally agreed upon a fortnight after the attack on the Medway and was finally signed at Breda in August, was thus a compromise enabling the Dutch and the English to stand ready in peaceful alliance to check the aggression of the French King. Each side was to retain its conquests—the Dutch secured West Africa and the East Indies, the English acquired New York (hitherto the New Netherlands and renamed after the Duke of York, the heir to the English throne) and New Jersey. Agreement was reached regarding the saluting of the flag and the English navigation acts were modified. But the Dutch paid no indemnity. They kept the English warships, which they had towed out of the Medway—evidence of England's humiliation. The *Royal Charles* was sold at public auction. These pin-pricks contributed to Charles II's determination to revenge himself on the Dutch. In 1672 England declared war on the United Netherlands, having procured a French offensive alliance. That war, too, proved inconclusive.

On July 12, 1667, Samuel Pepys recorded in his diary:

It is strange how everybody do nowadays reflect on Oliver Cromwell, and commend him, what brave things he did, and made all the neighbour princes fear him; while here a prince, Charles II, come in with all the love and prayers and good liking of his people, who have given greater signs of loyalty and willingness to serve him with their estates than ever was done by any people, hath lost all so soon, that it is a miracle what way a man could devise to lose so much in so little.

The Earl of Clarendon, as the King's leading minister, was made a scapegoat for the conduct of the Cavalier Parliament. He was forced to resign, was impeached and exiled to France. Gradually the majority in the House of Commons turned from being anti-Dutch to being anti-French and before the House was dissolved it tried to push the King into war against the French. It was unfairly implied in speeches and pamphlets that the King and his brother were being manipulated by the French. However, anti-French feeling remained latent until 1688 when Charles' brother James II was deposed and William of Orange, Stadholder of Holland, was invited to save England from Catholic tyranny. The humiliation in the Medway had been a decisive factor in the fall of the House of Stuart and the realization that France was a more dangerous rival than the Netherlands. Henceforth the colonial and commercial policies of England and Holland were united against France.

MAURICE ASHLEY

Cornelis de Witt, by Jan de Baen. He and his brother Jan worked out the plan to attack the English fleet at its bases.

Relative peace in Italy contrasts with

Italy

While central and northern Europe were fighting their religious, dynastic and civil wars, Europe south of the Po and the Danube remained relatively quiet —but not entirely at peace. Increasing numbers of travelers were crossing the Alps and sailing into the ports of the Adriatic and Tyrrhenian seas at that time, and those travelers returned home with ideas and tastes that were to have a profound effect on the character of the north in the next century. The Grand Tour had in fact already become an integral part of seventeenth-century aristocratic culture. The tour was not without its dangers, however, and travelers were often advised to alter their routes in order to avoid local insurrections.

Naples

Spain remained the dominant power in Italy until the beginning of the eighteenth century, when Austrian power began to grow. The Kingdom of Naples and Sicily—which comprised the whole of Italy south of the Abruzzi—was ruled by viceroys appointed by the Spanish kings. The oppressive character of their government provoked repeated uprisings, among them the 1598 rebellion in Calabria led by the philosopher Tommaso Campanella (1568–1639). His unsuccessful attempt to rid Naples of Spanish tyranny was put down with great

The signing of the Treaty of Nijmwegen, 1678, by which Louis XIV gave up his support for the rebels of Naples.

severity, and Campanella spent twenty-seven years in prison.

In 1647 there were widespread riots in Sicily, which forced the Viceroy to flee from Palermo, and that same year there was a rebellion in Naples that forced the Viceroy there to seek refuge in Castelnuovo. The Neapolitan rebels—who had been provoked to violence by a new tax on fruit, the staple food of the poor— elected Masaniello (Tommaso Aniello), a fisherman from Amalfi, to be their captain-general. And, when the tumult spread beyond the walls of the city and into the towns and villages of the hinterland, the Viceroy gave way and granted all the rebels' demands. The fruit tax and all other oppressive taxes were removed, various concessions were granted

and the citizens were permitted to remain in arms until the treaty was ratified by the King of Spain.

On July 16, 1647, however, the rebel leader was murdered while haranguing his followers in the market-place. When the tumult burst out afresh, the Viceroy was again compelled to seek refuge in Castelnuovo and a new rebel leader was found in Gennaro Annese (1604–48). When he learned that reinforcements had been dispatched from Spain, Annese appealed to France for help, and in response to the rebel's appeal the Duke of Guise landed in Naples with an expeditionary force. Following the unpopular Viceroy's recall, order was restored by his wily successor, Count d'Ognate, with the assistance of Don Juan of Austria (the

younger) (1629–79). After coming to terms with Annese, Ognate had him and all the other rebel ring-leaders executed.

Revolt in Sicily

Thirteen years after this popular revolution had almost ended Spanish contol over Naples, there was a similar uprising in Sicily. Like the Neapolitans before them, the Sicilians called upon the French to help them drive the Spanish out—while the Spanish, unable to quell the revolt, turned to the Dutch for help. Both countries responded to the call for aid; a French fleet commanded by the Duke of Vivonne and a Dutch fleet under Admiral de Ruyter set sail for Sicily.

Despite some success against the Spanish, Louis XIV abandoned the Sicilian rebels to the persecution of their Spanish masters, under the terms of the 1678 Treaty of Nijmwegen. The Spanish were able to remain in control of Naples until 1707 and of Sicily until 1713.

Northern and central Italy

North of the Kingdom of the Two Sicilies lay the Papal States. These were increased in size by the seizure of two important fiefs, Ferrara and Urbino, by the papacy. Clement VIII (1536–1605) invaded the former in 1598 and Urban VIII (1568–1644) the latter in 1631. Urban VIII's attempts further to expand his holdings by attacking the Duchy of Parma were checked by Tuscany, Modena and Venice, and after the Treaty of Westphalia (1648) no hope of extending the papal territories could be entertained.

The papacy continued to advance monarchical claims that were unacceptable even to Roman Catholic states, as the Venetian Interdict and the passing of the Gallican articles had shown. Outside Italy, the papacy's ability to influence events was declining rapidly. When in 1648 Innocent X (1574–1648) published *Zelo Domus Deo*, which condemned the Peace of Westphalia, his bull was universally ignored. The growth of arguments based on reasons of state dealt a death blow to any papal hopes that the seventeenth century would improve the position of the papacy inter-

A view of Naples, by Gaspar van Wittch.

increasing Turkish pressure

Pope Innocent XI.

nationally, and there is considerable irony in the fact that it was Richelieu, a cardinal and the chief minister of the most Christian King Louis XIII, who was the creator of the new politics. In 1682 the French clergy endorsed the four Gallican articles, which declared that in practice the pope had few rights in France and that in theory his opinions were subject to the decisions of general councils. Pope Innocent XI (1611–89) was only prevented from proclaiming an interdict in France by the intervention of the Archbishop of Cambrai, François Fénelon (1651–1715).

Outside Europe, Roman Catholicism continued to spread rapidly as it had done during the sixteenth century. The main impetus for this continued expansion came from Urban VIII, who set up the Congregation for the Propagation of the Faith in the first year of his pontificate. But after Urban's death most of the popes were men of very limited ability, elected mainly because they would be unlikely to cause offense either inside or outside the Papal States. As a result, for nearly two hundred years the Papal States remained notoriously ill-governed and were usually in a position of financial weakness.

The extensive Duchy of Milan had been a dependency of the Spanish crown since the death of

François Fénelon, Archbishop of Cambrai.

Francesco Sforza ended his family's reign in 1553. As in the rest of the Spanish territories, there was considerable discontent and in 1713 the Austrians succeeded in seizing power there.

Although repeatedly at odds with its neighbors, the Grand Duchy of Tuscany and the Duchy of Savoy, Milan managed to retain its independence. By the Treaty of the Pyrenees (1659), which ended the war between Spain and France, Charles Emmanuel II of Savoy was permitted to re-occupy most of the towns that the French had captured.

The other principal states of northern Italy were the duchies of Modena and Parma. The former continued to be governed by the Este family, even after the loss of their capital, Ferrara, in 1597, while the latter remained in the possession of the Farnese family.

Venice

Despite its golden period in art and music, the political and military importance of Venice continued to decline throughout the seventeenth century, and the Venetian economy showed itself unable to recover from its slump in the sixteenth century. In 1645 the Turks turned their attention to Crete, which had been a Venetian possession for four centuries. In 1646 they landed an army of 50,000 men on the island, occupied Canea and took Retimo. Two years later they were able to lay siege to the capital of the island, Candia. The siege lasted for more than twenty years, but Candia eventually fell—and in September, 1669, the whole island passed into Turkish hands.

There was a brief resurgence of Venetian power under Francesco Morosini, who was appointed as commander-in-chief of the Republic's army in 1684 amid renewed hostilities with the Ottoman Empire. With the help of German mercenaries, Morosini was able to reconquer much of Dalmatia and the region of southern Greece known as the Morea. The septuagenarian commander was elected Doge by a grateful senate, but after his death the territories that he had reconquered were allowed to revert to their Turkish masters, and the Republic ceased forever to be a threat to the Turks.

The Ottoman Empire

The uneasy peace that had existed between Turkey and Austria since 1569 was broken by a fresh outbreak of war in 1593. A treaty signed in 1606 brought an even more lasting peace. Austrian involvement in the Thirty Years War and the need for the Ottoman sultans to be vigilant along the Persian border and also to prevent rebellions meant that neither side was eager to pursue hostilities. The invasion of Crete signaled the outbreak of a new phase of hostilities with the West. In 1669, when Candia was finally captured, the Ottoman Empire had reached the greatest extent of its long history.

From 1648 to 1687 the Ottoman Empire was ruled by Mohammed IV. His Grand Vizier, a vastly energetic Albanian, Mohammed Kuprili by name, who had begun his career as a scullion in the palace kitchen before his rapid rise to power, was largely responsible for this resurgence in the Empire's power. Although lacking any formal education—he was totally unable to read or write—the aged Kuprili, past seventy when he gained power in 1656, proved to be a man of immense ability. He restored the fleet, recaptured the islands that had been taken by the Venetians and put down revolts against his harsh regime with great severity. His ruthless determination to enlarge the power of his master, the Sultan, was reminiscent of that of Richelieu in France. In 1661 he was succeeded by his son, Fazil Ahmed Kuprili, a more humane man, but no less capable as an administrator.

In 1663 Ahmed Kuprili attacked Austria, which represented a far greater threat to Turkey than did the Venetian Republic. Following a succession of victories, Ahmed's troops were eventually overwhelmed at the Battle of St. Gotthard Abbey, and he was forced to conclude a treaty at Vasvár on August 10, 1664. Despite his serious defeat, the terms of the truce, which was to last for twenty years, were surprisingly favorable. But before the truce had expired, war broke out again along the Hungarian border, and the Turks prepared to besiege Vienna.

Mohammed IV.

Vienna under Siege

Vienna—capital of the Hapsburg Empire, cultural hub of Austria's golden age and gateway to the heart of Europe—became the object of an enormous Turkish siege operation in July of 1683. By August of that year the city appeared doomed: its bastions were in ruins, its garrison was decimated by dysentery and cannon fire, and its supply line to Poland was threatened by a Hungarian-Turkish army. Mustering a relief force of more than 60,000 Polish and German troops, John III Sobieski, King of Poland, marched south to save the embattled city. Sobieski's followers arrived in Vienna on September 7, and five days later they met the Turks at Nussdorf in a bitterly contested battle that turned back the "invincible" Ottoman armies. The Sultan's forces would not threaten Europe again.

Suleiman I, whose victory at the Battle of Mohacs in 1526 created the threefold division of Hungary that still existed in 1683.

Opposite Mohammed IV's siege of Vienna, the high point of the Turks' advance into Europe.

At the Battle of Mohacs in 1526, Suleiman the Magnificent, the most famous of the Ottoman sultans, crushed the medieval kingdom of Hungary. The King of Hungary was killed in that battle, and his country fell under Turkish domination. The Hapsburgs of Vienna laid claim to the slain King's crown, and a long contention between Austria and the Ottoman Empire ensued. During the reign of Sultan Suleiman, three distinct Hungaries emerged: Ottoman Hungary, centered around the great fortresses of Belgrade, Buda and Esztergom on the middle Danube; Transylvanian, to the east of the Tisza and under the control of a prince dependent on Istanbul; and Hapsburg, the territories located to the far north and west of the realm. This threefold division was to undergo little change after Suleiman's death.

In 1664 the forces of the Hapsburg Emperor Leopold I overcame the Ottomans at St. Gotthard on the Raba River. That campaign was the first major field battle that the Christians had ever won against the formidable might of the Ottoman Turks. Despite his victory, the Emperor made peace with the Sultan at Vasvar in 1664 on terms unfavorable to himself. He surrendered several fortresses and recognized an Ottoman nominee as Vaivode of Transylvania.

The situation prevailing in the Emperor's Hungarian territories led the statesmen at Vienna to accept the agreement made at Vasvar. The Hungarian magnates and nobles in Leopold's domain were divided into a pro-Hapsburg element and a faction suspicious of the policies emanating from Vienna. Many of the nobles feared that the Hapsburg desire to impose more centralized administrative and political control would mean the loss of their own large privileges. There was friction, too, on religious grounds. Calvinism had won much success in Hungary, and the forces of the Counter-Reformation sought to end that Calvinist allegiance.

In 1678 Imre Thököly, who was to become a leader of Hungarian resistance to the Hapsburg regime, assumed command of a rebel army.

Thököly turned to Istanbul for aid, and the Grand Vizier Kara Mustafa Pasha sent some assistance to the Hungarian rebels in 1681. At this same time the Emperor, hoping to placate the malcontents, summoned a Hungarian Diet to meet at Sopron. But Kara Mustafa Pasha induced Thököly to repudiate Leopold's concessions and began to give the rebels much more active support.

Leopold I and his ministers, who seemed to be listening to the latter group, concentrated on the activities of Louis XIV. To the government in Vienna, nothing was more unwelcome than a renewal of conflict with the Ottoman Turks—and it was this outlook that led the Emperor to seek from the Sultan a prolongation of the Vasvar settlement, due to expire in 1684. The Austrian ambassador at Istanbul sought to achieve this aim in 1681, but without success. Nor was Albert Caprara, a special envoy sent from Vienna in 1682, able to secure a continuation of the peace. Kara Mustafa Pasha, the Grand Vizier, had now in fact reached the moment of decision. In August, 1682, Thököly received the title of King from Sultan Mohammed IV—a clear indication that the Grand Vizier had chosen war, not peace.

In October, 1682, the Grand Vizier left Istanbul for Edirne (Adrianople). The preparations for a great campaign continued throughout the ensuing winter. At the end of March, 1683, the Ottoman forces set off from Edirne for Belgrade, arriving there at the beginning of May and encamping at Zemun on the northern bank of the Sava. Rain and the need to repair the great bridge across the marshes at Osijek hindered their subsequent advance; not until late in June did the Ottomans reach Szekesfehervar. There the Grand Vizier revealed to a council of war his determination to attack Vienna; there, too, Tartar horsemen from the Crimea joined the army. By the beginning of July, Kara Mustafa had reached Raab, one of the few Hungarian fortresses still under Hapsburg control.

No effort was spared to secure aid from abroad. In January, 1683, the Elector of Bavaria agreed to

Vienna during the siege.

Right An allegorical picture of the Emperor Leopold, who had reduced Ottoman pressure on Europe by his victory at St. Gotthard in 1664.

Atti Bassa, the Governor of Buda, who was to be killed when the Christians recaptured the city, 1686.

send troops to assist the Emperor. More important still was the compact negotiated with Poland. The activities of Thököly and his rebels in the Carpathians, and the resulting suspicion that the Ottomans might be contemplating an attack on the lands around Cracow, induced the Polish King, John III Sobieski, to reach an agreement with Emperor Leopold in the autumn of 1682. The terms of the agreement were clear and simple: Austria would seek to hold the Ottomans on the Danube, and Poland would attack them in the Ukraine. If the Ottomans moved against Cracow, the Emperor would send troops to its assistance; the Polish King would perform a like service should the Ottomans decide to besiege Vienna.

In the spring of 1683 Charles of Lorraine concentrated his forces at Pressburg, and then moved down the Danube to the region of Raab and Komarno. He hoped to reach either Nove Zamky or Esztergom, two important fortresses under Ottoman control, but a divided high command, inexplicit orders from Vienna and a shortage of supplies and fodder doomed his campaign. Lorraine had to fall back toward Raab, and then still farther in the direction of Pressburg. Soon all prospect of holding back the Ottoman advance was gone. A messenger

126

was sent to Sobieski on July 5, telling him that Vienna was beyond all doubt the objective that Kara Mustafa Pasha had set for himself.

On July 7, the Emperor and his court withdrew westward to Linz and thence to Passau, leaving Commandant Ernst von Starhemberg to hold Vienna. Lorraine, with his cavalry, reached the capital on July 8 and most of his men encamped in the suburb of Leopoldstadt or on the islands in the Danube. His infantry, under General Leslie, began to arrive in Vienna on July 10. To defend the capital, Starhemberg would have eleven thousand regular troops and a number of civilian auxiliaries, amounting to perhaps five thousand additional men. On July 13 the embankment before the walls of Vienna was cleared of buildings that might give protection to the Ottomans. On the following day, Lorraine began to pull his cavalry out of Leopoldstadt, breaking down the bridges across the Danube and retiring to a new position north of the river. On that same day Grand Vizier Kara Mustafa Pasha reached Vienna. The long siege was about to begin.

The defenses of Vienna comprised a banked earthen grade behind which was a counterscarp with palisades and a covered road along its summit. That road was divided into sections, each defensible as a self-contained unit. To the rear of the counterscarp was a dry moat. Additional defenses—in the form of entrenchments and blockhouses—had been erected on its floor. Behind the moat lay the actual walls of Vienna, strengthened with large and formidable bastions. The main Ottoman assault was to be launched against the southern flank of the fortress. On their right wing the Ottomans faced the Burg bastion; their center stood opposite the Burg ravelin, located within the moat; and their left was over against the Löbel bastion.

The Ottoman siege works—an elaborate system of deep trenches covered with timber roofing and provided with gun emplacements—would later receive high praise from the Christians. Kara Mustafa had brought a considerable number of medium- and light-caliber cannon with him, but no large siege guns. The main instruments of attack would therefore be trenches and mines.

The Ottomans began digging their approach trenches on the night of July 14-15. Along the slopes behind these trenches the Ottoman batteries opened fire on the morning of the fifteenth. Kara Mustafa, eager to complete the encirclement of Vienna, sent a strong force across the "canal"—the southern arm of the Danube—with orders to seize Leopoldstadt and the islands in the river. From that vantage batteries soon came into action against the northern walls of the fortress. At the same time the Ottomans established bridges across the Danube, above and below the Viennese fortifications. It was now possible for the Turks to cut off the flow of supplies down the river.

On July 23 the first Ottoman mines exploded along the sector between the Burg bastion and the Löbel bastion. A whole series of assaults and counteroffensives followed thereafter. By August 3 the Turks had broken through the counterscarp opposite the Burg ravelin.

The Ottomans next directed their attack downward against the entrenchments and blockhouses in the moat. After nine days of furious conflict the Turks reached the edge of the ravelin. Starhemberg was forced to withdraw his large guns from the threatened area to the actual walls and bastions of the fortress. On August 12 the Ottomans fired a mine of exceptional size and launched a violent assault that secured them a lodgment on the ravelin itself.

The fighting continued stubborn and bitter throughout the second half of August. Nothing that the Christians could do sufficed to halt for more than a brief interval the steady advance of their foe. On September 3 Starhemberg abandoned the ravelin. Worse was to follow: on September 4 a great mine brought down some of the Burg bastion, and on September 8 two more mines inflicted serious damage on the Löbel bastion. Dysentery and battle wounds reduced the Viennese garrison to perhaps four thousand effective soldiers. If help did not come soon, the city would fall to the Ottomans.

Meanwhile, events of importance had been taking place outside the fortress. Upon the arrival of the Ottomans, Charles of Lorraine had left Leopoldstadt and withdrawn to Jedlesee. There news reached him that Imre Thököly and a mixed force of Hungarians and Turks were thrusting westward along the north bank of the river. That movement, if unchecked, might cut the lines of communication linking Vienna with Poland. It would also diminish the area still capable of providing supplies and forage for the Hapsburg troops in the field. Lorraine, recognizing the danger, advanced eastward to Pressburg and there, on July 30, drove back Thököly and his

Charles of Lorraine, the leader of the Christian army which fought the Turks.

A view of the siege of Vienna, by de Hooghe.

127

The siege of Belgrade, 1690. The defeat of the Turks at Vienna did not immediately shatter their hopes of making further conquests in Europe and they recovered much of the territory they had lost during the next few years, but the great threat to Europe was much diminished.

men. At Stammersdorf, on August 24, Lorraine was able to repel a second Turkish-Hungarian advance. The routes along which aid might come from Poland and the German lands remained free.

And at last help was indeed arriving for the relief of Vienna. Toward the middle of August some 11,000 Bavarian troops reached the area south of Krems. Soon about eight thousand soldiers from Franconia and Thuringia joined them. At the same time regiments that had hitherto been serving the Emperor

on the Rhine began at last to appear at Krems.

Meanwhile, the news had reached John Sobieski on July 15 that Kara Mustafa was moving against Vienna. Orders went out for troops from northern Poland to concentrate at Cracow, as well as forces from the Ukraine, experienced in warfare against the Turks from their service in the Podolian War. The Polish King entered Cracow on July 29; the Podolians, led by Nicholas Sienawski, arrived there on August 2, and the contingents from the north, under Stanislas Jablonowski, on August 8. Time was needed at this juncture to decide which routes should be followed through Silesia, Moravia and Austria, and to arrange with the representatives of Emperor Leopold for the procurement of supplies adequate to maintain the Poles during their advance toward Vienna. But by August 20 all the Polish forces stood waiting at Tarnowski to begin the great campaign. The march southward began on August 22. Nine days later, on August 31, Sobieski met Charles of Lorraine at Oberhollabrunn. Here the German troops also had been brought together—Bavarian, Hapsburg and Franconian, soon to be strengthened through the arrival, on September 6, of a Saxon contingent over 10,000 strong.

By September 7, all the relief forces (numbering more than 60,000 men) were concentrated south of the river near Tulln. On September 9 the fateful advance began eastward across the Wienerwald. On the Christian left stood the Hapsburg troops and the Saxons; the Bavarians and other German contingents held the center; on the right wing rode Sobieski with the Polish forces. By September 11 the army was on the Kahlenberg ridge, only five miles from Vienna.

Kara Mustafa Pasha had begun to suspect that all was not well on his western flank. On September 8-9 he held two councils of war, at which he decided to withdraw from the siege about six thousand infantry and a considerable number of guns. To these troops he added some 20,000 horsemen. It was a belated measure designed to make good a situation

The Decline of Turkey's European Empire

- ● Hapsburg Empire in 1683
- ▬ Frontier of Ottoman Empire in 1683
- ● Poland in 1683
- ○ Acquired by Hapsburg Empire in 1699
- ▪▪ Frontier of Ottoman Empire in 1699
- ◐ Acquired by Poland in 1699
- ◑ Acquired by Venice in 1699
- ○ Acquired by Hapsburg Empire in 1718

SILESIA

POLAND

● Cracow

MORAVIA

RUSSIA

AUSTRIA

Linz

Pressburg

HAPSBURG HUNGARY

PODOLIA

Krems

Vienna

Raab

Tisza River

Heiligenstadt

Budapest

Esztergom   TRANSYLVANIA

OTTOMAN HUNGARY

Mohacs

Karlowitz

Belgrade

Passau

Danube River

Adrianople

Istanbul

now becoming critical. For Kara Mustafa had committed a number of grave errors in the deployment and use of his forces. He had neglected patrols in the Krems-Tulln area, watches over the routes across the Wienerwald, occupation of the Kahlenberg and adequate defenses for the protection of the Ottoman encampments before Vienna. The price demanded for this negligence was high.

Vienna was saved on September 12, 1683. An Ottoman attack in the region of Nussdorf, below the Kahlenberg ridge, led to a stubborn and complicated battle in broken terrain. Most of the fighting, until noon, was on the left of the Christian line. The Ottomans at length withdrew from Nussdorf, leaving the road toward Heiligenstadt open. On the right the Polish advance was less rapid, but at last Sobieski and his men came out on the slopes above the Alsbach stream. Ahead was more level ground, not two miles distant from Vienna and from the headquarters of Kara Mustafa Pasha near St. Ulrich.

The Christian forces now formed themselves into two lines. It was the moment for a supreme effort. The Hapsburg and Bavarian troops, pushing forward on the left against a strong resistance, swung toward the right. So, too, did the Saxon and German troops attacking in the center. The whole tide of battle surged toward the south and east. And now Sobieski and his horsemen struck hard against the Ottoman center. The Turkish defense held out for a while, then weakened and degenerated almost at once into a total collapse.

Only a rapid pursuit would draw the fullest advantage from the new situation. The difficulties hindering such a pursuit were serious enough—the shortage of supplies at Vienna and the ravaged state of the lands lower down the Danube. Nonetheless, Lorraine and Sobieski wanted to press forward. On September 17 the campaign was once more in motion. By September 23 a bridge had been reconstructed over the Danube below Pressburg. Now the Christians would have access to the supplies and forage available in the district of Schütt. The advance continued thereafter toward Parkany, where a bridge to the great Ottoman fortress of Esztergom crossed the Danube. On October 9, at Parkany, the German and Polish troops, amounting perhaps to 25,000 men, confronted an Ottoman force some 16,000 strong. The Turks made a wild attack, failed to break through and found themselves driven to the bank of the river. A portion of the bridge over the Danube, weakened by the fire of the Christian guns, fell into the water. Unable to escape, about nine thousand Ottomans lost their lives. By October 19, pontoon bridges had been brought into position for a crossing of the Danube. On October 22 the Christians laid siege to Esztergom. The Turkish garrison, seeing no hope of relief, surrendered on October 27. This event brought to an end the operations of 1683.

The siege of Vienna was a great and famous event, celebrated throughout Europe. On the level of individual success or failure it raised men like Starhemberg, Charles of Lorraine and Sobieski to the summit of their personal fame, while to Kara Mustafa it brought death, at Belgrade, on the order of the Turkish Sultan.

Turkish troops in the mid-seventeenth century.

Its consequences were more notable still in the realm of politics and war. At Linz, in March, 1684, a *Sacra Liga* was formed between Austria, Poland and Venice against the Ottoman Empire. The war thus begun was not to end until 1699, at the Peace of Karlowitz. It brought to the Hapsburgs almost all the Hungarian lands; Venice received the Morea (only to lose it to the Ottomans in 1718); Poland acquired Podolia; and Russia, a late participant in the conflict, was given Azov.

It is debatable whether the relief of Vienna saved Europe from an Ottoman conquest. It can be argued that the last Turkish offensive that might perhaps have led to the subjugation of Austria occurred in the bitter conflict of 1593-1606, a war that underlined the fact that the Ottoman Empire had reached the viable limits of expansion. Now, problems of time and distance, of terrain, climate and logistics rendered dubious any enlargement of the already extended frontier.

Even in the realm of warfare, the tide of events was adverse to the Ottomans. Technological advance in Europe had brought about the elaboration of tactical systems that the Turks would find hard to meet. The Ottoman war machine might still be formidable in sieges—witness the assault on Candia in 1667-69 or even on Vienna itself in 1683. On the field of battle, however, the outlook for the Ottomans was grave. Further, the Austria of 1683 was not the Austria of 1526—it stood now on the verge of a golden age as one of the great powers in Europe.

Yet Kara Mustafa had almost achieved the conquest of Vienna. This simple fact will serve to explain how it was that Sobieski, only twenty-four hours after his cavalry had cut through the Ottoman defense, could write to Pope Innocent XI, on September 13, in a spirit of immense and pardonable jubilation, "we came, we saw and God conquered." So must other men have thought on that memorable September 12, 1683.   V. J. PARRY

Louis XIV's ambitions strain even

Mercantilism

At the root of many of the problems that most disturbed seventeenth-century government were problems connected with trade and colonialism. Europe's colonial powers, France, Holland, England, Spain and Portugal, developed what has come to be known as the mercantilist system. Historians argue about the precise nature of mercantilism, and a few deny its very existence. The term was first used by the eighteenth-century Scottish economist Adam Smith to describe the basically similar economic policies of Europe's main powers. In the words of Thomas Mun (1571–1641), a seventeenth-century writer on trade whose influential *Treasure by Forraign Trade* was posthumously published in 1644, "We must ever observe this rule; to sell more to strangers yearly than we consume of theirs in value." Mercantilism necessitated a relationship between the government and merchants little less close than exists today.

The colonial powers sought to encourage their own national trade with the colonies and to exclude outsiders from the benefits. Monopolistic navigation laws were the main means that they used to achieve this end. The main result of these mercantilist endeavors was to make governments aware of the benefits that interference could bring and to en-

courage a closer regulation of economic life generally.

There was another important result too. It is obvious that the balance of trade of all states cannot be in surplus at the same time. Because Holland, France and England were aware of the problem and at the same time were strong politically, economically and militarily they were the primary beneficiaries of mercantilism. Other, weaker states suffered. As a result the gap between the advanced and the more backward states widened steadily in the seventeenth and early eighteenth centuries. The trade surplus of the advanced countries could be used to bring social benefits to the community, although in practice it usually was not. It could also be reinvested in further trading and colonial ventures; the growth and development of stock markets and exchanges during this period were made possible by the wealth acquired from foreign trade. An alternative use of trading surpluses was in war; the Anglo-Dutch wars were wars made possible by trade as well as being wars about trade. The immediate occasion of these wars was the problem caused by the Navigation Acts.

The prosperity of British industry in the eighteenth century was made possible by its trading surpluses. Investment both in science and in technological improvement was built on the foundation of a trading surplus.

French expansionism

During the 1680s, while the main attention of the Holy Roman Emperor was diverted by the Turkish invasion of Austria, the French army had been making inroads along his western frontier. Louis XIV had ample reason to be proud of his army: composed of 200,000 well-trained officers and men—mostly infantry armed with wheel-lock muskets, bayonets and fourteen-foot pikes—it was well equipped and harshly disciplined. The name of one of its officers, Jean Martinet, a military engineer and renowned tactician, was to give a new word to the English language. The army's strength and efficiency was the work of Louis' war ministers, Michel Le Tellier, and Tellier's son, François Michel Le Tellier, who was created Marquis of Louvois. Marshal Vauban—whose fortresses, built as a cordon round France between 1678 and 1688, are masterpieces of the craft—was responsible for the army's skill in engineering and siege techniques.

The army had already captured Dunkerque, the Franche Comté and extensive territories along France's disputed eastern border with the Low Countries—whose towns, Louis confessed, were ever before his eyes. Those victories were confirmed in the 1684 Treaty of Regensburg. The treaty ratified French possession of a string of fortified Flemish towns and counties—Luxemburg, Alsace and Strasbourg—as well as the Franche Comté.

France under Louis XIV

The France of Louis XIV was at the height of its power, but the King had even greater ambitions. In 1683 death removed the constraining counsels of his great minister, Jean Baptiste Colbert, who had restored the country's finances and built up its powerful navy—and Louis' thoughts turned again to war. His opportunity came in 1685, when the Elector of the Palatinate died childless. Louis immediately claimed the country for France.

This claim, which aroused

The Royal Exchange in London.

Louis XIV at a siege, by Frans van der Meulen.

France's considerable powers

Colbert (center) with members of the court.

Europe against him, led to the foundation of the League of Augsburg (an alliance composed of Austria, Sweden, Holland and several German states) in 1686.

England did not join the League but, after William III's accession, supported it. Louis hurled his armies against the Palatinate, thus declaring war on the League. The members of the League were joined in war by Spain, Savoy and England.

War of the League of Augsburg

Despite the number and strength of his enemies, the war went well for Louis. The Duke of Luxemburg—a worthy successor to Condé and Turenne—decisively defeated the allied armies under the Prince of Waldeck at Fleurus in 1690 and under William III of England and Holland at Leuze in the following year. Mons was captured in 1691 and Namur was occupied after a siege in 1692. The Duke of Luxemburg won further victories over William at Steenkerke in 1692 and at Neerwinden in 1693. Meanwhile, Marshal Catinat captured Nice and overran Savoy, defeating the Duke of Savoy, Amadeus II, at Staffarda and Marsaglia. At sea the navy, which Colbert had built up with such tender care, took on the

English and Dutch fleets and forced them to retreat in disorder off Beachy Head in 1690.

The English and Dutch fleets bombarding Dunkerque.

Although the sea war was not totally one-sided, as the English sunk or captured fifteen ships from Admiral Tourville's fleet at the Battle of La Hogue, Tourville was able to inflict a crushing defeat on the allies in the Mediterranean in 1693.

Despite these early victories the war had so exhausted France's resources that Louis was compelled to bring it to an end in 1697. By the Treaty of Ryswick he surrendered nearly all the German territories—except for Strasbourg, which he had conquered earlier. Louis was compelled to allow the Dutch to garrison the frontier towns of the Spanish Netherlands and to recognize not only that William of Orange was King of England, but also that William's staunchly Anglican niece Princess Anne should succeed him.

The war on heresy

Louis had made another mistake in the 1680s—apart from his decision to go to war. His Queen, Maria Teresa, died in 1683, the year of Colbert's death, and left him free to marry Madame de Maintenon. The new Queen, granddaughter of the distinguished Huguenot, Theodore Agrippe d'Aubigné, had been converted to Roman Catholicism and was a devout member of the Church. She did not bear as much of the responsibility for Louis XIV's religious policies as her contemporaries supposed, but she made no attempt to conceal her satisfaction when those policies induced Protestants to recant. She was a woman of piety and felt that it was her duty to convert all those who had strayed from the paths of righteousness.

Although not a deeply religious man, Louis was scrupulous in his observance of the outward forms of religion; he heard Mass almost every day of his long life. As a Christian king and the head of the Roman Catholic Church in France, he believed that it was one of his principal duties to induce all his subjects to accept what he regarded as the true faith, and also to carry out the promise that had been contained in the coronation oath since the time of Henry IV: "Seriously to extirpate all heretics, so branded by the Church, out of my land."

To achieve that ambition, an energetic campaign was mounted against the religious minority, the country's million-or-so Huguenots. Missionaries were sent into Normandy, Poitou and Languedoc—areas of Huguenot strength—and proclamations excluding Huguenots from public office were issued.

Violence was proscribed, but it was inevitable when troops were forcibly billeted in the houses of Protestants that there should be some bloodshed. The poor could not afford to feed and lodge the soldiers; the rich could not bear rough troops ruining their homes. Reports soon reached Paris of dragoons driving Protestants to Mass, forcing them to listen to missionaries and sprinkling them with holy water.

These methods were strikingly successful. The population of some predominantly Protestant towns, following the example of the leading Huguenot families in the district, were converted to Roman Catholicism in large numbers. Other towns lost many of their Protestants as a result of emigration. By 1685 there were no more than a quarter of a million Huguenots in France. This minority, however, remained obdurate in its faith. The Protestants clung stubbornly to their Church councils and schools. They relied on the protection of the 1598 Edict of Nantes, which guaranteed their freedom of religion and gave them a recognized position. Louis determined to withdraw this protection.

The demolition of the Protestant church at Charenton in 1685, part of Louis XIV's campaign against the Huguenots.

royal households. Faced with this heavy barrage, the persecuted minority naturally moved to occupations still open to them. In Pau, for example, there were two hundred Huguenot, compared with only fifty Roman Catholic advocates; but, from July, 1685, this avenue was likewise blocked and the Huguenots turned in some cases to the medical profession. Then the King barred that as well, on the grounds that there would soon be too many doctors of the wrong faith. No wonder, then, that the Protestants began to feel trapped.

Education presented no happier prospects. Attempts were made to close down Protestant schools by renewing the ban on teachers in those establishments taking on more and more boarders. Schools located in the centers of towns were to be relocated close to temples, which were mainly in the suburbs. Protestant academies offering courses in the liberal arts and philosophic sciences were also banned. Because Huguenot children could not gain places in secondary schools and colleges approved by the state and were in fact restricted to primary education, they were often sent abroad until, in June, 1681, it was further decreed that parents must recall their offspring from lands where they might become infected with maxims contrary to the loyalty that they owed to France.

While education was thus being bombarded with vetos, more positive proselytizing was in full swing, sometimes with equally unpleasant results. In 1677, conversion offices had been set up and any Protestant wishing to turn his coat was paid a handsome sum of money. At the same time, central authority asked for lists of Protestants, with details of names, occupations and financial resources and word went round the clergy to keep a vigilant eye on the heterodox members of their parishes and report the slightest irregularity. Once again clerics were to be used as spies; nor did it matter much whether denunciations were properly justified or not. False testimony was common. If the state wanted evidence, then the vast legion of opportunists would be delighted to oblige. A good

example of this was furnished in 1680, when the First President of the Bordeaux *Parlement*, writing to the Secretary of State about a man condemned to the galleys, mentioned some detail of faulty evidence, adding nonetheless that "the zeal of the judges went beyond the rule in order to make an example." That was what mattered most: the deterrent value of the punishment.

But, if this seemed overtly zealous, it was nothing compared to the enthusiasm of Poitou, where, after 1681, the *intendant*, Marillac, distinguished himself and reserved a place in history by the extreme conversion methods he employed. Parish registers were divided into three columns. In the first appeared Roman Catholics, who were exempted from some taxes; in the second, the newly converted, who escaped taxation altogether; in the last, the obstinate Protestants, who were subjected to a surcharge. This last item was indeed daunting: those who had hitherto paid thirty *livres* now found themselves faced with the bill for 300 or even 500 *livres*—surely a compelling argument for changing one's religion. Marillac was particularly good at billeting troops on Huguenot families—the so-called *dragonnades*—who suffered cruelly from excesses condoned and encouraged by the *intendant*. After 1682, these *dragonnades* were extended and intensified. Now the poor Protestants were intimidated, not only by brutal soldiery but also by a fanatical priesthood in the form of Capuchin monks, who were also billeted in their homes. Many could not stand the strain. So successful were the *dragonnades* that Louvois organized them on a national scale and in the southwest alone some 60,000 conversions were obtained in a two-week period.

The year 1685 became the climacteric for a surprising number of reasons. The Assembly was meeting once more. Having had a quarrel with the Pope, and having limited papal power in France, Louis XIV was anxious to prove that he was still a good Roman Catholic. This was precisely what the Assembly demanded of him. Five months

The revocation ceremony at Fontainebleau, after a drawing by Jan Luiken.

Madame de Maintenon, mistress and second wife of Louis XIV. A convert to Catholicism, she exerted a strong religious influence over the King.

before the Edict of Fontainebleau deprived the Protestant minority of its few remaining rights, the Bishop of Valence, who in 1682 had thundered against Rome in defense of Gallican liberties, was vehemently urging the King to extirpate heresy. This eloquent priest, Daniel de Cosnac, was to play a vital role in pushing Louis over the brink. Economics were also tugging at the King's sleeve. The Church's free gift was more necessary than ever to ensure solvency, since the great palace at Versailles had cost and was still costing so much. France needed Roman Catholic funds; but it also cast a covetous eye upon charitable endowments administered by Huguenots, many of which would now fall into Roman Catholic hands. The moment was ripe in other ways too. England had papist James on the throne and, for the time being at least, France's nearest neighbor and keenest rival could be counted upon not to help a Calvinist faction across the Channel. Futhermore, the French monarch could promote a Roman Catholic Europe, declaring his firm intention to perfect in unity and strength the monarchical system of government; and, just as the Monmouth rebellion had been crushed in England, so would France's seditious group—who in 1683 had demonstrated so effectively in the south its potential for trouble-making—be ground into the dust.

There were, moreover, compelling personal reasons for putting on the pressure. The middle-aged monarch was changing. His mistress (and later spouse), Madame de Maintenon, noted his frequent recourse to God and recurrent thoughts concerning his own salvation. She also commented with evident satisfaction on his reading of the Bible, which he now judged to be the very best of books; upon the confession of his faults and his desire to convert others. As the Duke of Saint-Simon remarked, "Louis was the kind of man who

Madame de Montespan, Louis' mistress for nearly twenty years. The King's feelings of guilt over their relationship added to the pressure upon him to revoke the Edict of Nantes.

must do penitence on the backs of others," in this case, the Huguenots. In particular, he was expiating his adulterous relationship with Madame de Montespan, who had dabbled in devil-worship —and perhaps in poisoning too—and he was doing so in the arms of the respectable Maintenon, who conceived the role of royal mistress as that of a missionary keeping the King from wicked women.

All these reasons contributed to the persecution in 1685. In August and September, the number of conversions was particularly impressive. Louis, who either did not know, or did not very much care how such miracles had been effected, decided that since only a few hundred hard cases must now remain, the Edict issued by his benevolent grandfather was obviously redundant. On October 18 he signed the revocation. Compared with its liberal predecessor, the preamble was couched in terms both cold and laconic. Louis cynically recalled that three former kings had granted toleration only to withdraw it when it suited their purpose and, flying in the face of truth, declared that until 1684 he had been content merely to close down chapels and abolish tribunals composed of equal numbers of Roman Catholic and Protestant judges. Thus the act was accompanied by a document full of untruths and half-truths, unworthy of a great monarch and a great country.

It was nonetheless acclaimed with joy by many. Naturally it was welcomed by the bigoted who rejoiced in its harshness; surprisingly too by the educated and intelligent Madame de Sévigné, who called it "the greatest and finest thing ever imagined or brought about" and the even more intelligent La Fontaine, Racine and La Bruyère, who were in other ways progressive. Only Vauban, the fortifications expert, and Saint-Simon, the politician and memorialist, from the ranks of the famous registered their protests. Indeed, it was the former who hit on the truth when he explained that sovereigns may well be the masters of their subjects' lives and possessions, but they can never be the masters of their opinions.

The consequences of the revocation were bad for the minority and bad for France. More temples were destroyed. All ministers of the Reformed Church were to leave France within fifteen days or be sent to the galleys for life. Children would in future be brought up in the Catholic faith. Calvinists would be exposed to even more brutal *dragonnades* and, if they had refused a Roman Catholic sacrament during an illness, they would be sent to the galleys on their recovery. After 1687, Huguenots trying to escape were sent to the galleys too, if apprehended. Yet, despite all these dreadful possibilities, during the entire period of persecution about 300,000 had gone abroad and even between 1680 and 1700 some 175,000 fled to other lands. Generally speaking, the refugees were men of sound principle, who imparted backbone and sinew to their adopted countries. This might be regarded as a moral consequence of the revocation.

The economic consequences were more obvious. Many Huguenots were merchants, who thus left France precisely at a time when they were required at home to bring to fruition the nascent commercial and industrial revolution, so much the domain of the middle classes in any case. Other lands became richer for the change. As Britain, Holland and some German states were moving into boom conditions large numbers of industrious Protestant Frenchmen settled in these countries, thereby adding materially to the economic and political life of their new homes. Voltaire tells us that whole quarters of London in Spitalfields and Soho were suddenly peopled by French silk weavers and that, at the London mint, 60,000 guineas were struck from imported Huguenot gold. Amsterdam banks did particularly well in 1687, especially as the new arrivals had been obliged long before 1685 to convert their assets into gold. On the other hand, some arrived penniless and were consequently dependent on the charity of the English, who took collections in their churches, and the Dutch, who exempted them from paying many taxes.

In the South of France, the Protestant cause was to go underground, only to emerge later in unpleasant forms. For instance, in 1703 when France was at war, the Camisards, thus called because of their distinctive shirts, embarked on an insurrection which lasted for two years and tied down vast numbers of royal troops commanded by an outstanding general, Marshal Villars, just at

the moment when France sorely needed both. Abroad, too, France was to suffer. Much free-thinking was to stem from Holland and in particular from two French refugees, Pierre Bayle and Pierre Jurieu. These ideas were subsequently reimported and were spread by the celebrated *philosophes* of the mid-eighteenth century, for whom Bayle's *Dictionary* became a bible and arsenal. In its pages were discovered advanced and liberal notions, which became the very stuff of French revolutionary thought at the end of the eighteenth century. More immediate was the decree of the Great Elector, Frederick William of Brandenburg, whose Edict of Potsdam countered that of Fontainebleau and who, in October 1685, invited French Protestants to settle in German lands. Another European reaction came from Britain in 1688, for Louis' blunder may be regarded as one of the reasons for the downfall of the Stuart monarchy in England. The analogy was, after all, inescapable; and British Protestants felt that it was time to get rid of a king who might well imitate his repressive colleague across the sea. When James yielded the throne to William and Mary, a new European alliance was formed against Louis XIV, who now appeared quite clearly monopolistic and totalitarian. In the long run, then, the Treaty of Utrecht, by which France renounced its territorial ambitions in Europe, was the logical outcome of the Edict of Fontainebleau, signed with such pomp in the autumn of 1685.

JOHN LAURENCE CARR

Louis' monumental palace at Versailles. Erected in the midst of what had been a sandy waste Versailles became the wonder of Europe.

137

The Dutch Republic

On July 31, 1668, a treaty was signed at Breda, and the Second Dutch War with England came to an end. The treaty settled some vital differences between the two nations, but their quarrels were not yet over. Although a common fear of the ambitions of Louis XIV brought England and the United Provinces into temporary alliance against France, Louis had little difficulty in persuading Charles II that his real enemy was Holland, not France. In 1670, an alliance was signed between England and France that provided for an attack on Holland, the destruction of its commercial power and the partition of the country.

The middle years of the seventeenth century had been just as difficult in the United Provinces as they had been in England. There, too, the power of the prince was for a short time destroyed. After the death of William II of Orange in 1650, tension between the House of Orange and the province of Holland was renewed. As William's son, the future William III, was born after his father's death, the republicans, who were already influential, attempted to set up a republican regime in the United Provinces. The leading republican was Jan de Witt (1625–72), who became Grand Pensionary of Holland, which had been the most disaffected of the provinces since the time of Oldenbarneveldt.

When William III was eighteen he began to take an interest in politics, and de Witt's attempts to exclude him from the States-General failed. In 1670 William joined the Council of State, and it was clear that there was still support for the House of Orange even in the province of Holland.

The end of the Republic

The Dutch Republic showed great resourcefulness in the face of the danger from attack by the English and French. But the House of Orange provided a better rallying point than the Republic, and in 1672 William was appointed Stadholder of several of the provinces. De Witt was assassinated, and the United Provinces were once again united by the House of Orange. The English again failed in the fighting to defeat the Dutch navy, and the French, who attacked on land, failed to reach Amsterdam, as the Dutch opened the dikes and flooded the countryside. The war lasted from 1672 to 1678, and at its end Holland remained as much of a commercial threat to England as it had been before. During that period the Dutch became a dangerous rival to France also, as William III, a harsh, brilliant, asthmatic, unattractive prince, became the leading opponent of Louis XIV's aspirations and the chief architect of the European alliances against him. By the time the European wars were finally over, England had greatly increased both her share of world trade and the power of her navy. Holland was to emerge from the conflict weakened; the Dutch never regained their position as a world power.

The theater in England

While Racine was writing in French, the English theater, closed

The Battle of Schooneveld between the English and Dutch navies.

during the Commonwealth, reopened in London. It was no longer a national theater, as it had been in Shakespeare's time; indeed until the civil wars the most notable productions of the English stage were court masques —stylized, allegorical and spectacular pageants on which Ben Jonson and Inigo Jones (1573–

English models such as Ben Jonson. The comedy of manners, perfected by Molière, became popular in England, and its lightness of touch appealed to the cynical courtiers of Charles II.

Such plays as *She Would if She Could* (1668) and *The Man of Mode* (1676) by Sir George Ethridge (1634–91) as well as those of

Drawing by Inigo Jones for a court masque.

1652) lavished their respective talents as poet and stage designer.

With the exception of a few, English writers for the theater during the Restoration period were more successful in comedy than in tragedy. The major exceptions include John Dryden (1631–1700), Thomas Otway (1652–85), whose greatest work, *Venice Preserved, or a Plot Discovered*, appeared in 1682, and Thomas Shadwell (1642–92), whose comic work outnumbered although it did not outweigh his serious plays.

In comedy, Shadwell stood out in looking backward toward older

William Wycherley (1640–1716) had an immense if somewhat ephemeral popularity. The great architect of Blenheim Palace and Castle Howard, Sir John Vanbrugh (1664–1726), also wrote two popular plays, *The Relapse* (1696) and *The Provoked Wife* (1697). But Restoration drama, based as it was on ideas that appealed to "polite society" tended toward superficiality. Only William Congreve (1670–1729) managed to some extent to transcend the limitations of the comedy of manners, as Molière had so successfully done in French. Con-

A view of Amsterdam, by Ludolf Backhuysen.

ensure Parliament's subservience

greve's *Love for Love* (1695) and *Way of the World* (1700) are unquestionably the finest products of Restoration comedy.

Restoration comedy was attacked by contemporaries not so much for its superficiality as for its obscenity, and the publication of *A Short View of the Immorality and Profaneness of the English Stage* in 1696 by the nonjuring clergyman Jeremy Collier (1650–1726) seems to have been a major cause of the decline of Restoration comedy. It is interesting that this attack did not spring from a Puritan milieu, which had declined in influence by the end of the seventeenth century, but from a future nonjuring bishop. Nonjurors were those who refused to swear allegiance to William III on the grounds that James still was *de jure* King.

Charles II

The politics of the reign of Charles II (1630–85) and his successor James II (1633–1701) were dominated by constitutional crisis. The problems that had led England through the traumas of civil war, Commonwealth and Restoration had left the essential questions unanswered. The reigns of the last two Stuart kings brought the crisis to a head.

From 1660 onward Charles' chief minister, the brilliant Edward Hyde (1609–74), Earl of Clarendon, sought to restore the royal power to what it had been before the outbreak of the civil wars. His attempts, however, brought him great unpopularity in the country. Despite Clarendon's services to the crown, the King disliked his refusal to abandon constitutional methods. In 1667 Charles used the Dutch attacks, as well as the rather unfair criticism caused by the plague and the fire of London, as an excuse to dismiss Clarendon. The Earl retired to write his *True Historical Narrative of the Rebellion and the Civil Wars*, which even 300 years later remains one of the best and liveliest accounts of the period.

Charles left the government in the hands of the "Cabal"—Clifford, Ashley (Ashley-Cooper), Buckingham, Arlington and Lauderdale—but played off its members against each other. Increasingly, the King felt drawn

Charles II, by Samuel Cooper.

toward alliance with France, despite the unpopularity that this policy was sure to bring in a country that would have preferred an alliance with Protestant Holland. Religious motivation certainly played a part in this; two members of the Cabal were Roman Catholics, as was the heir to the throne, James, Duke of York. Charles himself became a secret Roman Catholic. In 1670 Charles and Louis XIV signed the secret Treaty of Dover, which gave Charles a large subsidy to continue the war with Holland. In 1672 Charles issued a Declaration of Indulgence for all nonconformists, including Roman Catholics, but was forced to withdraw it, as it was obvious that the only real intention was to benefit Roman Catholics.

Parliament became increasingly hostile toward Roman Catholics, and in 1673, a Test Act, banning them from office, became law. Anglican fears of popery were fanned in 1678 by the Popish Plot, when Titus Oates (1649–1705), a perennial liar, revealed the almost entirely fictitious details of a plot to overthrow Church and State. As a result of this, and of Louis XIV's revelation of details of the Treaty of Dover, Roman Catholics were excluded from Parliament, and the House of Commons began pressing unsuccessfully for the exclusion of the Duke of York from the succession to the throne. Suspicions of Rome became so acute that Charles' new chief minister, Thomas Osborne (1632–1712), Earl of Danby, was almost impeached, although he was an Anglican.

The last two years of Charles' reign were more successful as far as his plans were concerned. He began a large-scale remodeling of constitutional institutions and procedures, including the electoral process, in order to ensure the election of parliaments that would favor the energetic use of the royal prerogative. By now it was becoming increasingly clear that there were two parties, the "Tories," who in general favored an extension of the royal power, and the "Whigs" who wanted rule by parliamentary oligarchy. The Tories favored the succession of the Duke of York; the Whigs, led by Anthony Ashley-Cooper (1621–83), now Earl of Shaftesbury, preferred Charles' illegitimate son, James Scott (1649–85), Duke of Monmouth. An attempted rebellion in favor of Monmouth petered out, however.

James II

When Charles died in 1685 it looked as if the Stuarts had at last been able to achieve their ambition of rule through a subservient parliament. Even the justiciary, whose independence under Charles I had helped the parliamentary cause, had been muzzled by such political appointments as that of George Jeffreys (1644–89) as Lord Chief Justice.

It was the considerable achievement of the honest but foolish James II to throw away the heritage of his dishonest but prudent brother within three short years. The heritage of goodwill that made a servile parliament grant substantial revenues to the King for life and led the country to overthrow the Duke of Monmouth's rising was soon exhausted. James' misuse of the funds that he had been voted and the immense cruelty shown by Judge Jeffreys "the hanging judge" to Monmouth's defeated supporters after the Battle of Sedgemoor (1685)—300 were executed and 800 exiled to the West Indies as serfs—lost the King much popularity.

Even more serious was James' attempt to infiltrate Roman Catholics into the Church and the universities. Scholars—at least at Oxford—and clergymen were the traditional supporters of the monarchy and it could be said with more truth in the seventeenth century than it could in the nineteenth that the Church of England was the Tory party at prayer.

James sought to appoint individual Roman Catholics to secular office by dispensing them from the Test Act. To deal with the Church and the universities he set up an ecclesiastical commission, which suspended the Bishop of London for refusing to punish an antipapist preacher, deprived the Vice-Chancellor of Cambridge for refusing to allow a monk to receive a degree and replaced all twenty-five fellows of Magdalen College, Oxford, with Roman Catholics.

By now James' unpopularity was enormous. He could still have ruled if he had moved slowly to achieve his wishes, but in 1688 he threw all caution to the winds. He summoned a new parliament, whose members, often illiterate and poor men, would be likely to support him. He suspended the laws against Roman Catholics and noncomformists, and ordered the clergy to read his declaration at sermon time. Seven of the bishops, including William Sancroft (1619–93), Archbishop of Canterbury, refused to accept the royal power to suspend the law. A more intelligent monarch would have realized the danger of antagonizing the clergy, but James had the bishops tried—and was surprised when they were aquitted.

The final blow, which turned unpopularity into rebellion, was the birth of a son to the King. Popular hopes of a Protestant succession were shattered. The Glorious Revolution began.

Titus Oates.

The Glorious Revolution

In November, 1688, a time of year when the English Channel can be at its most treacherous, William III of Holland set sail with a small army to claim the throne of England for his wife, Mary, daughter of the reigning King James II. Awaiting him, if the fleet could navigate the difficult waters, was James with an army three times as large. Incredibly the fleet made the passage, the army landed, and England succumbed without a drop of blood being shed. James fled the country and William and Mary were acclaimed joint sovereigns.

William of Orange, King of England, after Lely. The crown was offered to William together with the Declaration of Rights, thereby asserting the political supremacy of Parliament in Britain.

On November 1, 1688, Prince William III of Orange, Captain-General of the Republic of the United Netherlands, ordered a Dutch armada to sea. Consisting of some fifty warships, guarding over two hundred military transports, it set out across the North Sea on an invasion of England. William was both the nephew and the son-in-law of the English Roman Catholic monarch, James II; his mother was a daughter of Charles I, while his wife Mary was James' elder daughter by his first marriage. In a declaration addressed to the English people, published on September 30, William had given the reasons for his proposed entry into England:

We cannot any longer forbear to declare that, to our great regret, we see that those counsellors who have now the chief credit with the King [James II] have overturned the religion, laws, and liberties of those [British] realms and subjected them in all things relating to their consciences, liberties and properties to arbitrary government.

The declaration proceeded to describe the favoritism shown to "papists," the plots against the Protestant religion and the breach or perversion of the laws of the land. William claimed to act on behalf of his wife who was, he asserted, the rightful heiress to the English throne. His intention was to defend the English people against the violence of James' "evil counsellors." He therefore invited all the English people, from the peers of the realm to commoners, to assist him in the execution of his altruistic design to save their kingdom from "arbitrary government" and "slavery."

The military expedition was daring in the extreme. It was launched in the late autumn when the weather was likely to be a major hazard (an earlier attempt to set sail had been abandoned because of storms). James II, himself an experienced

Opposite The apotheosis of William and Mary. Louis XIV of France lies underfoot, symbolizing the triumph of Protestantism.

soldier and sailor—the invasion was really aimed against him and not his "evil counsellors"—had at his disposal a navy, equal to that of the Dutch, stationed near Harwich to meet the invasion fleet. He also had a professional army three times as large as his nephew's. All the principal ports along the east and southeast coasts were adequately garrisoned. James hoped that his fleet would either win a victory at sea or disrupt the military transports. Failing that, he was confident that his army, whose central reserve was concentrated at Salisbury and could be moved either eastward or westward, would easily overpower and vanquish William's expeditionary force after its landings, even if it were supported by discontented elements in England. The Church of England, which had always been loyal to the House of Stuart, would, James believed, exert its moral influence on his side. He had expected the invasion for at least three months. For his part he had made concessions to the malcontents at home and had promised that a new parliament would be elected to meet after an interval of three years. As a politician and military man, James could not imagine that William's foolhardy adventure stood the smallest chance of success.

Yet, incredibly, it succeeded and even more incredible not a drop of blood was shed. William had given orders to his English naval commander, Admiral Herbert, that his task was not to fight James' navy but to protect the transports and ensure a safe disembarkation. For a time a fog hid the movements of the Dutch fleet from the English naval commander-in-chief, Lord Dartmouth. The original intention had been to make a landing somewhere on the east coast. But Herbert was against this. In any case heavy winds prevented the expedition from turning north and the resolution was taken to pass through the straits of Dover and land the troops at Torbay in unguarded

A song written in honor of the birth of James II's son, the Old Pretender. The fear that James might be succeeded by a Catholic heir finally turned the court (Tory) party against him.

THE

Princely Triumph:

Or, Englands Joy in the BIRTH of the

Young Prince of WALES:

Born on the 10th. of June, 1688. to the great Content and Satisfaction of all LOYAL SUBJECTS.

To the Tune of, Packington's Pound.   This may be Printed, R. P.

A song written in honor of the birth of James II's son, the Old Pretender. The fear that James might be succeeded by a Catholic heir finally turned the court (Tory) party against him.

Opposite A satire of James' second wife, the Catholic Princess Mary of Modena, confessing to the Jesuit Father Edward Petre. Popular suspicions aroused by Mary's devotion to her religion were to contribute to James' downfall.

Devonshire. Dartmouth moved too late to intercept the Dutch fleet and the landing on November 5, was unopposed. Four days later William set up his headquarters at Exeter.

For the next two weeks there was a lull, but what happened proved decisive. William stayed at Exeter to discover how the landing of his small army would be received by the English people. James, having failed to persuade the leaders of the Church of England to express their abhorrence of William's declaration, left London on November 17 to join his army in Salisbury. Here he learned that some of the officers were already deserting to join William. In the north of England, at Chester, Derby and York, rebels in full sympathy with William's aims rose in arms against the King. The English navy gave up any attempt to interfere with the Dutch ships lying at anchor.

James was palsied by doubt and alarm. When he was at Salisbury his nose bled profusely and he was terrified he would be kidnapped by mutinous soldiers. On his return to London he learned that his younger daughter, Princess Anne, and her husband had already gone over to William. The King's policy was now purely defensive. He simply aimed at keeping his capital and his army intact while he waited on events. Finally, at the end of November, he announced that a parliament would be called and he opened negotiations with William, who had left Exeter on November 21, and was slowly advancing toward London, for an armistice and for agreed conditions on the safeguarding of the meeting of a free parliament to settle all the grievances urged against the government.

William's answer reached London on December 11. His terms were stiff but not unreasonable. They included the demand that all James' fellow Roman Catholics should be removed from their offices. William's army, swollen by deserters from James, was now only eight days march from the capital. James now decided to abandon his kingdom. Early the following morning he secretly left the Palace of Whitehall, threw the Great Seal into the Thames River, and rode to Sheerness, lower down the river, to board a boat for France. When Lord Dartmouth learned of the King's withdrawal from London, he handed over his fleet to William. With the wholesale desertion of James' fleet and army and the successful completion of the rebel risings in northern England the bloodless revolution against King James II was to all intents and purposes at an end.

How did the revolution come about? It was not a class struggle, which the earlier English civil war is sometimes supposed to have been. It had two principal characteristics, one religious, the other political. The tradition of antipopery in England dated back at least a hundred and thirty years: the burning of Protestants, including Archbishop Cranmer, at the stake in the reign of "Bloody Mary," the Pope's condemnation of her Protestant sister, Elizabeth I, the Gunpowder Plot organized against James I by Roman Catholic conspirators, the widespread belief that Charles I, influenced by his Roman Catholic Queen, intended to reintroduce popish ritual into the Church of England, and finally an imaginary popish plot disclosed by lying clergymen in the reign of King Charles II all combined to fill zealous Protestants and upholders of the established Church with fearful apprehension. During the reign of King Charles II the majority in three different Houses of Commons voted to exclude his brother James, an avowed Roman Catholic with a Roman Catholic wife, from succession to the throne. Only the shrewd, skillful and unscrupulous efforts of the superficially lackadaisical Charles II preserved the hereditary monarchy and enabled his brother James to come peacefully to the throne in 1685.

James, who was fanatical, humorless and over-sexed, had at first proceeded cautiously and at once promised "to preserve this government in Church and State as it is now by law established." Yet he was in his heart determined to use every resource not only to free his fellow Roman Catholics from the penal laws introduced by the Tudors, but to give them and other nonconformists or dissenters from the Church full civil rights. That meant the repeal of two Test Acts passed by Parliament during the previous reign, the first in 1673 forbidding those who refused to take the sacrament according to the rites of the Church of England from holding any public office, the second in 1678 banning them from sitting in either House of Parliament. To achieve his ends James II would have, on the face of it, been obliged to persuade Parliament to repeal these two Test Acts. Otherwise he might dispense with the acts, or suspend their operation, by exploiting the prerogative powers inherent in the crown. The precedents for doing so, however, were not good. Charles II who, like his brother, believed in liberty of conscience for all Christians, had tried to grant Declarations of Indulgence both in 1662 and 1672; but in each case he had been compelled by Parliament to withdraw them.

James was less resilient than his brother. He thought that since he had come peacefully to the throne, since an abortive invasion in 1685 by "the Protestant Duke," his nephew the Duke of Monmouth, had been easily crushed, and since the House of Commons—elected at the outset of his reign—had been loyal and friendly, he could take action without consulting Parliament. So he suspended the penal laws. In June, 1686, a collusive case, known as Godden v. Hales, brought before the King's Bench resulted in eleven out of twelve judges ruling that the King had the right to dispense with the Test Act of 1673 and thus permit Roman Catholics and other nonconformists to accept any office. On this basis James had proceeded to appoint Roman Catholic officers in the army and navy, to admit them to membership of his Privy Council and to put them into academic posts.

In the first half of 1687, the King issued royal proclamations in Scotland and England giving,

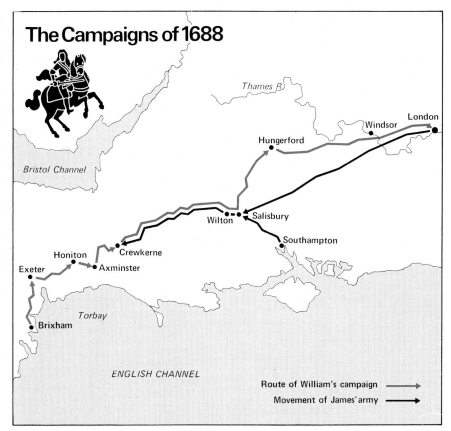

The Campaigns of 1688

Route of William's campaign →
Movement of James' army →

A Dutch painting of William's successful landing at Torbay.

Right James II, by Godfrey Kneller. James was the last English King to claim kingship by Divine Right.

as he explained, "liberty of conscience to all dissenters whatsoever, having ever been against persecution for conscience sake." A year later James reissued this proclamation and gave orders that it was to be read out in every church in England on successive Sundays in May and June. The leaders of the Church of England, who had hitherto been loyal, if restive, under a Roman Catholic monarch, at last struck. On May 18, the Archbishop of Canterbury and six other bishops presented a petition to the King in which they said that they could not obey his instructions because the dispensing power had been declared illegal by Parliament during the previous reign. James was furious and exclaimed: "This is the

standard of rebellion." The bishops were first sent as prisoners to the Tower of London and then put on trial before the King's Bench for seditious libel. Early in the morning of June 30, the bishops were acquitted by a jury which had sat all night, and the London mob rejoiced, burning effigies of the pope in the streets. On the same day, a letter was secretly carried over to Holland by Admiral Edward Russell inviting William of Orange to land in England to help preserve the religion, liberties and properties of Englishmen. The letter was signed by Russell, five peers and the Bishop of London, traditionally known as "the Immortal Seven." William told Russell that he would come over in the autumn.

The gist of the charges against James II was not merely that he showed favoritism toward Roman Catholics, but that he employed arbitrary methods, backed by force, to attain his ends and ignored the rights of Parliament. Yet James himself realized that to procure civic equality for all nonconformists he would in the long run require the cooperation of Parliament. For that reason much of his time and that of his trusted minister, the Earl of Sunderland, was occupied throughout 1687 and 1688 in trying to pack a parliament committed to the repeal of the Test Acts. So their objective was common knowledge. It made the Anglicans afraid that the repeal of the Test Acts was only a first step toward overthrowing the Elizabethan Church and toward restoring the kingdom to allegiance to the pope in Rome. Their fears were understandable, if irrational; and were reinforced when on June 10, 1688, James' Roman Catholic Queen gave birth to a son—to be known as the Old Pretender—and the Pope was named as his godfather. The birth of a Roman Catholic heir to the English and Scottish thrones and the trial of the seven bishops were important factors in drawing up the letter of invitation to William of Orange and the promise included in it that "the most considerable" of the nobility and gentry in the kingdom would "venture themselves with your Royal Highness at your first landing."

It is necessary to distinguish the motives of William from those of the conspirators who invited him over. William wanted to ensure that the English kingdom would not again closely ally itself with France, as it had done in 1670, to destroy the Dutch Republic and enhance the overweening power of Louis xiv. He was genuinely afraid that James ii would seek French aid not only to force an unpopular religious policy upon England but also to make himself as absolute a monarch as the French King. William also feared that should James call a parliament in 1688 civil war would follow, as in 1642, transforming the English government into a cipher of European politics. That was why during the winter of 1687–88 William had decided to intervene in England in the name of his wife who—until the birth of the Old Pretender—was the heiress presumptive to the throne, provided that the political conditions were favorable to such an attempt and that he received a letter of invitation from important representative Englishmen. After James, outmaneuvered in every way, fled the country, William and his wife Mary were duly acclaimed joint sovereigns. William was then able to exercise his new authority by persuading the English Parliament to unite with the Dutch States-General in a grand alliance to resist the aggressions of Louis xiv. As a contemporary statesman observed, "he took England on the way to France."

The Glorious Revolution of 1688 was significant in two respects: first in its effects upon England and Scotland constitutionally; second in its implications for Europe as a whole. Some historians have argued that revolution is a misnomer, claiming that what happened in 1688 was an invasion of England resulting simply in a change of dynasty, and that the rights of the monarchy were not seriously impaired. It was not even a change in dynasty because both William and Mary were Stuarts, as was their successor, Queen Anne. Sir Winston Churchill, on the other hand, described the revolution as "a national conspiracy." The Immortal Seven in their letter of invitation wrote: "There are nineteen parts of twenty of the people who are desirous of a change and who, we believe, would willingly contribute to it." Indeed men like the Earl of Danby, a signatory of the letter, hoped that William would arrive with a big fleet but only a few soldiers, confident that with his backing James would be obliged by his subjects to alter his behavior. Their intention had certainly not been to make William King. The small success of the elaborate lobbying, in which James and Sunderland had engaged in order to obtain the election of a House of Commons willing to

A contemporary engraving of James' flight after William's landing.

repeal the Test Acts, had shown conclusively that a large part of "the political nation" was unwilling to be persuaded or bribed into committing themselves to the King's policy. Although after William's victory some leading men, including bishops and nobility—to be known as Jacobites—remained loyal to their exiled "King over the water" in France, the chances of James ii's restoration to power or, later, of his two sons, was impossible without foreign assistance. Never were there enough Jacobites in England or Scotland to compel the kingdoms to resume their allegiance to a Roman Catholic king.

As to whether the rights of the English monarchy were reduced by the revolution, it is true that the Declaration of Rights which was read to William and Mary before they were offered the crown was curiously phrased. It claimed that much done by James ii had been "utterly and directly contrary to the known laws and statutes of the realm." His behavior was deplored, but the constitution was not altered in so many words. However, when the Declaration was embodied into a Bill of Rights passed by Parliament, clause nine stated that henceforward no English monarch could be a Roman Catholic or be married to one. The Declaration of Rights thus opened the road toward a limited monarchy. The Scots, for their part, elected William and Mary as joint monarchs, though the precedent for an elective monarchy was not to be followed. As to Europe, England, which had been the ally of Louis xiv both during the Cromwellian Protectorate and the reign of Charles ii, in 1689 became the enemy of France. A "second Hundred Years War" then began, which was only to end in 1815 with the defeat of Napoleon on the battlefield of Waterloo.

MAURICE ASHLEY

The Quakers

One of the main consequences of the Glorious Revolution was the increase in religious freedom in England. When the Stuart kings had offered Declarations of Indulgence to the nonconformists they had been treated with suspicion, as their aim was obviously mainly to benefit the Roman Catholics. But the Act of Toleration passed by the Convention Parliament was open to no such suspicion, since it excluded Roman Catholics and Unitarians. The main beneficiaries in practice were the Quakers, as most of the other dissenting Protestants had been accorded a large measure of toleration, since they had been willing to meet in private, while the Quakers had insisted on holding public prayer meetings.

The Friends of the Truth—known, particularly by their enemies, as Quakers, mainly because their founder George Fox (1625—91) had told a judge to tremble at the name of the Lord—had been organized in 1668 and had a large following both in England and in America. The American Quakers were mostly concentrated in Pennsylvania which had been founded by William Penn (1644–1718), himself an ardent convert.

Other religious groups, the bishops in Scotland and the Tory clergy in England, were less pleased by the arrival of William, and because they refused to accept the deposition of James, the Scottish Church was dis-

established, while the seven bishops who had been tried by order of King James were dismissed from their sees by order of King William—a sad fate for a loyal and consistent group of priests. It was to be many years before the nonjuring schism (the bishops refusing to swear the oath of fealty to the new King) eventually died out, and the supporters of episcopacy in Scotland remain an influential religious minority today.

Sweden

Sweden retained the commanding position in northern Europe that Gustavus Adolphus had won for it during the reign of Queen Christina, his strange and gifted daughter who came to the throne when she was eighteen. She was a patron of the arts and encouraged education. Her court attracted foreign scholars and intellectuals such as Grotius and Descartes. But the wayward, extravagant and self-centered Christina soon wearied of government. Aware of the unrest that her unusual personal behavior was causing in Sweden, she abdicated in 1654 in favor of her cousin Charles Gustavus who became King Charles x. Christina became a Roman Catholic and went to live in Rome where her irregular life caused little less scandal than it had done in her native land. Before her death in 1689 she twice tried unsuccessfully to recover the Swedish throne.

Within a year of his coronation Charles persuaded the *Riksdag*

Charles X at the Battle of Ivernaes against the Danes.

that a campaign against Poland would be to Sweden's advantage. Leading an army of 50,000 men into Poland in July, 1655, he occupied Warsaw, forced the Polish King, John Casimir, to seek refuge in Silesia and captured Cracow. The brutality of Charles' troops, most of whom were mercenaries, the arrogance of his rapacious officers and his own ill-concealed contempt for their national and religious feelings aroused the Poles to rebellion. Charles lost Warsaw and more than half of his troops in a protracted campaign against large bands of guerrillas and a reorganized Polish army led by John Casimir. Only by buying the help of the Elector Frederick William of Brandenburg was his army able to reoccupy Warsaw and defeat the forces of the Polish King. The Poles refused his peace terms and war was resumed. In June, 1657, the Danes gave Charles an excuse to extricate himself from his exhausting and profitless war by declaring war on Sweden.

Charles' early military successes against Denmark were astonishing; a powerful thrust carried him across Jutland to Fredericksodde, and across the frozen expanse of the Great and Little Belts to Zeeland. Although the treaties of Taastrup and Roskilde in 1658 ceded almost half of Denmark to Sweden, Charles was still greedy for more territory and still greater military renown. He resumed the war but met with little success due to the intervention of Holland, France and England, who feared a total Swedish domination of the Baltic and the obliteration of Denmark. Upon the King's premature death in 1660, the Council of Regency signed two peace treaties. By the terms of the Peace of Oliva, Sweden's possession of Livonia was confirmed, but the Elector of Brandenburg acquired the Duchy of Prussia; by the Treaty of Copenhagen, Sweden obtained the southern part of the Scandinavian Peninsula in return for the island of Bornholm.

Charles XI

During the years of Charles xi's minority, Sweden's strength rapidly declined, war with Denmark broke out again and Sweden was defeated by Brandenburg at Fehrbellin in 1675. When the young King came of age in 1672, he set out to revive Sweden's power. Boorish and ill-educated, but determined and brave, Charles followed the advice of his shrewd minister John Gyllenstjerna. He reorganized the national arma-

George Fox, founder of the Quakers, in court.

Queen Christina of Sweden.

their power in Eastern Europe

ments and his demoralized army, recovered the alienated crown lands, deprived the corrupt *Riksdag* of its control over finance and administration and converted the government of Sweden into a semi-absolute monarchy. The treaties of Nijmwegen and St. Germain in 1679 ended the wars and confirmed Sweden's possession of Finland, Ingria, Estonia, Livonia, numerous islands in the Baltic and large parts of present-day Denmark, Germany and Poland. Those vast territories were poor and sparsely populated by a variety of races with their own languages and customs. More than three-quarters of Sweden's three million people were peasants, most roads were little more than footpaths, and few cities were worthy of the name—yet Charles XI made the army a powerful, well-trained and well-equipped force once more.

Poland

The raising of the siege of Vienna in 1683 was largely due to the intervention of the Polish army

John Sobieski; determined to revive the greatness of Poland.

under John Sobieski. Poland had been at war with the Turks since 1672, when Mohammed IV had declared war on Poland's King, Michael Wisniowiecki, who had set himself up as the champion of the Sultan's rivals in the Ukraine. The Turkish army had captured Kamenets, Lemberg and Lublin, and the Poles had been forced to cede Podolia, the area between Moldavia and the Ukraine, to Turkey by the Treaty of Buczacs. Led by Sobieski, Poland had set out to retrieve her fortunes; the war against Turkey had been resumed, and on November 11, 1673, John Sobieski had won his first great victory at Choczim, a victory that brought him the Polish crown. From the time of his election to the throne in 1674, when he triumphed over the candidates assisted by the Hapsburg, French and Brandenburg factions, he showed a ruthless determination to stop the steady decline of Poland's international position, as well as the decline of royal power within the kingdom. But Sobieski's energy was in fact an additional factor in Poland's decline. While war continued, as it did for almost the whole of his reign, the country's economic position was bound to deteriorate further. Even before Sobieski's election, the wars with Sweden, Russia and the Turks in the 1650s and 1660s had weakened the economy, and Poland's population is estimated to have fallen by one-third during the third quarter of the seventeenth century.

Sobieski saw that he could not hope to destroy Turkish power in the Ukraine, and in 1676 he agreed to a compromise, which allowed the Turks to retain most of the areas that they had already captured. He did this mainly in order to free his energies to deal with Brandenburg, which he wrongly regarded as a greater threat to his power. It was only when war broke out in 1682 between the Ottoman and Hapsburg empires that Sobieski, in alliance with Hapsburg Austria, began an all-out effort to destroy Turkish power in the Ukraine and Hungary.

In order to prosecute his war against the Turks unhindered, Sobieski was forced to conclude a humiliating treaty with Russia. He was also obliged to make substantial concessions to the diet, including the right of *liberum veto*,

which allowed a single vote to sabotage what would otherwise have been a unanimous decision. More than anything else, this was to cripple effective government in Poland during the eighteenth century.

Yet even these sacrifices were not enough. In 1699, two years after Sobieski's death, the Treaty of Karlowitz gave the Turkish Ukraine and Podolia to Poland. But the provinces of Moldavia and Wallachia were irretrievably lost. As a result Poland entered the eighteenth century weakened both internally and externally. The second series of Swedish invasions from 1700, the rivalry between the Saxon Augustus II and the Pole Stanislas Leszczynski and, later, the civil wars and the rise of Russian influence, paved the way for the disastrous war of Polish succession in 1733 and for the final eclipse of Poland as a major power in Eastern Europe.

Hungary

The failure of imperial policy in the Thirty Years War and the defeat of the Turks in 1683 show a basic paradox in the history of the Austrian Hapsburgs. The imperial title, for which the Hapsburgs had fought so hard and so long, came to mean less and less in terms of power and authority, and became no more than a meaningless honor. At the same time, the Hapsburg emperors and archdukes were able to consolidate their power in Austria and the other lands that they ruled directly and to expand their territories both in Eastern Europe and, from the beginning of the eighteenth century, in Italy.

The defeat of the Turks at Vienna was the signal for the resurgence of Christian aspirations in Eastern Europe and the Balkans. Polish successes in Podolia and the Ukraine and Venetian reconquests from the Turks on the Dalmatian coast were only part of the Christian gains. The Turkish client King of Hungary, Imre Thököly, lost ground steadily from 1685. In 1686 Buda was captured by Leopold of Austria's army, and in the following year Leopold's son Joseph was crowned King of Hungary. Troubles in Istanbul did nothing to help the Turkish cause; Mohammed IV was deposed in 1687. Transylvania,

which had for a century been a tributary of the Turks, acknowledged Hapsburg suzerainty in 1688, and in the same year Belgrade was captured.

In 1690 the power of the Turks showed signs of reviving and Belgrade was recaptured. During the next eight years the war continued inconclusively. The decisive victory of Eugene of Savoy at Zenta in 1697 transformed the situation, and in 1699 the Turks finally acknowledged their losses to the Christian powers by the Treaty of Karlowitz, which gave Hungary, Croatia, Transylvania and Slavonia to the Hapsburgs.

It was, however, to be many years before the Hapsburgs could regard their power in Hungary as being assured. This was largely due to the rebellion of Francis II Rakoczy (1676–1735) in 1703. The inefficient and Austrian-dominated government of Joseph had led to widespread social discontent, which Francis' followers succeeded in channeling into rebellion. At first Francis carried all before him, and Joseph was formally deposed. But Francis showed little capacity as a military leader, and the Austrians were gradually able to win back control. In 1711 Austrian rule was confirmed by treaty, and for the next two centuries Hungary was to be a main center of the "dual monarchy" of Austria-Hungary.

Russia

Austria was not the only state in Eastern Europe to expand its power. Despite its internal weakness, Russia for centuries the most energetically expansionist power in Europe, continued its rapid growth. War with Poland and the Turks brought some territory—Azov was granted to Russia by the Treaty of Karlowitz—but Russia's expansion in the east was more important. As early as 1689 Russia and China had come into conflict in the Far East, but fighting had been avoided by the Treaty of Nerchinsk. In 1696 the Russians expanded their holdings on the Pacific Ocean by annexing the Kamchatka peninsula. But there was a real danger that territorial expansion would lead to even greater internal difficulties than existed already, and the young Tsar Peter saw the need to modernize his backward country.

A Window on the West

The Grand Embassy that set out from Moscow in 1695 was officially led by François Lefort, tutor to Russia's young Tsar, Peter I. Lefort's entourage included a twenty-three-year-old soldier of imperial mien who called himself Bombardier Peter Mikhailov. Mikhailov—as every member of the Embassy and every crowned head in Europe knew—was Tsar Peter himself. Traveling "incognito" through Western Europe, the young ruler obtained interviews with the Emperor of Austria, the kings of Poland and England, and numerous German princes. As the Embassy made its slow circuit of Europe's capitals, Peter studied Western industries at first hand—and by the time he returned to Moscow he had mastered fourteen specialized technical skills. His extensive knowledge of European technological advances enabled Peter to Westernize his nation and his army in less than a decade—and helped him achieve the age-old Russian dream of "a window on Europe."

At a time when London, Paris, Rome and Vienna were already flourishing capitals, Moscow was little more than a small village, lost in the forested wilderness of northern Russia. The city is first mentioned in official chronicles in 1147; a century later it became the fief of Prince Daniel, younger son of the famous Alexander Nevski. Under his descendants the small princedom was transformed—through treaties, marriages and territorial purchases—into a powerful state whose rulers, the grand dukes, succeeded in shaking off the yoke of the Mongols. Assuming the title of tsar, the Muscovy princes organized a centralized government which eventually administered a vast area that included part of Siberia.

The period of troubles that began with the extinction of the House of Rurik in 1598 and ended with the election of the new dynasty of the Romanovs only temporarily interrupted the evolution of a young and already promising nation. But during the period of Asiatic domination (1223-1380) there had been little contact between Russia and the civilization of the West, and during the troubles that occurred early in the seventeenth century, Muscovy was deprived of all access to the sea. It remained an underdeveloped, feudal country, populated by some 10 million pious but ignorant peasants and dominated by an autocratic monarch who considered himself an heir to the Byzantine emperors. These tsars found only feeble supporters in a fanatical clergy and in a class of indolent noblemen, the boyars. The West remained as much a closed book to them as it did to their subjects. Nevertheless, national defense and urgent commercial considerations dictated a closer connection with the feared and despised West. The idea of an outlet to the sea began to haunt the best minds of a nation that, until then, had kept its eyes fixed on the steppes. Peter the Great, the tsar-reformer, was the man who realized that dream.

Born in Moscow in 1672, Peter led a stormy childhood amid dynastic quarrels, clan rivalries and popular uprisings. His father, Tsar Alexis, pious and easygoing, had two unpromising sons by an earlier marriage: the sickly Fëdor and the partially blind and feebleminded Ivan. When Alexis died in 1676, Fëdor inherited the throne. His reign lasted only six years, and upon his death the incompetent Ivan and ten-year-old Peter were proclaimed joint sovereigns of all the Russias under the regency of their half sister Sophia, an intelligent and ambitious virago of fifty. Although she was frequently compared to Elizabeth I of England—and although she consciously modeled herself on the Empress Pulcheria of Byzantium—Sophia was unable to maintain order in her own country. Relegated to the background, the adolescent Peter witnessed scenes of bloodshed that gave him a horror for the atmosphere of the Kremlin and for the traditional habits of the old Muscovy.

The young prince was brought up by his mother, Natalia Naryshkin, in a country setting on the outskirts of Moscow. There he supplemented an adequate education through contacts with the humble foreign artisans who lived in the nearby German quarter. Peter, who had a passion for soldiering (a list of his early toys includes pistols, carbines, bows and arrows, drums and cannon), organized his companions—gentlemen's sons, stableboys and street ragamuffins—drilled them and learned with them how to handle arms. Other boys joined the ranks, and the games grew more ambitious. Using boats, they mounted a full-scale assault on a small fortress that Peter had had built on a little island not far from his home. At the end of a few years he had two well-trained battalions of several hundred men each. With this nucleus of what was to become a famous army, he executed a coup d'état in 1689 to free himself from the hampering tutelage of Princess Sophia, put an end to her dangerous intrigues and take over actual power.

At this time two remarkable men became his tutors in the military profession and in the art of Western living: an old mercenary, Patrick Gordon,

The Empress Natalia Naryshkin, mother of Peter the Great.

Opposite Emperor Peter the Great as a shipbuilder at Deptford during his stay in England. His interest in the sea led him to attack the Turkish port of Azov, so that Russia would have an outlet to the sea.

Peter the Great as a child with his elder half-brothers, Fëdor and Ivan, patriarch Adrian and a metropolitan.

scion of an illustrious Scottish family, and young François Lefort, another soldier of fortune and a native of Geneva. Under the influence of these two friends Peter revived the old dream of giving Russia access to the sea. In 1695 he flung himself into a war against Turkey and captured Azov, at the mouth of the Don. But even in the moment of victory he realized that his land and naval forces were inadequate to gain him mastery of the Black Sea. He decided to send a "Grand Embassy" to various Western countries, not only to secure the help necessary to continue the war or to conclude an advantageous peace, but also to build up a corps of specialists by initiating young representatives of his nobility into European science.

To everybody's astonishment Peter himself joined the embassy, traveling incognito. For eighteen months the Tsar of All the Russias traveled with his apprentices through the Baltic countries, the German states, Holland and England, vainly attempting to escape notice under the borrowed name of "Bombardier Peter Mikhailov." Officially, the embassy was led by François Lefort, seconded by two Russian dignitaries. But all eyes were naturally turned to the young sovereign, who was taller by a head than any of his companions and distributed lavish gifts and was received at every court.

At Königsberg he met the Prince-Elector of Brandenburg; at Koppenbrugge, the princesses of Hanover. In Holland he had his first interview with William of Orange, King of England, whom he was to meet again in London. In Vienna he was on intimate terms with Emperor Leopold of Austria. And on his way back to Russia, at Rawa Ruska, he made friends with Augustus of Saxony, who had just been elected King of Poland.

Diplomatically, the results of Peter's Grand Embassy were rather slight, since none of the European cabinets was ready to support the Russian plans for a crusade against the Turks. But the royal traveler had other interests. His goals included developing his naval building program, organizing a powerful artillery, inviting selected specialists—from among the captains, seamen and engineers he met—to Russia, and building up a corps of his countrymen instructed in the most recent scientific and technological methods. He wanted to superintend the apprenticeship of the young noblemen that he had brought with him, and he cherished the ambition of serving as their model. His biographers never fail to point out that he ended by mastering fourteen skills, not counting that of statesman: at various times he functioned as engineer, cannoneer, carpenter, boatman, armorer, drummer, blacksmith, joiner and tooth-puller.

Peter even spent a week with his old friend Gerrit Kist (who had been a blacksmith in Moscow) in the little Dutch village of Zaandam, working in Master Rogge's yard under the name of Master Peter, exploring the canals and visiting the local spinning mills, sawyards and oil works.

In Amsterdam, where he was to spend more than four months, the Tsar concentrated on increasing his knowledge of shipbuilding. Although he slighted neither the museums nor the laboratories nor the dissecting rooms, he spent the greater part of his time in the East India Company shipyards. But it was in England, in the yards of Deptford and the arsenals of Woolwich, that he completed his apprenticeship and became an accomplished master of the art of shipbuilding. "If I had not come here," he was to say later, "I should never have been more than a plain carpenter." He also perfected the technique of navigation, spent hours rowing and sailing, attended

The *streltsy* fighting Peter's troops, who are led by Patrick Gordon. The *streltsy* were regarded by Peter as his chief enemy as they supported the Regent, Princess Sophia.

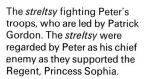

A boyar or Russian noble.

Left An Easter procession outside of the Kremlin in Moscow.

Below Cutting the boyars' beards; Peter's reforms affected the lives of all his subjects, but the beard cutting was of symbolic importance.

the maneuvers at Spithead and revived the courage of British sailors during a storm by asking them: "Have you ever heard of a tsar being drowned?" Later, remembering this period in his life, he often said to his courtiers, "The life of an English admiral is infinitely happier than that of a ruler of Russia."

When he was not on the water, Peter inspected the collection of weapons at the Tower of London; visited the Mint and the Greenwich Royal Observatory; went to a masked ball, the theater, a bear fight and a cock fight; paid court to an actress; and incidentally wrecked the elegant house that he and his party were living in. He even found a moment to watch, through an attic window, the opening of Parliament (thus giving a wit the chance to remark: "Today I saw something unique in the world—one sovereign on the throne and another on the roof").

A few months later, as Peter was finishing his conversations in Vienna, he was suddenly obliged to return to Moscow because of an uprising of the *streltsy*, the undisciplined, turbulent and reactionary local militia guards. The *streltsy* were survivors of the old Muscovite regime. Armed with muskets and sabers, unadapted to modern warfare, they occupied separate quarters near the capital and in frontier towns. They had been partisans of Princess Sophia, had participated in all the recent upheavals and were prepared to fight to the last for the maintenance of the old order of society, which they felt was being menaced by an "ungodly tsar" who had gone abroad for unknown reasons. Determined to reestablish Sophia on the throne and to exterminate the nobles and the boyars, they had marched on Moscow—and nothing but the courageous intervention of General Gordon had prevented the success of their plan. With remarkable speed he had dispersed isolated detachments of the *streltsy* before they had had time to concentrate, had encircled their main forces and had ended the revolt. By the time Peter returned to

Moscow on August 25, 1698, there was nothing left for him to do but to act as judge.

Peter returned to his country the possessor of intellectual and technical equipment such as no Russian before him had commanded. He knew that his nation was at the crossroads, and that it would be unable to maintain its role in the world without the radical reforms that he was prepared to accomplish. The *streltsy* were barring his way and he considered it his duty to finish with them once and for all. He subjected them to terrible reprisals, participating personally in the interrogations that took place in torture chambers. Three hundred and forty-one rebels were condemned to death, brought in carts to Red Square and hanged from the crenelated walls of the Kremlin, where their emaciated skeletons remained exposed to the horror of passersby.

More executions followed during the ensuing weeks; the number of victims finally reached 799. The sixteen *streltsy* regiments were disarmed and disbanded; the families of the condemned men were turned out of their homes. Princess Sophia, considered responsible for the whole upheaval, was deprived of her rank and obliged to take the veil.

At last Tsar Peter was free: he had broken with the past and was now prepared to lead his country into a gigantic military and reforming enterprise. The horrors of the executions were soon overshadowed by the glory of his victories and of his reforms.

On August 8, 1700, Peter made his historic decision to declare war on Sweden, in order to open a road from Russia to the West by the conquest of the Baltic littoral. He had secured the collaboration of Poland and Denmark, but his alliance with these two rivals of Sweden was to prove ineffectual. With nothing to rely on but his own forces, Peter was defeated at Narva by the valiant Swedish King, Charles XII. Refusing to be discouraged by this defeat, Peter raised and equipped new armies; he put immense effort into creating a good artillery; he worked with his own hands on the construction of the frigates that were to give him mastery of the

Baltic. Then his disciplined and well-trained regiments seized the mouth of the Neva and entrenched themselves along the coveted littoral. On June 27, 1709, in a battle at Poltava, he put his great adversary, Charles XII, to flight.

To achieve this brilliant success, Peter had been obliged to subject the entire structure of his country to a basic transformation. In a certain sense Russia emerged completely "Europeanized" and "Westernized." Even before venturing into war, Peter had undertaken to change the outward aspects of his fellow countrymen, or, more precisely, of his own entourage. During his journeys in western Europe he had observed how ridiculous the long medieval gowns and long beards of the Muscovites looked to the outside world. The day after his return from abroad, Peter received the boyars who came to greet him with a large pair of scissors in his hand—and chopped off the beards of the most eminent among them. At a banquet later in the same week, the Tsar's jester (an ancestor of the novelist Turgenev) circled the table and cut off the beards of all the

Eudoxia, wife of Peter the Great. The Tsar did not get on with his wife who was the daughter of a court official.

Above right Bust of Peter by Rastrelli.

Below right A plan of a battle between Denmark and Sweden; Peter's keenness to have an outlet on the Baltic led him into continuous wars with Sweden, in which the Danes were usually his allies.

One of the *streltsy* soldiers.

Peter the Great Square and the Senate in St. Petersburg. Peter built St. Petersburg as a new capital for his kingdom, perhaps because of its proximity to the sea.

Above left The Battle of Poltava, 1709, at which Russia won a decisive victory over the Swedes. This victory secured for Peter Livonia and Estonia as well as a Baltic foothold.

guests who had not yet adopted the new fashion. Three days later nearly all beards had disappeared from the court. Within a few months Peter was also wielding the scissors on the exaggeratedly long sleeves of his attendants. "With these full sleeves," he said, "accidents are always happening: sometimes they get dipped in the soup, sometimes they break windows."

Resistance, of course, was greater in the case of more serious reforms, but Peter nonetheless had his way. He established conscription as a means of recruiting a permanent and regular army with an adequate number of specialists, and he did the same for the fleet. He subjected a recalcitrant Church to his authority by replacing the all-powerful patriarch by an ecclesiastical body, the Holy Synod, which was given strictly limited functions. He replaced the hereditary aristocracy by a "nobility of service" open to all deserving officers and functionaries. And to put an end once and for all to the old customs and habits, he left Moscow and the Kremlin and moved his residence to a swampy, deserted region at the mouth of the Neva, newly conquered from Sweden. There he built his new capital, St. Petersburg (renamed Petrograd in World War I and Leningrad by the Communists in 1924)—"a window on Europe," as he put it.

Permanent connection with the West—the final goal of all his efforts—was not easily established. For long years the cabinets of Europe turned a cold shoulder to the upstart Tsar who took no interest in the great Spanish problem then in the limelight, and who persisted in fighting the "invincible" King of Sweden in what was considered a perfectly "useless" war. Russia's prestige was very low at Versailles, Vienna and The Hague. It was only after the victory of Poltava that all Europe turned its eyes to the East.

Following Poltava, the French cabinet expressed interest in a rapprochement with Russia and in acting as mediator between Russia and Sweden. Peter set off for Paris immediately and soon entered into a friendship with the French regent. His second appearance in the countries of the West was as pregnant with consequences as the first had been. By directing his ministers to sign the Amsterdam Agreement with France and Prussia in 1717, Peter inaugurated a system of interchangeable alliances that was to be employed by his successors on a great scale. By submitting to the admiration of the Parisian populace, by showing a charming affection for the boy king, Louis XV, and by visiting Madame de Maintenon, Louis XIV's durable mistress, Peter laid the foundation for his fame throughout the world.

In Russia that fame was marred by Peter's treatment of his son and heir, the Tsarevich Alexis. The two men could hardly have been more different: while Peter was creating a new Russia, Alexis preferred the old Russia, with its indolent quietism and its horror of innovation. Incapable of leading a revolt himself, he became—quite without premeditation—a symbol around whom all the malcontents in Russia rallied. The contest between the two came to a climax in 1718 when Peter imprisoned Alexis and appointed a supreme court that condemned him to death. It was one of Peter's few—but lasting—blunders.

As the years wore on, he had many victories. The surrender of the Swedish fleet after the naval battle of Hangö in 1714, the military occupation of Finland, and two raids into Skane in southern Sweden led to the signing—on August 30, 1721—of the Treaty of Nystad. That document ceded Russia all of Estonia, Livonia, Ingria and Karelia, and part of Finland, including the fortress of Vyborg.

Peter's triumph was complete. He had conquered the Baltic littoral, his coveted objective. He had further succeeded in establishing a sort of veiled protectorate over Poland and in setting up a series of duchies along the western Baltic. On October 22, 1721, three years before his death, he was proclaimed "Emperor of All the Russias," and the senate bestowed upon him the title of "the Great."

Like a warship launched from the ways, Russia had made her entrance into Europe to the clang of hammers and the thunder of guns.

CONSTANTINE DE GRUNWALD

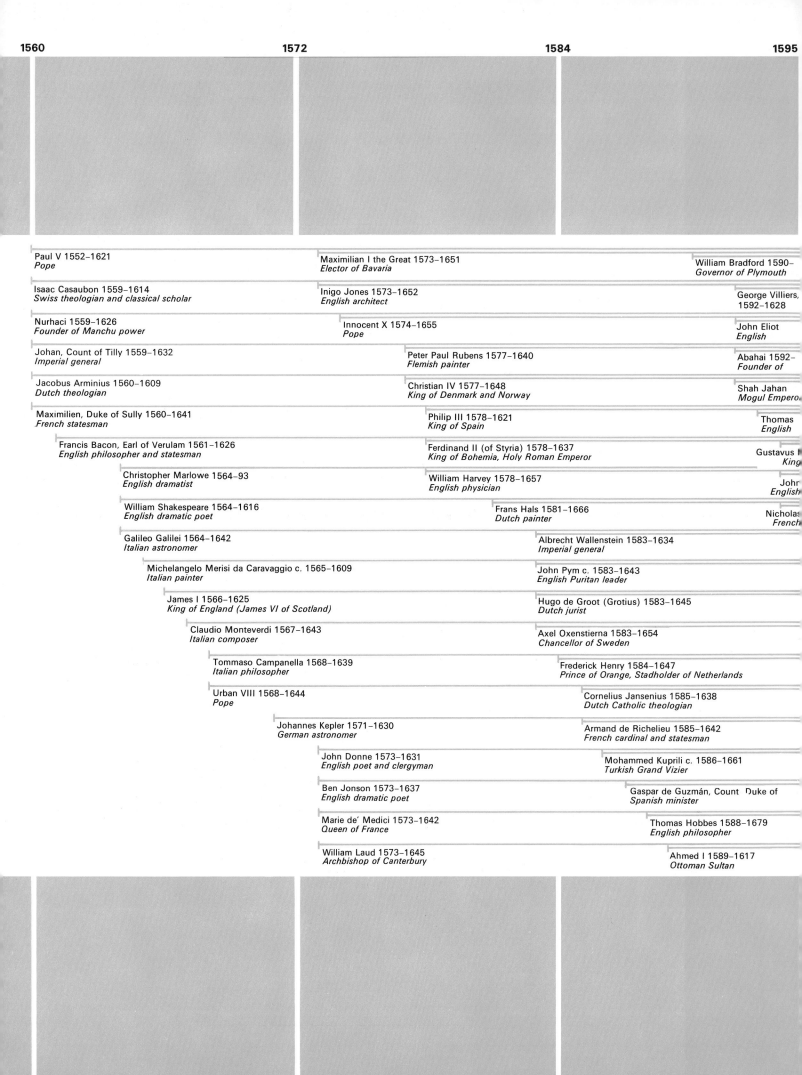

Paul V 1552–1621
Pope

Isaac Casaubon 1559–1614
Swiss theologian and classical scholar

Nurhaci 1559–1626
Founder of Manchu power

Johan, Count of Tilly 1559–1632
Imperial general

Jacobus Arminius 1560–1609
Dutch theologian

Maximilien, Duke of Sully 1560–1641
French statesman

Francis Bacon, Earl of Verulam 1561–1626
English philosopher and statesman

Christopher Marlowe 1564–93
English dramatist

William Shakespeare 1564–1616
English dramatic poet

Galileo Galilei 1564–1642
Italian astronomer

Michelangelo Merisi da Caravaggio c. 1565–1609
Italian painter

James I 1566–1625
King of England (James VI of Scotland)

Claudio Monteverdi 1567–1643
Italian composer

Tommaso Campanella 1568–1639
Italian philosopher

Urban VIII 1568–1644
Pope

Johannes Kepler 1571–1630
German astronomer

John Donne 1573–1631
English poet and clergyman

Ben Jonson 1573–1637
English dramatic poet

Marie de' Medici 1573–1642
Queen of France

William Laud 1573–1645
Archbishop of Canterbury

Maximilian I the Great 1573–1651
Elector of Bavaria

Inigo Jones 1573–1652
English architect

Innocent X 1574–1655
Pope

Peter Paul Rubens 1577–1640
Flemish painter

Christian IV 1577–1648
King of Denmark and Norway

Philip III 1578–1621
King of Spain

Ferdinand II (of Styria) 1578–1637
King of Bohemia, Holy Roman Emperor

William Harvey 1578–1657
English physician

Frans Hals 1581–1666
Dutch painter

Albrecht Wallenstein 1583–1634
Imperial general

John Pym c. 1583–1643
English Puritan leader

Hugo de Groot (Grotius) 1583–1645
Dutch jurist

Axel Oxenstierna 1583–1654
Chancellor of Sweden

Frederick Henry 1584–1647
Prince of Orange, Stadholder of Netherlands

Cornelius Jansenius 1585–1638
Dutch Catholic theologian

Armand de Richelieu 1585–1642
French cardinal and statesman

Mohammed Kuprili c. 1586–1661
Turkish Grand Vizier

Gaspar de Guzmán, Count Duke of
Spanish minister

Thomas Hobbes 1588–1679
English philosopher

Ahmed I 1589–1617
Ottoman Sultan

William Bradford 1590–
Governor of Plymouth

George Villiers,
1592–1628

John Eliot
English

Abahai 1592–
Founder of

Shah Jahan
Mogul Empero

Thomas
English

Gustavus
King

Johr
English

Nicholas
French

1601
A Play for All Seasons –
William Shakespeare's reworking of a familiar folk legend gives the stage its most famous tragedy

1609
Revolt of the Netherlands –
After eighty years of determined resistance, the Dutch win their independence from Europe's mightiest monarch, Philip II of Spain

1628
Harvey Explains the Circulation of the Blood –
By observation and experimentation, William Harvey explains the circulation of the blood thereby helping inaugurate the "Scientific Revolution"

1630
The Day of the Dupes –
Richelieu's victory over Marie de' Medici frees the French monarchy from the influence of family feuds and the power of the great nobles

1620
The Pilgrims at Plymouth –
An intrepid band of expatriate Englishmen establishes a new atmosphere of religious diversity in the New World

1657
Colony

Duke of Buckingham
Favorite of James I

1592–1632
statesman

1643
Ch'ing dynasty

1592–1666

Wentworth, Earl of Strafford 1593–1641
statesman

Adolphus 1594–1632
of Sweden

Hampden 1594–1643
statesman

Poussin 1594–1665
painter

Frederick V "the Winter King" 1596–1632
Elector Palatine, King of Bohemia

Michael Romanov 1596–1645
Tsar of Russia

René Descartes 1596–1650
French philosopher

Marten Harpertszoon Tromp 1597–1653
Dutch admiral

Giovanni Bernini 1598–1680
Italian sculptor

Anthony van Dyck 1599–1641
Flemish painter

Robert Blake 1599–1657
English admiral

Oliver Cromwell 1599–1658
Lord Protector of England

Olivares 1587–1645

Diego Velásquez 1599–1660
Spanish painter

Alexander VII 1599–1667
Pope

Charles I 1600–49
King of England, Scotland and Ireland

Pedro Calderón 1600–81
Spanish dramatist

Louis XIII 1601–43
King of France

Anne of Austria 1601–66
Queen, regent of France

Jules Mazarin 1602–61
Italian cardinal and French minister

Abel Tasman c. 1603–59
Dutch explorer

Li Tzu-ch'eng c. 1605–45
Chinese bandit leader

John IV 1605–56
King of Portugal

Philip IV 1605–65
King of Spain

Rembrandt van Rijn 1606–69
Dutch painter

Pierre Corneille 1606–84
French dramatist

Michel de Ruyter 1607–76
Dutch admiral

George Monck, Duke of Albemarle 1608–70
English general

John Milton 1608–74
English poet

John II Casimir 1609–72
King of Poland

Edward Hyde, Earl of Clarendon 1609–74
English statesman and historian

Henry, Viscount of Turenne 1611–75
Marshal of France

Henry Vane 1613–63
English Puritan administrator

André Lenôtre 1613–1700
French landscape gardener

Jean, Cardinal de Retz 1614–79
French politician

Nicholas Fouquet 1615–80
French statesman

Bartolomé Murillo c. 1617–82
Spanish painter

Francesco Morosini 1618–94
Venetian commander and Doge

Aurangzeb 1618–1707
Mogul Emperor

Prince Rupert of the Rhine 1619–82
General and admiral

Jean Baptiste Colbert 1619–83
French statesman

Frederick William "the Great Elector" 1620–88
Elector of Brandenburg

Jean de La Fontaine 1621–95
French poet

Masaniello (Tommaso Aniello) 1622–47
Neapolitan rebel leader

Charles X 1622–60
King of Sweden

Jean Baptiste Molière 1622–73
French comic dramatist

Blaise Pascal 1623–62
French scientist and philosopher

Cornelis de Witt 1623–72
Burgomaster of Dordrecht

John III Sobieski 1624–96
King of Poland

Jan de Witt 1625–72
Grand Pensionary of Holland

1598
Edict of Nantes

1604 ●
Peace settlement between Spain and England

c. 1600 ●
Invention of microscope

1600–1868 ●
Tokugawa period in Japan: capital Tokyo

1602–27
Persian-Turkish Wars

1605
Gunpowder Plot: failure leads to Catholic persecution in England

1605
Publication of Cervantes' *Don Quixote*

1609 ●
Moriscos expelled from Spain

1613 ●
Accession of Romanov dynasty in Moscow

1619 ●
First African slaves brought to North America

1618 ●
Defenestration of Prague: beginning of Thirty Years War

1621 ●
Resumption of Dutch War of Independence

1622 ●
English take Ormuz and gain influence in declining Persian Empire

1624 ●
Virginia becomes a royal colony

1621–29
Swedish-Polish War

1627–28 ●
Siege of La Rochelle by Richelieu

1629–40 ●
Charles I of England rules without Parliament

1630
Colonization of Massachusetts

● **1626**
New Amsterdam (New York) founded

1631 **The Rape of Magdeburg** –
The Protestant citizens of Magdeburg defy their Catholic Emperor and spark a religious war that engulfs the Continent

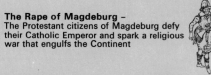

1640
The Meeting of the Long Parliament –
After eleven years of personal rule England's Charles I is forced to call Parliament, setting the stage for civil war and a revolutionary change in government

1644 **Foundation of the Ch'ing Dynasty** –
The Manchus win the struggle for supremacy in China, establishing a dynasty that will last nearly three hundred years

1649 **"A Cruel Necessity"** –
Decades of bitter dissension between Parliament's Puritan radicals and England's fumbling monarch culminate in the execution of Charles I

1661
"L'état c'est moi" –
Declaring that he *is* the state, Cardinal Mazarin's astonishing pupil, Louis XIV, guides the French nation through its golden age

---

George Fox 1625–91
Founder of Society of Friends

Christina 1626–89
Queen of Sweden

Marie de Sévigné 1626–96 *French noblewoman and writer*

Sivaji Bhonsle 1627–80
Maratha leader

Robert Boyle 1627–91
British physicist and chemist

John Bunyan 1628–88
English writer

François, Duke of Luxemburg 1628–95
French general

Alexis I 1629–76
Tsar of Russia

Don Juan of Austria (the younger) 1629–79
Spanish general

Christiaan Huyghens 1629–95
Dutch mathematician and physicist

Charles II 1630–85
King of England

John Dryden 1631–1700
English poet

Jan Vermeer 1632–75
Dutch painter

John Locke 1632–1704
English philosopher

Thomas Osborne, Earl of Danby 1632–1712
English statesman

Anthony van Leeuwenhoek 1632–1723
Dutch natural historian

Christopher Wren 1632–1723
English architect and mathematician

Baruch Spinoza 1632–77
Portuguese-Dutch philosopher

James II 1633–1701
King of England, Scotland and Ireland

Marshal Vauban 1633–1707
French military engineer

Ahmed Kuprili 1635–76
Turkish Grand Vizier

Johan Gyllenstjerna 1635–80
Swedish minister

Françoise de Maintenon 1635–1719
Second wife of Louis XIV

Shun-chih (Fu-lin) 1638–61
First Ch'ing Emperor

Michael Wisniowiecki 1638–73
King of Poland

Louis XIV 1638–1715
King of France

Maria Teresa 1639–83
Queen of France

Jean Racine 1639–99
French tragic poet and dramatist

Leopold I 1640–1705
Holy Roman Emperor

Michel de Louvois 1641–91
French statesman

Mohammed IV 1641–91
Ottoman Sultan

Anthony Heinsius 1641–1720
Grand Pensionary of Holland

Isaac Newton 1642–1727
English physicist

Charles V of Lorraine 1643–90
Imperial general

William Penn 1644–1718
English Quaker

Jules Hardouin Mansart 1645–1708
French architect

Gottfried Leibnitz 1646–1716
German mathematician and philosopher

Pierre Bayle 1647–1706
French philosopher and critic

William III (of Orange) 1650–1702
King of Great Britain and Ireland

Thomas Savery c. 1650–1715
English military engineer

John Churchill, Duke of Marlborough 1650–1722
English general and statesman

François de La Mothe Fénelon 1651–1715
French writer and theologian

André Hercule de Fleury 1653–1743
French cardinal and statesman

Sheng Tsu (K'ang Hsi) 1654–1722
Manchu Emperor

Charles XI 1655–97
King of Sweden

Edmund Halley 1656–1742
English astronomer

Sophia Alekseevna 1657–1704
Regent for Peter I of Russia

Frederick I 1657–1713
First King of Prussia

George I 1660–1727
King of Great Britain and

Charles II 1661–
King of Spain

Robert Harley, Earl
English statesman

Mary II 1662–
Queen of Great

George
English

Prince
Imperial

John
English

Giulio
Italian

1633 Galileo condemned by the Inquisition

1635 ●
Treaty of Prague between Holy Roman Emperor and Elector of Saxony

1641 ●
Dutch capture Malacca and establish supremacy in East Indies for 150 years

1640 ●
Accession of Braganza dynasty in Portugal

1640–59 ●
Revolt in Catalonia supported by France

1642–46 ●
Civil war in England

1645–64
Turkish-Venetian War

● **1643**
Battle of Rocroi: French defeat Spaniards

1648 ●
Peace of Westphalia: end of Thirty Years War

1648 ●
Treaty of Münster divides Netherlands

● **1651**
First Navigation Act gives English shipping monopoly, causing First Anglo-Dutch War

● **1648–53**
Fronde revolt in France

● **1652**
Capetown founded by Dutch settlers

1658
Battle of the Dunes: French and English defeat Spaniards

● **1659**
Treaty of the Pyrenees between France and Spain

1660 ●
Stuart Restoration

Royal Society of London founded ● **1662**

1664 ●
Treaty of Vasvár: twenty-year Austrian-Turkish truce

1667 The Dutch in the Medway –
England's humiliation in the Medway
paradoxically leads to the realization that her
real rival is France—not the Netherlands

1667 John Milton Publishes *Paradise Lost* –
Blind and disappointed, the Puritan poet
withdraws from political life and writes his epic
on the fall and redemption of man

1666 Cambridge's Young Genius –
One of Trinity College's least promising
graduates, Isaac Newton, lays the foundation
for modern physics

1688 The Glorious Revolution –
William of Orange achieves a bloodless victory
over numerically superior forces to gain the
English throne

1685 The Revocation of the Edict of Nantes –
By reversing the policy that had made her a
leader in religious toleration for almost a
century, France drives out many of her most
valuable citizens

1683 Vienna under Siege –
Kara Mustafa leads the "invincible" armies of
the Ottoman Sultan in a final—and nearly
successful—assault on Vienna

1698 A Window on the West –
Traveling incognito through Europe, Peter the
Great learns technological skills that enable him
to westernize his Empire

Frederick Augustus (the Strong) 1670–1733
Elector of Saxony, King of Poland

Peter 1 the Great 1672–1725
Tsar of Russia

Louis, Duke of Saint-Simon 1675–1755
French soldier, statesman and writer

Robert Walpole 1676–1745
English Whig statesman

Stanislas Leszczynski 1677–1766
King of Poland

Charles XII 1682–1718
King of Sweden

Philip V 1683–1746
King of Spain

George II 1683–1760
King of Great Britain and Ireland

Johann Sebastian Bach 1685–1750
German composer

George Berkeley 1685–1753
Irish philosopher and bishop

George Frederick Handel 1685–1759
German-English composer

Balthasar Neumann 1687–1753
German architect

Alexander Pope 1688–1744
English poet

Nadir Shah 1688–1747
Turcoman Shah of Persia

Charles de Montesquieu 1689–1755
French political philosopher

François Marie Voltaire 1694–1778
French philosopher

William Hogarth 1697–1763
English painter and engraver

Antonio Canaletto 1697–1768
Italian painter

Ireland

1700

of Oxford 1661–1724

94
Britain and Ireland

Byng 1663–1733
admiral

Eugene of Savoy 1663–1736
general

Vanbrugh 1664–1726
dramatist and architect

Alberoni 1664–1752
cardinal and statesman

Anne 1665–1714
Queen of Great Britain and Ireland

Ivan V 1666–96
Joint Tsar of Russia

Jonathan Swift 1667–1745
English satirist

William Congreve 1670–1729
English dramatist

1670 Secret Treaty of Dover
between Charles II and
Louis XIV against Holland

1673 Test Act: Catholics excluded
from public office in
England (till 1828)

1667
Treaty of Breda ends Second
Anglo-Dutch War

1668
Spain recognizes
Portuguese independence

1669
Aurangzeb prohibits
Hinduism in India

1678–79 Treaties of Nijmwegen end
Franco-Dutch and Franco-
Spanish Wars

1679 Habeas Corpus Act:
protection against arbitrary
arrest in England

1689
Bill of Rights gives political
supremacy to Parliament in
Britain

1690 Battle of the Boyne:
conquest of Ireland by
William III

1694
Bank of England founded

1694
Gold discovered in Minas
Gerais, southern Brazil

Treaty of Ryswick: Louis XIV **1697**
recognizes defeat by League
of Augsburg

Treaty of Karlowitz: Austria **1699**
obtains Hungary, Poland
regains Podolia from Turks

1700–21
Great Northern War

1701
Elector of Brandenburg
becomes King of Prussia

1701–14
War of Spanish
Succession

Acknowledgments

The authors and publishers wish to thank the following museums and collections by whose kind permission the illustrations are reproduced. Page numbers appear in bold, photographic sources in italics.

12 *Mansell Collection*
13 *Mary Evans Picture Library*
14 (1) *Mary Evans Picture Library* (2) National Portrait Gallery, London
15 (1) National Portrait Gallery (2) Duke of Portland
16 (2) *Mary Evans Picture Library* (3) Dulwich College, London: *Radio Times Hulton Picture Library*
17 (1) *Mansell Collection* (2, 3) National Portrait Gallery
18 (1, 2) National Portrait Gallery (3) *Mansell Collection* (4) *Mary Evans Picture Library*
19 (1) National Museum, Stockholm: *Anderson* (2) Prado, Madrid: *Mansell Collection*
20 *Mary Evans Picture Library*
21 *Radio Times Hulton Picture Library*
22 (1, 2) *Mansell Collection*
23 (1, 2) *Mary Evans Picture Library*
24 (1) Rijksmuseum, Amsterdam (2) *John Freeman*
25 National Gallery, London: *Michael Holford*
26 (1, 2) *Radio Times Hulton Picture Library*
27 (1) *Roger-Viollet* (2) Reproduced by gracious permission of Her Majesty The Queen – crown copyright reserved: *A. C. Cooper* (3) *Radio Times Hulton Picture Library*
28 Plimouth Plantation, Plymouth, Mass.
29 Pilgrim Hall, Plymouth, Mass.
30 (1) *Mary Evans Picture Library* (2) *Radio Times Hulton Picture Library* (3) *Mansell Collection*
31 (1, 2) *Mansell Collection*
32 British Museum, London
33 (2, 3) *Mansell Collection*
34 (1) New York Public Library (2, 3) *Radio Times Hulton Picture Library* (4) *Michael Holford*
35 (1) Collection of the Library Company of Philadelphia (3) *Radio Times Hulton Picture Library*
36 (1) British Museum: *John Freeman* (2, 3) *Mary Evans Picture Library*
37 (1) National Gallery (2) *Mansell Collection*
38 National Portrait Gallery
39 Wellcome Institute, London
40 (1) *Mansell Collection* (2) British Museum: *John Freeman*
41 (1, 2) *Mansell Collection*
42 Royal College of Physicians, London
43 *Transworld Feature Syndicate Inc.*
44 (1, 2) *Mansell Collection*
45 (1) *Phoebus Picture Library* (2) *Mansell Collection* (3) *Photo Bulloz*
46 Louvre, Paris: *Photo Bulloz*
47 Musée de Versailles: *Photo Bulloz*
48 (1) *Mansell Collection* (2) *Photo Bulloz*
49 Musée Carnavalet, Paris: *Photo Bulloz*
50 Musée de Versailles: *Photo Bulloz*
51 (1) Louvre: *Photo Bulloz* (2) *Photo Bulloz*

52 *Mansell Collection*
53 (1) *Mary Evans Picture Library* (2) *Photo Bulloz*
55 *Swedish Institute for Cultural Relations*
56 (1) *Mansell Collection* (2) *R. B. Fleming*
57 (1) *Mansell Collection* (2) Germanisches National Museum, Berlin
58 (1, 3) *Blainel*
60 (1) *Roger-Viollet* (2) *Mansell Collection*
61 (1) *Mary Evans Picture Library*
62 (1, 2) *Mansell Collection*
63 (1) National Portrait Gallery (2) *Radio Times Hulton Picture Library* (3) National Army Museum, London
64 National Portrait Gallery
65 British Museum: *John Freeman*
66 (1) *Mansell Collection* (2) British Museum: *Phoebus Picture Library*
67 British Museum
68 Reproduced by gracious permission of Her Majesty The Queen – crown copyright reserved
69 (1) National Portrait Gallery (2) Victoria and Albert Museum, London: *Angelo Hornak*
70 (2) *Novosti Press Agency* (3) *Mansell Collection*
71 (1) *Radio Times Hulton Picture Library* (2) Chester Beatty Library, Dublin
72 British Museum
73 British Museum
74 School of Oriental and African Studies, London University; National Palace Collection
75 Collection of the National Palace Museum, Taipei, Taiwan, Republic of China
76 Gulbenkian Museum of Oriental Art and Archaeology, Durham: *J. Teasdale*
77 Victoria and Albert Museum: *Michael Holford Library*
78 British Museum
79 British Museum
80 (1) *Mary Evans Picture Library*
81 (1) National Gallery (2) *Mansell Collection*
82 *Mansell Collection*
83 Earl of Radnor
84 (1) British Museum: *John Freeman* (2) National Portrait Gallery
85 (1) *Mansell Collection* (2) National Portrait Gallery
86 (1) British Museum (2) *Mansell Collection* (3) *John Freeman*
87 *John Freeman*
88 Victoria and Albert Museum
89 (1) Scottish National Gallery, Edinburgh, on loan from Lord Rosebery (2) British Museum
90 (1) Comédie Française: *Photo Bulloz* (2) *Photo Bulloz*
91 (1) Bibliothèque Nationale, Paris: *Photo Bulloz* (2) *Mary Evans Picture Library* (3) *Radio Times Hulton Picture Library*
92 Musée de Versailles: *Mary Evans Picture Library*
93 *Giraudon*
94 *Photo Bulloz*
95 (1) *Mansell Collection* (2) *Giraudon* (3) *Mary Evans Picture Library*

96 (1) *Mansell Collection* (2) *Photo de Musées Nationaux*
97 *Giraudon*
98 (1) *Michael Holford* (2) *Giraudon*
99 By permission of the trustees of the Wallace Collection, London
100 (1) *Mansell Collection* (2) Apsley House, London: *Editions Robert Laffont*
101 (1) By permission of the trustees of the Wallace Collection (2) *Mansell Collection*
102 Royal Society, London
103 Royal Society
104 (1, 2) *Mansell Collection*
105 (1) *Mansell Collection* (2) Science Museum, London (3) *Mary Evans Picture Library*
106 (2) *Ronan Picture Library*
107 (1) *Mary Evans Picture Library* (2) National Portrait Gallery (3) *Ronan Picture Library*
108 (1) *Giraudon* (2) *Mansell Collection* (3) National Portrait Gallery
109 (1) *Mansell Collection* (2) National Maritime Museum, Greenwich
110 (1) Victoria and Albert Museum: *R. Todd-White*
111 *Radio Times Hulton Picture Library*
112 British Museum: *Phoebus Picture Library*
113 (1) British Museum: *R. B. Fleming* (2) *Michael Holford*
114 (1) Exeter Cathedral Library (2) *John Freeman*
115 *Mansell Collection*
116 National Maritime Museum, Greenwich Hospital Collection
117 National Maritime Museum
118 (1) *Mansell Collection* (2) National Portrait Gallery
120 By permission of the Masters and Fellows of Magdalene College, Cambridge
121 (1, 2) Rijksmuseum, Amsterdam
122 (2) Pecci Blunt Collection, Rome: *Radio Times Hulton Picture Library*
123 (1, 2) *Mansell Collection* (3) Topkapi Museum, Istanbul: *Sonia Halliday*
124 *Sonia Halliday*
125 *Sonia Halliday*
126 (3) *Mary Evans Picture Library* (4) *John Freeman*
127 (1) *Mary Evans Picture Library* (2) National Bibliothek, Vienna
128 *Sonia Halliday*
129 (1) *Mansell Collection* (2) *Sonia Halliday*
130 (1) British Museum: *John Freeman* (2) Apsley House: *Editions Robert Laffont*
131 (1) Apsley House: *Editions Robert Laffont* (2) *Roger-Viollet* (3) *Editions Robert Laffont*
132 Louvre: *Scala*
133 Archives Nationales, Paris: *Photo Bulloz*
134 (1, 2) *Mansell Collection*
135 *Mansell Collection*
136 (1) Musée de Versailles: *Photo Bulloz* (2) Palazzo Pitti, Florence: *Scala*
137 Musée de Versailles: *Photo Bulloz*
138 (1) Apsley House: *Editions Robert Laffont* (2) *Radio Times Hulton Picture Library* (3) *Courtauld*

Institute, London
139 (1) *Radio Times Hulton Picture Library* (2) *Mansell Collection*
140 National Portrait Gallery
141 British crown copyright—reproduced with the permission of the Controller of Her Britannic Majesty's Stationery Office
142 *Mansell Collection*
143 British Museum: *John Freeman*
144 (1) Reproduced by gracious permission of Her Majesty The Queen – crown copyright reserved (2) National Portrait Gallery
145 *Mansell Collection*
146 (1) Society of Friends: *Su Gooders* (2, 3) National Museum, Stockholm
147 *Mary Evans Picture Library*
148 Hermitage, Leningrad
149 *Novosti Press Agency*
150 (1) British Museum (2) *Novosti Press Agency*
151 (1) British Museum (2) *Mary Evans Picture Library* (3) *Mansell Collection*
152 (1) *Mary Evans Picture Library* (2) Hermitage: *Novosti Press Agency* (3) *John Freeman*
153 (1) *John Freeman*

Managing Editor *Jonathan Martin*
Assistant Editors *Geoffrey Chesler*
                  Francesca Ronan
Picture Editor *Julia Brown*
Consultant Designer *Tim Higgins*
Art Director *Anthony Cohen*

Index